Graphics Programming with JFC™

Graphics Programming
with JFC™

David Wall
Arthur Griffith

Wiley Computer Publishing

John Wiley & Sons, Inc.
NEW YORK • CHICHESTER • WEINHEIM • BRISBANE • SINGAPORE • TORONTO

Publisher: Robert Ipsen
Editor: Robert M. Elliott
Assistant Editor: Pam Sobotka
Managing Editor: Brian Snapp
Electronic Products, Associate Editor: Mike Sosa
Text Design & Composition: Benchmark Productions, Inc.

Designations used by companies to distinguish their products are often claimed as trademarks. In all instances where John Wiley & Sons, Inc., is aware of a claim, the product names appear in initial capital or ALL CAPITAL LETTERS. Readers, however, should contact the appropriate companies for more complete information regarding trademarks and registration.

This book is printed on acid-free paper. ∞

Published by John Wiley & Sons, Inc.

Published simultaneously in Canada.

This publication is designed to provide accurate and authoritative information in regard to the subject matter covered. It is sold with the understanding that the publisher is not engaged in rendering professional services. If professional advice or other expert assistance is required, the services of a competent professional person should be sought.

Java and all Java-based trademarks and logos are trademarks or registered trademarks of Sun Microsystems, Inc. in the United States and other countries.

This publication is designed to provide accurate and authoritative information in regard to the subject matter covered. It is sold with the understanding that the publisher is not engaged in rendering legal, accounting, or other professional service. If legal advice or other expert assistance is required, the services of a competent professional person should be sought.

Library of Congress Cataloging-in-Publication Data:
Graphics programming with JFC / David Wall, Arthur Griffith.
  p. cm.
"Wiley Computer Publishing."
Includes index.
ISBN 0-471-28307-X (pbk. : CD-ROM : alk. paper)
1. Computer graphics. 2. Java (Computer program language)
3. Java foundation classes. I. Griffith, Arthur. II. Title.
T385.W352 1998
006.6'633—dc21
                                                        98-29270
                                                          CIP

Printed in the United States of America.

10 9 8 7 6 5 4 3 2 1

CONTENTS

Acknowledgments   ix

Introduction   xi

Chapter 1   Introduction to Java Graphics   1
          Understanding the Java2D Package   2

Chapter 2   Discovering Java2D   15
          Coordinate Spaces   16
          Paths   17
          Text   17
          Fonts   18
          Layout   18
          Images   19
          Rendering   19
          Complex Fills   20
          Strokes   20
          Transformations   20
          Transparency   21
          Compositing   21

Chapter 3   Understanding Points, Coordinates, and Transforms   23
          Using a Transform to Move Points   24
          Transforming from the World to a Window   28
          Degrees and Radians   31

Chapter 4   Getting a Grip on Colors and Textures   33
          Creating a Color Object from RGB Values   33
          The Predefined Color Objects   36
          Using a Graphics Object to Display Colors   38
          Simple Shading   40
          A Color Gradient   42
          A Diagonal Color Gradient   44
          The Acyclical Color Gradient   45
          A Cyclical Color Gradient   48
          Filling with an Image   49

Chapter 5   Positioning and Rotating in Two Dimensions   53
          SimpleLine   53
          SimpleLine2   56
          MoveDownRight   58
          Tilt   60
          Spin   62
          Circularity   64

		Circularity2	65
		CircularPlacement	68
		ScaleUp	70
		ScaleUp2	72
		ScaleDownTurn	74
		ScaleDownTurn2	75

Chapter 6	**Line Drawing**	**79**
	The Basic Line Drawings	79
	The Default Stroke	81
	Wide Lines Rounded Off	82
	The Corners Are Mitered and the Ends Are Squared	83
	Wide Lines with Bevelled Corners and Butted Line Endings	86
	Dashed Lines	87
	Drawing Figures with Dashes: Part I	90
	Drawing Figures with Dashes: Part II	91

Chapter 7	**Making Shapes and Fitting Curves**	**93**
	Building a Rectangle with GeneralPath	93
	Transforming with Graphics2D	95
	Scaling Lines	97
	Dynamic ZigZag	98
	The Winding Rule	100
	Arcs	103
	Scaling an Arc Another Way	106
	Variations on Scaling	108
	Ellipse	111
	Quadratic Curves	112
	Drawing Asymmetrical Quadratic Curves	115
	Symmetric Cubic Curves	117
	Asymmetrical Cubic Curves	119
	A Double Cubic Curve	122
	Drawing Square-Cornered Rectangles	124
	Drawing Round-Cornered Rectangles	125
	Using a GenPath Object to Append Shapes	127
	Connecting Shapes	131
	Using an Area Object to Combine Shapes	133

Chapter 8	**Fitting Text**	**137**
	All the Font Families	138
	All the Fonts	141
	Showing All Fonts	143
	Basics of String Drawing	147
	Basic Operations with TextLayout	151
	Mixing Text Attributes	155
	Drawn Letters	158
	Drawn Letters II	160

Letters with Pictures 162
Dynamic Resizing 166

Chapter 9 **Performing Animation** **169**
A Pong Applet 170
A Pong Application 173
Electrons 177

Chapter 10 **Plotting and Graphing** **181**
Reading Data Files 182
A RAM-Resident Trace 185
Multiple Traces in One Window 190
Filling a Trace 193
Fill Above and Draw Lines Below 196
Scattergram with Least Squares 199
A Single Data Item 203
Bar Graph 205
A Pie Chart 209

Chapter 11 **Exploring Bitmapped Images** **211**
Loading and Displaying an Image 211
Scaling an Image with Replication 213
Scaling an Image with Area Averaging 217
Pixel by Pixel 219
Convolving 222
Image Transformation 230
Compositing 241
Cross Fading with Transparency 247

Chapter 12 **Understanding the Mouse** **251**
Reading Mouse Events 251
Mouse Motion 254
Dissecting Mouse Events 255
Changing Mouse Cursors 259
Locating and Dragging 261

Chapter 13 **A Set of Basic Tools for Three-Dimensional Operations** **267**
A Point in Space 268
The Edge of a Shape 268
A Plane in Space 270
A Face of an Object in Space 271
Describing a Shape in a File 273
Loading a Three-Dimensional Shape 274
An Oblique Cubelike Thing 279

Chapter 14 **Rotating Wire Frame Shapes in Three Dimensions** **283**
An Adjustable Wire Frame 283
An Automatic Rotater 286
Manual Rotater 292

Chapter 15   **Hidden Line Suppression**   **295**

XYZPoint   297

A Line Segment   300

Link   304

TriangleMetrics   305

The Line Splitter   308

Obscuring Lines behind a Triangle   315

TriangleFace   322

HiddenLineWireFrame   326

A Triangulation Demonstration   329

ManualHide   334

AutoHide   338

Chapter 16   **Perspective**   **343**

Vanishing Points   343

Screen Projection   344

PerspectiveWireFrame   346

AutoPerspective   349

Chapter 17   **Exploring the Advanced Imaging API**   **357**

How It Fits into Java   358

Design Goals   359

Reviewing AWT Image Processing   360

Comparing Java2D Imaging   361

How the Advanced Imaging API Differs   362

Advanced Imaging API Resources   364

What's on the CD-ROM?   **365**

Hardware Requirements   365

Installing the Software   366

User Assistance and Information   366

Index   **367**

ACKNOWLEDGMENTS

The authors extend their warmest thanks to everyone involved with the development and production of this book. Bob Elliott, Emilie Herman, Brian Calandra, Brian Snapp, and the others at Wiley deserve high praise, as do Margot Maley and Carole McClendon at Waterside Productions. We owe a special debt of thanks to Sun Microsystems and the communities of experts on the early-access JFC mailing lists.

David Wall would further like to thank Adam Bergman, Melissa Salva, and Diana Yap for their friendship and support.

—David Wall
Round Hill, Virginia

—Arthur Griffith
Homer, Alaska

The Java™ programming language is just beginning to come into its own as a fully capable software development tool. Just as the early days of air travel were more concerned with (and constrained by) technology, the first months of Java programming had to do with working out bugs in the language's basic functioning. Now, the language has more features, it runs more reliably, tools for working with it have improved, and it's time to start developing serious software with Java.

Certain serious software has to do with graphics. The recent release of Java2D™ as part of the Java Foundation Classes (which are in turn part of Java™ 2) dramatically increased the number of graphics tools available within the core Java distribution. For the first time, it was relatively easy to do things like font manipulating, wire-frame modeling, ray tracing, curve fitting, and perspective changing. The tools were starting to catch up with programmers' imaginations.

With this book, we want to show you how to use the graphics tools that are part of the core Java distribution as of Java 2 (formerly code-named JDK 1.2). We also want to introduce you to some additional packages, such as Java3D™ and the Advanced Imaging API.

How This Book Is Organized

We've organized this book as a series of texts and commentaries. The texts are the programs we've written to illustrate Java graphics programming concepts; the commentaries are the words we've written to explain how we've gone about solving particular problems. The idea is that you can look at our code if you prefer to learn that way, or consult our commentary if there's something you don't understand on your own.

Chapter 1 explains some of Java's newfound graphics capabilities in general terms. You'll find out about some of the things you can do with the new Java2D classes, and you'll learn a thing or two about how Java deals with shapes, lines, fills, vectors, bitmaps, and the like.

Chapter 2 goes into a little more depth on the concepts you must understand in order to do Java graphics programming. You'll find out what it means to perform a transform, for example, and how User Coordinate Space differs from Device Coordinate Space.

Chapter 3 has nothing to do with Java directly. Rather, Chapter 3 provides an introduction to the mathematics that are relevant to graphics programming. Mainly, this chapter is an introduction to performing transforms on planes and in space.

Chapter 4 explains colors and texture. You'll get the goods on the various Java2D color models, the objects that hold colors, and the means of applying colors (and gradients) to shapes. (You'll need to load images from the accompanying CD-ROM to view the color images that correspond with this book.)

Chapter 5 gets back to transforms, with a thorough discussion of the mechanics of actually moving points around in two-dimensional space with Java. You'll find out about linear transforms (moving things along a line), rotations, and scaling.

Chapter 6 reveals the mechanisms Java2D provides for drawing lines, including the options available in terms of joins, end caps, and thickness. You also find out about dashed lines and the specific considerations they require.

Chapter 7 goes a step beyond lines, detailing the special capacities Java2D has to handle shapes and regions. Here, you'll find out about arcs, curves, irregular paths and other "baskets" for holding multiline information. You also find out about the winding rule, which defines how regions and shading work when a path overlaps itself.

Chapter 8 shows how Java2D treats text as graphical regions, capable of undergoing transformation, distortion, and other modifications before being rendered to an output device. This chapter deals with one of the largest changes in Java from JDK 1.1 to Java 2—you'll probably want to read this chapter closely, even if you're not working specifically with styled strings.

Chapter 9 can be summed up in one word: Pong. This chapter explains how to write animation routines, using everyone's favorite bouncing-ball game as an example. You'll find out how to write both a Pong applet and a Pong application.

Chapter 10 shows how Java2D graphics techniques apply to plotting points and lines. You'll see how to create a monitoring program that regularly checks a data file and updates a graph based on the file's contents. For you scientific types, there's a program that fits a line to a series of data points using the least-squares method, plus bar-graph and pie-chart demonstrations.

Chapter 11 addresses raster images and the means by which Java2D displays and modifies GIF, JPEG, and other kinds of image files. We explain compositing, convolution, and transparency, as well as the peculiarities of affine transforms as they apply to images.

Chapter 12 is where we squeak in some mouse information, explaining how to trap mouse events (sorry) and modify the mouse pointer. You'll also find out how to implement drag-and-drop functionality as you write a program that enables users to scoot shapes around a field.

Chapter 13 gets into surfaces, faces, polygons, and three-dimensional modeling. You'll learn how to make a program read point information from a file and convert those points into an image. You're effectively learning how to do three-dimensional graphics within the constraints of Java2D—which is important if you want to do any three-dimensional work with the core distribution.

Chapter 14 deals with wire-frame constructions, which are key to rendering objects that appear to have three dimensions on flat screens and pages. Though you don't find out about suppressing hidden lines here, you do learn how to make three-dimensional objects "spin."

Chapter 15 adds the next level of complexity—hidden line suppression. The algorithms in this chapter show you how to prevent lines that are "behind" surfaces from being rendered, thereby making your three-dimensional images that much more believable. Naturally, you find out how to create the surfaces themselves, and this chapter is filled with information on identifying and positioning polygons in three-dimensional space.

Chapter 16 adds perspective to the mix, showing you how to use point of view and vanishing points to make your renderings more realistic. Taking a Java approach and a math approach, this chapter provides some useful classes you'll probably be able to re-use in your own software.

Chapter 17 provides a quick introduction to the Advanced Imaging API, which is a standard (though not core) package that provides tools for specialized image editing and hooks for writing other tools. This API creates a special relationship between image sources and image sinks. This chapter isn't much more than a cursory overview of the Advanced Imaging API—it will help you decide whether you should look into the API further.

Who Should Read This Book

This book is for experienced Java programmers. You don't have to be an expert to use the material in this book, but you should have considerable experience writing and debugging Java programs. You will especially appreciate what we've written here if you have some graphics programming experience, in Java or another language.

How should you approach this book? We recommend you read it straight through to develop a complete mental picture of the state of the Java graphics art. However, if you want to skip right to a chapter that addresses a problem you're having, you should be able to get away with that, since the chapters are mostly free-standing. The later chapters, dealing with three-dimensional work, depend more upon one another than earlier chapters. Think of Chapters 13 through 16 as a unit, to be read together in sequence.

Tools You Will Need

You're a programmer; you know what you need to program. All you really need is a text editor and a Java 2 compiler. The rest is frosting. Really.

A Text Editor

If you're in the market for a new text editor, you might want to check out WinEdit from Wilson WindowWare (www.winedit.com). It's a good shareware package. Also, many of the commercial publishers of editing software provide demos on their sites. And of course, there's always Notepad.

A Java 2 Compiler

To convert source code into executable Java bytecodes, you need a Java compiler. We've provided a copy of JavaSoft's Java 2 on the CD-ROM that accompanies this book—you'll find installation instructions in an appendix.

You can check for future releases and updates to Java 2 at the JavaSoft site (www.javasoft.com).

What's on the CD-ROM?

The CD-ROM that accompanies this book contains all the code we wrote (that which appears in the chapters, plus some extra) and all the relevant supporting files, such as GIFs and JPEGs. Programs appear on the CD-ROM in compiled form, along with their source code.

You'll also find a copy of JavaSoft's Java 2 for Windows 95, 98, and NT on the CD-ROM. This will save you the trouble of downloading your own copy.

Summary

Good luck! We hope you enjoy this book, and that your Java graphics skills improve as a result of reading it. Let us know what you think—we're Arthur Griffith (arthur@belugalake.com) and David Wall (david@davidwall.com).

CHAPTER 1

Introduction to Java Graphics

In this chapter, you'll get a feel for what you can do with Java, in terms of graphics. More specifically, you'll learn about how advanced Java graphics programming has changed since the days of the bouncing Duke image so often downloaded from Sun's site in the language's early days.

This chapter concentrates on the Java2D and Java3D packages. Java2D comes with Java™ 2 (formerly code-named JDK 1.2) and is used to render vector images, raster images, and text—particularly decorative text. Java3D is distinct from the core Java distribution, so anyone who wants to run a program that calls the Java3D API must have that package installed on his or her machine.

Though this book is about graphics under the JFC (Java Foundation Classes), we pretty much ignore the Swing Set here, since programming graphical user interfaces stands as a discipline completely apart from that of writing programs that work with vector and raster images. There are many other fine books that deal with Swing—we'll let them keep that part of the spotlight. Instead, we focus on Java2D and Java3D, which is quite enough material for one book of reasonable length.

On with the show! Let's start with Java2D, since it's part of the core Java 2 distribution and therefore is available on every Java machine.

Understanding the Java2D Package

Java2D provides the programmer with a set of tools designed to ease the process of rendering images on an output device, such as a video screen or a printer. Java2D helps you *render* images, (i.e., make images appear) on output devices. At the lowest level, the Java2D classes are an interface between the programmer and the grungy video routines that actually make pixels light up and cause dots to appear in certain patterns on paper. You'll use the Java2D tools to orchestrate the behavior of pixels on an output device—a video screen in most of the examples in this book.

The classes in Java2D help you draw shapes—rectangles (including squares), ellipses (including circles), other shapes that we can define mathematically, and irregular shapes that we can't define easily with equations. Further, Java2D gives you ways to alter the appearance of the rendered shapes. You can, for instance, cause a square to be drawn with rounded corners, or draw a circle with a dashed perimeter—you can even define the dash pattern (long, long, short, long, etc.) to suit your needs. If you want, you can give a region a colored or textured surface. That's useful if you're writing games or other virtual reality applications.

The Java2D classes also provide mechanisms for moving shapes around in space and for rotating them about points. Using some math tricks you'll learn in Chapter 3 (but which you won't have to understand deeply unless you want to), Java2D makes it possible to scoot a shape across the screen or turn it upside down with just a few easy-to-understand lines of code.

This chapter walks you through, in general terms, the capabilities of Java2D and other graphical parts of the Java programming language. Read this chapter with Chapter 2, which explains elementary graphics concepts, and Chapter 3, which details some of the math you'll encounter in this book.

Drawing Lines and Shapes

The heart of any graphics programming language is its ability to make pixels distinguish themselves from their neighbors. You need the ability to specify pixels to be highlighted and the ability to make the highlighting happen (we use the term *highlighting* here because color is another matter that we'll soon address).

Typically, you'll want to make pixels distinguish themselves in patterns—shapes, lines, and the like. Java gives you several ways to create such pixel patterns.

Lines

You can draw lines easily with Java2D, simply by specifying—in the case of straight lines—the coordinates of a starting point and the coordinates of an ending point. Alternately, you can create segments of ellipses, Bezier curves, or quadratic curves. Figure 1.1 shows some examples of lines.

Regular Shapes

Java2D has built-in classes you can use to define shapes that are mathematically easy to define. Shapes like ellipses and rectangles—don't forget that perfect circles and squares are special kinds of ellipses and rectangles, respectively, and are mathematically definable as such—get their own classes in Java2D.

Figure 1.1   Various lines.

You can use an instance of the java.awt.geom.Rectangle2D class to define a square, for example. Such an object contains, in one form or another, the coordinates of the upper-left corner of the square, the square's height, and its width.

The same thing goes for the Ellipse2D, Line2D, QuadCurve2D, and Point2D classes and the other shape-holding objects. You're now able to treat shapes as modules that you can easily feed to rendering routines, transformations, or other pieces of code. Figure 1.2 shows some examples of regular shapes.

Irregular Paths and Shapes

Java2D also has an object, GeneralPath, that's designed to hold irregular shapes. These shapes may be defined mathematically, albeit not with an easy equation. Creating one isn't hard, either. All you do is instantiate an object, specify a starting point, then draw lines and/or Bezier curves to other points you specify. You can close up the path at the end if you like, or leave the path open. Figure 1.3 shows an irregular shape created with a GeneralPath object.

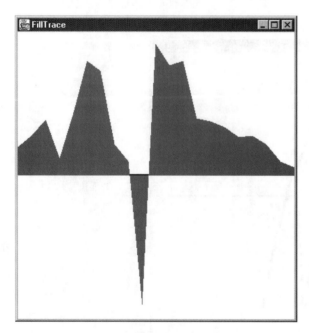

Figure 1.2   Regular shapes based on special objects.

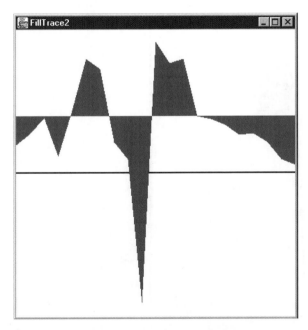

Figure 1.3   A shape stored in a GeneralPath object.

Creating Special Appearances

Java now provides the programmer with ways to perform special tricks with graphics. For example, you can specify that lines be dashed in a certain way, or that lines be of a certain thickness. You also can fill regions in a variety of ways. Here are some examples of ways you can create special appearances.

Line Styles

You can use Java2D's various drawing objects to cause lines to be rendered in different thicknesses, colors, or dash patterns. You can even fill a line with a texture, or define any dash pattern you want. Figure 1.4 shows some special lines created with the help of Java2D.

Caps

When you terminate a line, something has to be done with the end. It can be left square, rendered with a rounded end, or given beveled corners. These line-end decorations are called *caps*. Figure 1.5 shows the caps you can attach to your lines in Java2D.

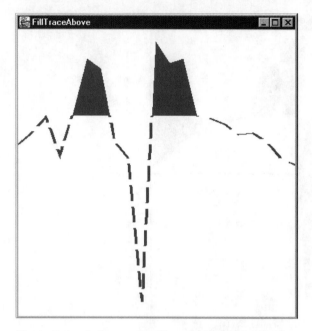

Figure 1.4   A shape stored in a GeneralPath object.

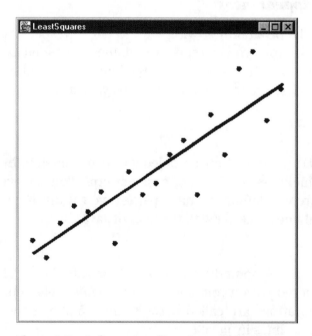

Figure 1.5   A shape stored in a GeneralPath object.

Joins

Java2D makes it easy to attach adornments to the angles formed when two lines—either independent line segments or parts of shapes—form a corner. You can put a rounded bead in the angle, or fill the angle with a straight fillet. These line attributes are called *joins*, and are shown in Figure 1.6.

Colors

You can render lines and other regions in any color you can define with a color triplet. You also can give lines and regions transparency.

Gradient Fills

Sometimes you'll want to decorate a region with a gradient fill—a gradual transition from one color to another. Java2D's rendering engine does the hard work of figuring out the shading for you—all you have to do is specify the colors between which you wish to fade. Figure 1.7 shows a rectangle filled with a red-to-white color gradient.

Figure 1.6 Joins.

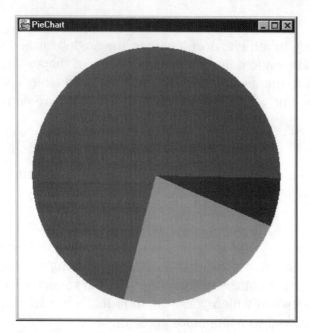

Figure 1.7 Painting a region with a gradient fill.

Textures

Not only can you paint a region—or a line—with colors and gradient fills, you can fill regions with textures. Figure 1.8 shows a rectangle filled with a texture. This image appears in color on the CD-ROM.

Compositing Images

Java makes it relatively easy to *composite* images; that is, to stack them atop one another. The language gives you precise control over how you superimpose one image on another (or several others) and takes into account transparency—if you paint one image, then place another, partly transparent image on top of the first, the first image will show through the second one. Of interest to those doing what-you-see-is-what-you-get page-layout tools is the fact that text can be treated as just another layer in a compositing operation.

Working with Text

Frequently, text plays a big part in the overall appearance of a graphical display. To live up to the demands placed on it by graphic artists and page designers, text must be able to be rendered in many different ways.

Figure 1.8 Painting a region with a texture.

The days of teletype output passed long ago, and modern text output must serve as both a decorative function and a communicative one.

Fortunately, Java2D provides the programmer with a whole suite of objects well-adapted to displaying text in visually appealing ways. With these classes, you can render text in all kinds of different fonts, and position text anywhere you want on a display in much the same way you can position lines and shapes on a display.

A note about fonts and typefaces: A *font* is a particular set of appearance attributes, such as "Garamond Bold Italic 36 point." A *typeface*, in contrast, is a particular way of rendering an alphabet's glyphs—"Garamond" is a typeface. You need complete font information in order to render text, not just a typeface. You'll learn more about that later.

This section provides a rundown of Java2D's text-management capabilities.

Strings

Strings have been part of the Java language since the beginning, and they haven't changed as a result of Java2D. This section appears here just to remind you of what strings are . . . and of what they are not.

Strings—objects that contain a series of characters—cannot be written to the screen without first being run through some sort of graphics object. Strings provide programmers with the greatest benefit when they're regarded as thingies floating around in memory, free to be manipulated content-wise or however. Don't think of the human-readable stuff you paint to the screen as strings, because that's not what they are.

What *are* they, then? Read on.

Characters

You'll work with characters under Java2D in the same way you've always worked with characters. Nothing changes here. We bring them up here only to highlight the fact that you'll have to think about characters slightly differently when the time comes to render them graphically.

Think for a minute about characters. In English, we have 26 letters, 10 digits, and 13 traditional punctuation marks (period, comma, colon, semicolon, hyphen, dash, question mark, exclamation point, opening double quote, closing double quote, opening single quote, closing single quote, and apostrophe). Additionally, there are some other characters, such as the dollar sign ($), the ampersand (&) and the "at" or "shell" character (@), that we see in text now and then. We regard each of those entities as characters, and if we added them to a Java string, they'd each add one to the length of that string.

You must realize, however, that one character does not necessarily correspond to one region that will be drawn to the screen in a text-painting operation. This is less obvious in English than it is in other languages that include accent marks. Even in English, there are examples. The exclamation point (!) stands as a good one. That punctuation mark is one character with two regions to be filled (the long part and the dot). These parts are called *glyphs*.

Glyphs

Glyphs are shapes that form part of a language character. The two dots in the umlaut above the character Ä are glyphs. The dot in the character "i" is a glyph—the main part below the dot is another glyph. The character "R" is a glyph.

More specifically, the character "R," rendered in this font, is a glyph. The character "R" in another font would be another glyph. The same with the other glyphs in the preceding list.

Consider also situations in which multiple characters are combined into a single glyph. Many typefaces, for example, combine certain pairs of letters into *ligatures*. The common letter sequence "tt" is rendered in lots of typefaces as a single glyph, as are "fi" and "ff." Ligatures are purely aesthetic—they're built into typefaces by their designers—and they have no impact on the way the characters are interpreted or pronounced.

Fonts

A *font* is a collection of glyphs with which you can form interpretable written statements. When preparing to render a piece of text, you'll want to attach a Font object to the text. Font objects incorporate information about the typeface, point size, weight (such as bold or light), and posture (such as italic or oblique). Font objects also include information about text transforms, which are pieces of positioning information that apply to text rendered under the Font object.

Text Transforms

It is possible to apply affine transforms to text, just as it is possible to apply such transforms to vector images, raster images, or anything else drawn with Java2D. Text transforms enable you to move text around relative to the origin (more on that in the next chapter) or to some other point. They also make it possible to rotate text, turning it to run vertically or at some other angle.

Special Layout Capabilities

The Java2D API includes a cool new object called GlyphSet. A GlyphSet object is the set of glyphs used to render a piece of text. With access to these shapes, you can write routines to distort them, for example. That's a handy feature if you're planning to do advanced typography work under Java.

Rendering Bitmapped Images

Java2D imbues the language with new capacity to work with *bitmapped* (or *raster*) images. Such images—usually in the form of .GIF or .JPEG files—can be used to store such things as true-color photographs, screen captures, icons, or other pictures that are defined pixel-by-pixel. True, Java always has had the ability to work with .GIF and .JPEG files, but Java2D has some highly excellent new methods for manipulating them.

A brief overview of what you can do with raster images under Java2D follows.

Buffering

Java2D includes a new extension of java.awt.Image—the BufferedImage object. A BufferedImage object resides in memory and allows you to access individual pixels in a raster image—before and after the image is written to the screen for the first time.

Tiling

Java2D institutes the concept of tiling, in which filters are applied to one image before it's repainted with alterations. What filters can you apply? Any you can create, plus these standard ones.

Affine Transforms. It's possible to apply affine transforms—which perform relocation and rotation tasks—to raster images, just as it's possible for vector images and text.

Scaling. You can make a raster image larger or smaller, simply by applying a scaling factor.

Lookup-Table Modification. The new Java2D raster image capabilities include the power to diddle with the values that affect the colors displayed in such images. By modifying images' lookup tables, it's possible to do such things as edge detection, sharpening, softening, and adjustment of brightness and contrast. Finally, Java raster image displays have the same power to fine-tune color and contrast as a 1975-vintage television. Such TVs have special "Brightness" and "Contrast" knobs that facilitate picture adjustment.

Color Conversion. You can convert colors in an image to other colors during the process of translating the image.

Convolution. This is the process of examining a pixel and its surrounding pixels, then using the collection of data to make some change. Convolution is used in softening and sharpening filters, and in edge detection.

Color

Every graphics environment needs a way to handle color. The color model included in Java2D makes it easier to define and otherwise work with colors and transparency.

Color Definition

Java2D provides you with several ways to define colors, both device-dependent and device-independent. You'll learn more about these means of defining colors in the next chapter, but realize now that Java2D supports three principal means of defining colors, one device-independent and two device-dependent.

The RGB Color Model. Java2D can define colors in terms of red, green, and blue. This model is device-dependent.

The CMYK Color Model. Java2D can define colors in terms of cyan, magenta, yellow, and black. This model is device-dependent.

The CIEXYZ Color Model. Defined by the International Commission on Illumination (CIE), this device-independent color model can be used to specify any color based on its position in a three-dimensional hypothetical color space.

Transparency

Java2D also supports colors with transparency values, allowing programmers to define colors that show their backgrounds to some degree. This comes in handy during compositing operations.

Graphics Hardware Support

Every computer has what Java calls a *graphics environment*. The graphics environment includes information on the video screens and printers attached to the computer, and about the fonts the system is able to support. Information about the graphics environment is stored, logically enough, in a GraphicsEnvironment object.

The GraphicsEnvironment object holds a series of GraphicsDevice objects. These objects describe the hardware capabilities of the system to render images.

On a particular system, there is one GraphicsDevice object for each graphics output device. Each video screen, each printer, and each plotter get one GraphicsDevice object—certain video screens, those attached to certain non-Windows and non-MacOS computers, can have different characteristics in different windows. In such situations, each window gets its own GraphicsDevice object.

What's in a GraphicsDevice object? You'll learn more about them later, but most importantly, these objects contain information about pixel resolution and color depth.

Doing 3-D Work with Java2D

One of the greatest things about Java2D is that its designers gave it sufficient power to do a decent job of rendering three-dimensional objects. Developers regard this as a boon because the Java3D package—discussed next and in great depth toward the end of this book—isn't part of the core Java distribution. It's possible to do three-dimensional renderings with classes built for two-dimensional graphics.

Pay attention to Part III of this book for a deep discussion of doing 3D work with 2D tools. What you can do without installing Java3D is pretty amazing.

CHAPTER 2

Discovering Java2D

P art of the Java Foundation Classes (JFC), Java2D is the portion of the Java programming language that facilitates the conceptualization and depiction of two-dimensional shapes. Developed jointly by JavaSoft and Adobe Systems, the Java2D API is a subset of the java.awt and java.awt.image packages.

Since Java2D is part of the JFC, it is therefore part of the core Java distribution as of Java 2. Any browser or other environment that supports Java 2 also supports Java2D, and there is no need to install special packages or other components in such environments in order to use programs that make reference to Java2D features. Both Microsoft Internet Explorer 5.0 and Netscape Navigator 5.0 are expected to support Java 2, including Java2D.

Java2D makes it easy to create and manipulate shapes (both regular and irregular), images (in several formats), and stylized text (characters with font, weight, and other characteristics). The API also makes it relatively easy to perform transformations, including rotation and scaling, on shapes. You can create composite images with Java2D, and use several rendering techniques to generate visible representations of shapes and images on a screen or on a printer. This book devotes much of its ink to the mathematics that underlie drawing and imaging, and the Java implementation of those mathematics. That's not to say that you have to be a math wizard to generate good graphics with Java, but it helps if you put your brain into conceptualization mode and start visualizing the relationships of objects in space.

Color support is extensive, too. You'll find facilities in Java2D for representing colors in any of several color models, including some that address alpha channels. You can convert colors from one color space to another easily and accurately. For the first time, Java has the kind of color support that's required for creating high-level renderings and professional-quality color output.

Further, Java2D makes it possible to address a variety of output devices. You'll find it possible to send images to video screens and printers with a great deal of accuracy and control, making it easier to create what-you-see-is-what-you-get applications.

The rest of this chapter provides more detailed information on what Java2D is good for, and supplies you with some handy background information.

Coordinate Spaces

You can think of the plane defined by a video monitor or a sheet of paper in a printer as a Euclidean plane, defined by axes running horizontally and vertically. Further, you can imagine the space in which shapes are created (before they're rendered to the output device) as another coordinate plane. The two planes do not have to be identical—they can have different origins and other characteristics. Java2D translates the contents of the User Coordinate Plane into the Device Coordinate Plane when it's time to render.

The physical rendering plane is called the Device Coordinate Space; the conceptual pre-rendering space is called the User Coordinate Space.

User Coordinate Space

You can conceptualize the two-dimensional space in which your shapes are rendered as any two-dimensional coordinate plane, with whatever origin and other characteristics best fit your conceptual needs.

Device Coordinate Space

The Device Coordinate Space represents the visual surface of a rendering device, such as a video screen or a sheet of paper that runs through a printer. Device Coordinate Spaces have their origins in their upper-left corners, with x coordinates increasing from left to right and y coordinates increasing from top to bottom.

One of the characteristics of a Device Coordinate Space is a definition of a transform that translates the graphics objects in a User Coordinate Space into the Device Coordinate Space. Translation from one coordinate space to the other occurs automatically at rendering time.

Paths

The Path object, part of Java2D, can be used to contain definitions of irregular shapes. There are several ways to define the contents of a Path object, but one useful way to do this is to define the series of points, in sequence, that define the perimeter of the shape.

Alternately, you can use a combination of straight lines and Bezier curves to define a BezierPath object. Though it's less easy to understand how Bezier curves work, the BezierPath object allows you to define shapes with curved boundaries.

Objects that contain paths also can be endowed with attributes that define where they exist in the User Coordinate Space.

Text

Java2D provides the Java programmer with advanced text manipulation and rendering tools for the first time. With the tools Java2D provides, it's possible to render text characters in any style imaginable, with accurate layout. You also can use the pixels that define a rendered piece of text as a graphics object like any other, meaning you can use text in layering, compositing, and clipping operations.

Fonts

Java2D supports a Font class that's superior to the one defined in the old AWT. Whereas under the AWT you were limited to getting and setting just a few font traits, under Java2D you can manipulate fonts and the characters rendered with them with very high degrees of power and precision.

For instance, Java2D allows you to get BezierPath objects that represent the shapes of individual characters in a font's collection. Furthermore, you can access plenty of font attributes, like the font's name, weight, and size. Even the metrics of individual glyphs are exposed. The attributes appear in an array called FontFeatures, which you can examine easily to get all the details on a font. The Font object also includes lots of convenient methods to ease access to attributes. You also can apply transforms to fonts, which means you can scale characters with plenty of precision.

Layout

Java2D provides the programmer with a great deal of control over where and how text is rendered in User Coordinate Space and Device Coordinate Space. Using these capacities, you'll find it easier to render complicated text in Java than in other programming languages. You'll even find it relatively easy to deal with multiple languages, multiple character sets and multiple text directions. If you want English text running from left to right on one part of a page and Chinese text running from top to bottom on another, you can do that. If you want to add some Hebrew—which is written from right to left—on another part of the page, you can do that, too. Special effects, such as English-language labels that consist of a series of characters stacked vertically, are made possible by these capabilities as well.

Java2D's layout capabilities also include the ability to manipulate glyph sizes (for example, in creating small-caps effects), kerning tables (getting subsequent characters to move under the crossbar in a capital "T"), and ligatures (replacing the "f" and "t" characters in the word *rift* with a special character representing a joined "f" and "t"). By exploiting these capabilities, you can gain near-absolute control over what gets rendered—something you might not get from your system by default.

Images

In expanding Java's capacity for handling and manipulating raster images such as JPEG and GIF files, Java2D has made some changes to the way images were handled in the old system. For example, it's now possible to conceptualize colors in several different models, not just RGB. You also can use an instance of the new BufferedImage object to determine exactly how pixels are oriented before they're rendered.

For people who really need a ton of image-handling capability, JavaSoft has supplemented Java2D with the Advanced Imaging API, which provides lots of high-powered image-manipulation tools. The main drawback of the Advanced Imaging API is that it's not part of the core Java distribution, which means you'll have to make sure it's installed on any machine on which you want to use an advanced imaging program. If you're concerned about an intranet, extranet, or other controllable environment, that may not be such a tall order—the Advanced Imaging API may do you a ton of good. Read all about it in Chapter 17.

Rendering

When a shape or other drawable entity (such as a piece of text) is rendered, several settings the programmer has specified are taken into account and used to affect the appearance of the final rendered entity. You can specify such characteristics as:

Stroke width. The breadth of the lines used to trace a path.

Join types. What happens when two lines join? Is the corner rounded, beveled, or what?

Color and texture fills. You can determine what fills in the region defined by the path.

Anti-aliasing. Are any steps taken to avoid the jaggies?

When something is rendered, here's what happens:

1. The contents of the User Coordinate Space are translated into the Device Coordinate space, using the transform designated for translating between the two spaces. At the same time, if several paths are

to be rendered, they're combined into a single BezierPath. Stroke and other attributes are taken into account.

2. Clipping is figured out. You can use any Path object to distinguish what should be rendered from what should not be rendered. Clipping is especially relevant when you're doing lots of repetitive rendering, as in the case of animation.

3. Color is processed. If an image is being rendered, color information comes from the image data. If a shape is being rendered, color information comes from settings the programmer has made. The color is then applied to the object to be drawn.

Complex Fills

You can fill shapes to be rendered with complex patterns, such as gradients. By applying a complex fill to a region, you save yourself the trouble of manually defining a fill pixel by pixel.

Strokes

When a path is rendered, it is first stroked. To stroke a path is to "draw" the segments that are included in its definition. The "pen" that draws the segments has certain characteristics—thickness of its nib chief among them—and it is these characteristics that are defined by the Stroke object. You can use Stroke objects (or the related BasicStroke objects) to specify the width, end-cap style, join style, and dashing pattern of Path-defining line segments.

Transformations

As you know, entities to be rendered are moved from the User Coordinate Space to the Device Coordinate Space by means of a mathematical mechanism known as a transform, typically encoded in a Transform object. But that's not the only use of transforms. You'll use them frequently to move, rotate, and scale shapes and images in your graphical compositions. You might, for example, set up a transform that moves by one degree of arc the line segment defining the second hand of an analog clock.

You also can use the transform to provide perspective to your images, regardless of the fact that perspective requires the use of nonlinear transforms.

Transparency

In Java2D, images hold alpha-channel information that defines their transparency. Each pixel in an image can have a different alpha-channel value. Alpha-channel values define a pixel on a continuum from totally opaque—that is, rendered with its own color value—to totally transparent—that is, rendered using the color value or values of the layers that underlie it in a composition.

Compositing

Java2D supports the creation of composite renderings, which are renderings that are composed of layers containing other individual shapes, images, or pieces of text. You can think of composites as the results of stacking layers of clear plastic on which images have been drawn. However, composites created with Java2D have the advantage of enabling you to blend the colors and transparencies in the various layers in whatever way you want. You can make the layers blend evenly, you can make one layer show particularly strongly, or you can let the uppermost layer in a stack dominate the others.

When creating a composite image, color blending rules are defined by a Composite object. An AlphaComposite object dictates how various images' alpha channels work together to create a composite image. For example, if you create an AlphaComposite object that specifies SRC_OVER transfer mode and an alpha value of 0.5, the upper layer in the composition will be rendered on top of the lower layer, with 50 percent of the lower layer's color showing through to the upper surface. This works even if the lower layer's color derives from some other definition of transparency that makes the lower layer's color a show-through of the color of some still lower layer in the composite.

You can use the Composite and CompositeContext interfaces to define easily reusable composition styles. CompositeContext objects spawn as many Composite objects as are needed to do multiple compositing operations in a multithreaded environment.

CHAPTER 3

Understanding Points, Coordinates, and Transforms

A t the most basic level, there are *points*—identifiable locations in space (two-dimensional space, three-dimensional space, or twelve-dimensional space, it does not matter yet). Points are the most basic elements in geometry and therefore in computer graphics. They are the atoms that make up everything graphical.

Coordinates are numbers we use to identify points. In a one-dimensional universe (a line segment), we could identify individual points in the universe with single numbers—(5) would uniquely identify the point five units from the origin. In a two-dimensional system, two coordinates are required to identify each point in the system—one for each axis, since axes denote dimensions. The point (5,–2) is the unique point five units in the positive direction along one axis and two units in the negative direction along the other. You can have coordinate systems for universes of infinite dimension, though in this book and in life you'll rarely see anything more elaborate than (x,y,z) coordinates identifying points in three-dimensional space.

Transforms are the mathematical mechanisms that you use to relocate points—particularly groups of them. You might use a transform to move a group of points five units to the right, or rotate them π/2 radians clockwise along a circle ringing the origin. Naturally, manipulating points with transforms involves working with their coordinates.

This chapter goes into detail on the mathematics behind transforms. Although this chapter isn't Java-specific, the things you learn here will prove valuable in the upcoming chapters as you begin to explore the AffineTransform object and the various drawing methods.

Using a Transform to Move Points

To move something from one location to another on a display is simply to move all the points that describe it. This can be rotation (moving the points along a circle surrounding another point), or it can be a simple linear offset (moving the points along a line). There is a convenient method for defining this sort of point transformation. The action needed to move a point from one location to another is defined as a regular algebraic equation. Once the equations are defined, they are translated into a matrix, called a transform, that can be used to process all the points defining the object to be moved.

The Origin

Java does its drawing in the form of pixels. To place a pixel two pieces of information are required: the color of pixel and its location. You tell Java your required location by placing the point in relation to the *origin*. Whenever groups of pixels are painted to the display, they are located relative to one another to form the desired image, and the entire group is positioned relative to the origin. The origin, remember, is the upper-left corner of the frame in which you're drawing.

A pixel is positioned by being a certain distance, vertically and horizontally, from the origin. The value of x determines the horizontal distance from the origin, the value of y determines the vertical distance. The values can be positive or negative to determine the direction from the origin. A positive value of x is always a point to the right of the origin, and a negative value of x is a point to the left of the origin. A positive value of y is below the origin, and a negative value of y is above the origin. These two numbers, the x and y, are the two values required to define a location—these numbers are known as the *coordinates* of the point.

It may seem odd at first to be able to have negative coordinates since they will be outside the display area of the window, but the fact is that you can, by using *transforms*, have coordinate points repositioned anywhere you want, and some of the otherwise invisible locations will be moved into the display area. The Java mechanics of doing this will be described later. The balance of this chapter covers the mechanism used by Java to transform coordinate points from one position to another.

From Equation to Matrixes

A rule that moves a point from one location to another is called a *transform*. A simple pair of equations will do this. The equations that move x to x' and y to y' look like this:

$$x' = x + a$$
$$y' = y + b$$

By setting the values of a and b to appropriate values, we can move x and y in any direction. This works fine for any linear transformation (that is, a simple repositioning of an object on the display), but not all transformations are linear. Say, for example, we want to rotate a point, or group of points, about the origin through the angle ϕ. The equations look like this:

$$x' = x \cos\phi - y \sin\phi$$

$$y' = x \sin\phi + y \cos\phi$$

The two actions (rotation and translation) can be combined into one set of equations. Combining the two actions we get these equations:

$$x' = x \cos\phi - y \sin\phi + a$$

$$y' = x \sin\phi + y \cos\phi + b$$

This combination happens a lot. So much, in fact, that there is a special notation that can be used to write down these equations and manipulate them. As it turns out, it is much easier to work with these equations if they are written in the form of a matrix this way:

$$\begin{bmatrix} x' \\ y' \\ 1 \end{bmatrix} = \begin{bmatrix} x \\ y \\ 1 \end{bmatrix} \begin{bmatrix} \cos\phi & -\sin\phi & a \\ \sin\phi & \cos\phi & b \\ 0 & 0 & 1 \end{bmatrix}$$

This is no different than the earlier equations, it's just a different way of writing them. You can think of the matrices on the right side of the equation as being the definition, a machine that will the matrix on the left side of the equation. This is done with a matrix multiply.

To operate this transform, you plug in values for x and y in the column matrix. Next, the column matrix is rotated on its side (by rotating it counter-clockwise) and applied to each of the rows in the 3×3 matrix. The result is exactly the same as if you had calculated the values from the previous two equations. This matrix multiplication—or transform, if you prefer—can be programmed in Java as an object that can be constructed when the values for the 3×3 matrix are supplied. The transform can then be used to transform as many points as is needed. The class that does this is defined in Java as the java.awt.geom.Affine-Transform class.

The term *affine* does not come from someone's name. It comes from the word affinity (in fact, in math the word *affinity* is another word for an affine transform). Strictly speaking, from the mathematical point of view, an affine transform is one that does linear transformations. However, the Java AffineTransform class also has the ability to do scaling, too. The matrix can be set up to do it quite easily, and it certainly doesn't hurt to have a little extra capability thrown in.

The Identity—A Transform That Does Nothing

The identity transform is one that will return, unchanged, any coordinate points given to it. This can be useful at times. It looks like this:

$$\begin{bmatrix} x' \\ y' \\ 1 \end{bmatrix} = \begin{bmatrix} x \\ y \\ 1 \end{bmatrix} \begin{bmatrix} 1 & 0 & 0 \\ 0 & 1 & 0 \\ 0 & 0 & 1 \end{bmatrix}$$

As you can see, it has no values to be added and there is no angle to be taken into consideration. Well, actually, the angle is zero degrees, which has a cosine of 1 and a sine of 0. No rotation and no translation. When you first instantiate an AffineTransform object, it is an identity transform. You will have to do things to it before it will have any effect on coordinates when it is applied.

Translation Moves Coordinates in a Straight Line

Using the matrix form to do a simple nonrotational translation—that is, moving a point in a straight line from one location to another—the matrix takes this form:

$$\begin{bmatrix} x' \\ y' \\ 1 \end{bmatrix} = \begin{bmatrix} x \\ y \\ 1 \end{bmatrix} \begin{bmatrix} 1 & 0 & a \\ 0 & 1 & b \\ 0 & 0 & 1 \end{bmatrix}$$

It is simply the identity matrix with a distance value specified for x and y. Here, the letters a and b represent the distance the point is to be moved, either positive or negative, in the x and y directions. For example, to move a point 12 pixels to the right and 9 pixels down, the matrix would look like this:

$$\begin{bmatrix} x' \\ y' \\ 1 \end{bmatrix} = \begin{bmatrix} x \\ y \\ 1 \end{bmatrix} \begin{bmatrix} 1 & 0 & 12 \\ 0 & 1 & 9 \\ 0 & 0 & 1 \end{bmatrix}$$

Rotation Moves Coordinates in a Circle

To perform a simple rotation of coordinates about the axis, it is necessary to fill in the values of the sine and cosine of the angle at four locations in the matrix. The coordinate system is positive down and to the right, causing positive angles to rotate in a clockwise direction and negative angles to rotate in a counterclockwise direction. A simple rotation transform looks like this:

$$\begin{bmatrix} x' \\ y' \\ 1 \end{bmatrix} = \begin{bmatrix} x \\ y \\ 1 \end{bmatrix} \begin{bmatrix} \cos\phi & -\sin\phi & 0 \\ \sin\phi & \cos\phi & 0 \\ 0 & 0 & 1 \end{bmatrix}$$

For example, if you wished to rotate all points in a clockwise direction around the axis by 30 degrees, the matrix would look like this:

$$\begin{bmatrix} x' \\ y' \\ 1 \end{bmatrix} = \begin{bmatrix} x \\ y \\ 1 \end{bmatrix} \begin{bmatrix} \frac{\sqrt{3}}{2} & -\frac{1}{2} & 0 \\ \frac{1}{2} & \frac{\sqrt{3}}{2} & 0 \\ 0 & 0 & 1 \end{bmatrix}$$

Scaling Changes the Size of the Figure

There is another operation that can be done with the matrix. It is possible to scale the figure up to make it larger and down to make it smaller. This expansion is something like the rotation in that it happens around the origin. That is, a figure is made large by having its coordinates move away from the origin, or made smaller by having its coordinates move toward the origin. The actual distance that a point moves is determined by its distance from the origin—the further away the point is from the origin, the further it will be moved. Scaling values greater than one will make the figure larger, and values less than one will make it smaller. This sample transform will reduce the size of a figure by one half:

$$\begin{bmatrix} x' \\ y' \\ 1 \end{bmatrix} = \begin{bmatrix} x \\ y \\ 1 \end{bmatrix} \begin{bmatrix} 0.5 & 0 & 0 \\ 0 & 0.5 & 0 \\ 0 & 0 & 1 \end{bmatrix}$$

The scaling does not have to be the same along each dimension. This transform will double the size of the figure horizontally and triple it vertically:

$$\begin{bmatrix} x' \\ y' \\ 1 \end{bmatrix} = \begin{bmatrix} x \\ y \\ 1 \end{bmatrix} \begin{bmatrix} 2.0 & 0 & 0 \\ 0 & 3.0 & 0 \\ 0 & 0 & 1 \end{bmatrix}$$

The Inverse Transform

Every transform has an inverse. The inverse of a transform is one that will undo exactly the action of another transform—these two are said to be inverses of one another. It is straightforward to construct an inverse transform—just undo whatever the other transform does. If the original transform rotates a figure 45 degrees, its inverse rotates the figure −45 degrees.

The Java AffineTransform class has a method that can be used to produce its inverse automatically.

Transforming from the World to a Window

To display data on the screen, it is necessary to translate the points from one coordinate system to another—that is, from those of the real world to the pixel world of Java. This can be done with one AffineTransform by setting the values into it.

First to define the variables: We want to convert from the data values of x and y to the pixel values, so they are named this way:

x — The world value of x

x' — The pixel value of x

y — The world value of y

y' — The pixel value of y

The size of the world window, the maximum and minimum values displayable in the window, are defined as being these four values:

xub — The beginning (leftmost) value of x

xue — The ending (rightmost) value of x

yub — The beginning (topmost) value of y

yue — The beginning (bottommost) value of y

You will notice that the origin for the data is at the upper left corner of the window, the same as it is for pixels. This is a matter of convenience in notation. If you wish to have your real world data with its origin in the lower left (which is most common for graphs and such), you just need to reverse the beginning and ending values for yub and yue when you are defining your graph sizes.

The size of the pixel window is defined with these variables:

xpb — The beginning (leftmost) value of x

xpe — The ending (rightmost) value of x

ypb — The beginning (topmost) value of y

ype — The beginning (bottommost) value of y

Under normal circumstance, the values of xpb and ypb will be zero, but you can set them to other values if you wish to move your data frame to another location within the window.

We begin by defining a couple of factors. These are numbers, constants for the duration of the life of the window, that will be used to create the affine transform. There is one for each axis and they are created with these equations:

$$fx = \frac{xpb - xpe}{xub - xue}$$

$$fy = \frac{ypb - ype}{yub - yue}$$

As you can see, these factors are constructed from the ratio of the sizes of our two coordinate systems and can be used as multipliers to scale the size of one to the other. To convert a pair of individual points from the world coordinate system to the pixel coordinate system, these two equations can be used:

$$x' = xpb + fx(x\text{-}xub)$$
$$y' = ypb + fy(y\text{-}yub)$$

Now that we know the relationships required to convert a point to the pixel coordinate system, it is simply a matter of converting this to a form that is appropriate for an affine transform. The affine transform is internally made up of this pair of equations:

$$x' = a * x + b * y + c$$
$$y' = d * x + e + y + d$$

So we simply need to come up with the constant values for a through d that will give us the same effect as the two equations we have derived. We need to determine the values of a, b, and c. Since there is no rotation involved—which would involve y—there is nothing to be done with b, so it becomes zero. The value of a is the constant that is multiplied by x and the value of c is the constant that is added. Reorganizing the equations we derived above, we get this:

$$x' = fx * x + (xpb - fx * xub)$$
$$y' = fy * y + (ypb - fy * yub)$$

We have the constants we need:

$$a = fx$$
$$b = 0$$
$$c = xpb - fx * xub$$
$$d = fy$$
$$e = 0$$
$$d = ypb - fy * yub$$

Finally, using these values as the constructor of an AffineTranform, we get this:

```
at = new AffineTransform(a,b,d,e,c,d);
```

All that is left is to set the AffineTransform into the Graphics2D object with setTransform() and all the world coordinate points that are drawn will be automatically mapped to the pixel coordinates.

Degrees and Radians

There are places in the API where degrees are used to represent angles, and other places where radians are used. There are a pair of convenience methods in java.awt.geom.Arc that can be used to convert from one to the other. They are static methods so there is no need to instantiate the object to be able to use the methods. To convert 45 degrees to radians, just do this:

```
double radians = java.awt.geom.Arc2D.toRadians(45.0);
```

and to convert the same angle from radians to degrees, do this:

```
double degrees = java.awt.geom.Arc2D.toDegrees(Math.PI / 4.0);
```

These are utility methods provided for exactly this purpose, and they're especially handy. This is where math intersects with Java code, which is convenient because the rest of this book is oriented toward code. You've passed the preliminaries!

4

Getting a Grip on Colors and Textures

This chapter talks about color and how it can be manipulated in Java2D. The exercises show you how to create Color objects, attach them to various interface components, and alter them on the fly. You'll also get the goods on the mechanics of various kinds of shading and gradients, which you can use to make your graphics look smoother and less cartoonish.

Color can be confusing. The best way to get a feel for how things look in real life is to actually run these programs and play with them. Also, be sure to test programs that use color on several systems, as implementation of color varies widely from platform to platform, and even among various video cards on the same platform.

Creating a Color Object from RGB Values

A Color object to be used in a display can be constructed with red, green, and blue values. This example shows how to create Color objects from RGB components.

The Code

```java
import java.awt.*;
import java.awt.event.*;
class SelectRGB extends Frame
        implements AdjustmentListener {
    ColorCanvas cc;
    int index = 0;
    int[] rgb = new int[3];
    String[] tagname = new String[3];
    Scrollbar[] scrollbar = new Scrollbar[3];
    TextField[] textfield = new TextField[3];
    public static void main(String arg[]) {
        new SelectRGB();
    }
    SelectRGB() {
        super("SelectRGB");
        addWindowListener(new WindowAdapter() {
            public void windowClosing(WindowEvent e)
                { System.exit(0); } } );
        setLayout(new BorderLayout());
        cc = new ColorCanvas();
        add(BorderLayout.CENTER,cc);
        add(BorderLayout.SOUTH,controlPanel());
        pack();
        show();
    }
    private Panel controlPanel() {
        Panel panel = new Panel();
        panel.setLayout(new BorderLayout());
        panel.add(BorderLayout.NORTH,scrollerPanel("R"));
        panel.add(BorderLayout.CENTER,scrollerPanel("G"));
        panel.add(BorderLayout.SOUTH,scrollerPanel("B"));
        return(panel);
    }
    private Panel scrollerPanel(String tag) {
        Panel panel = new Panel();
        tagname[index] = tag;
        scrollbar[index] = new Scrollbar(Scrollbar.HORIZON-
TAL,0,10,0,264);
        scrollbar[index].addAdjustmentListener(this);
        scrollbar[index].setName(tag);
        panel.setLayout(new BorderLayout());
        panel.add(BorderLayout.WEST,new Label(tag,Label.CENTER));
        panel.add(BorderLayout.CENTER,scrollbar[index]);
        textfield[index] = new TextField("0",3);
        textfield[index].setName(tag);
        textfield[index].setEditable(false);
        panel.add(BorderLayout.EAST,textfield[index]);
```

```
            rgb[index++] = 0;
            return(panel);
    }
    public void adjustmentValueChanged(AdjustmentEvent e) {
        Scrollbar bar = (Scrollbar)e.getAdjustable();
        for(index = 0; index<3; index++) {
            if(bar == scrollbar[index]) {
                rgb[index] = e.getValue();
                String valString = Integer.toString(rgb[index]);
                textfield[index].setText(valString);
                cc.setValues(rgb);
                break;
            }
        }
    }
    class ColorCanvas extends Canvas {
        ColorCanvas() {
            setSize(350,150);
            setBackground(Color.black);
        }
        public void setValues(int[] rgb) {
            setBackground(new Color(rgb[0],rgb[1],rgb[2]));
            repaint();
        }
    }
}
```

The Commentary

This example creates Color objects from the RGB values specified with the slider bars. Each value is a number in the range 0 to 255. The actual values of RGB in a Color object are immutable, so it is necessary to create a new object to change the color.

Depending on some systems, you will notice that the displayed color does not change with every move of a slider. That is, the displayed color will stay the same across a range of values as you move the slider. This is because of the limited number of colors available on your system's *palette* or color vector. The color displayed is the palette's nearest approximation of the specified color.

The actual drawing is done by the ColorCanvas class at the very bottom of the listing. An object of this class is displayed at the top of the Frame window. All it does is display its background color (the default paint() method of the Canvas class simply clears its window and fills it with the background color). The setValues() method receives new RGB values,

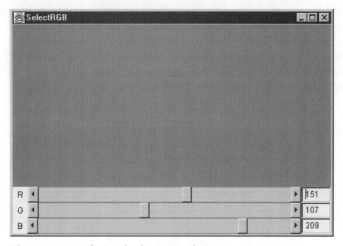

Figure 4.1 Select color by RGB values.

creates a Color object, and sets the background color accordingly. The repaint() method is called so the JVM will call the paint() method, causing the window to be filled with the color.

There are three scroll bars, one for each of the color values. The class SelectRGB implements AdjustmentListener so it can receive the AdjustmentEvent objects from the scroll bars. The method adjustmentValueChanged() is called each time a scroll bar value changes and, in turn, the setValues() method of the ColorCanvas object is called to update the color values and redraw the canvas. The output appears in Figure 4.1.

The Predefined Color Objects

The Java API contains a collection of predefined Color objects. These are convenient for use when you need the basic colors. They are all defined as static members of the Color class and can be addressed directly.

The Code

```
import java.awt.*;
import java.awt.event.*;
class SelectColorName extends Frame
        implements ItemListener {
    private ColorCanvas cc;
```

```
private String[] colorName;
private Color[] color;
private Choice choice;
public static void main(String arg[]) {
    new SelectColorName();
}
SelectColorName() {
    super("SelectColorName");
    addWindowListener(new WindowAdapter() {
        public void windowClosing(WindowEvent e)
            { System.exit(0); } } );
    buildColorArray();
    setLayout(new BorderLayout());
    cc = new ColorCanvas();
    add(BorderLayout.CENTER,cc);
    add(BorderLayout.SOUTH,colorChoice());
    cc.setColor(color[0]);
    pack();
    show();
}
private Choice colorChoice() {
    choice = new Choice();
    for(int i=0; i<colorName.length; i++)
        choice.addItem(colorName[i]);
    choice.addItemListener(this);
    return(choice);
}
public void itemStateChanged(ItemEvent e) {
    int index = choice.getSelectedIndex();
    cc.setColor(color[index]);
}
private void buildColorArray() {
    colorName = new String[13];
    color = new Color[13];
    colorName[0] = "black";
    color[0] = Color.black;
    colorName[1] = "blue";
    color[1] = Color.blue;
    colorName[2] = "cyan";
    color[2] = Color.cyan;
    colorName[3] = "darkGray";
    color[3] = Color.darkGray;
    colorName[4] = "gray";
    color[4] = Color.gray;
    colorName[5] = "green";
    color[5] = Color.green;
    colorName[6] = "lightGray";
    color[6] = Color.lightGray;
    colorName[7] = "magenta";
    color[7] = Color.magenta;
    colorName[8] = "orange";
```

```
                color[8] = Color.orange;
                colorName[9] = "pink";
                color[9] = Color.pink;
                colorName[10] = "red";
                color[10] = Color.red;
                colorName[11] = "white";
                color[11] = Color.white;
                colorName[12] = "yellow";
                color[12] = Color.yellow;
        }
        class ColorCanvas extends Canvas {
            ColorCanvas() {
                setSize(150,150);
            }
            public void setColor(Color color) {
                setBackground(color);
                repaint();
            }
        }
    }
```

The Commentary

The Color objects are all declared static and public, so they can be addressed directly by using the name of the Color class, as in Color.black.

This example is the same as the previous one except in the way the Color objects are derived. This example creates a pair of arrays: one of the Color names and the other of the Color objects. The names are all added to the Choice list and, when the user makes a selection, the Color object that corresponds to the selection is passed to the displayed ColorCanvas object. The ColorCanvas object uses the Color name to define its background color and calls repaint() to make the default paint() method clear the display area to its background color. The output is shown in Figure 4.2.

Using a Graphics Object to Display Colors

This example demonstrates setting the color for a Graphics object and using it to draw on the display.

Figure 4.2   Select color by name.

The Code

```java
import java.awt.*;
import java.awt.event.*;
class ShowColor extends Frame {
    public static void main(String arg[]) {
        new ShowColor();
    }
    ShowColor() {
        super("ShowColor");
        addWindowListener(new WindowAdapter() {
            public void windowClosing(WindowEvent e)
                { System.exit(0); } } );
        setSize(300,300);
        show();
    }
    public void paint(Graphics g) {
        g.setColor(Color.blue);
        g.fillRect(50,100,150,100);
        g.setColor(Color.pink);
        g.fillOval(25,150,100,100);
        g.setColor(Color.orange);
        g.fillOval(25,150,100,100);
        g.setColor(Color.black);
        g.fillRoundRect(75,175,100,50,25,15);
        g.setColor(Color.lightGray);
        g.fillOval(175,130,100,50);
    }
}
```

Figure 4.3 Various shapes in various colors.

The Commentary

This example isn't complicated. It extends the Frame class to get a window to draw into, and causes the paint() method to be called by the JVM whenever the window needs to be drawn, and, in the body of the paint() method, a series of solid shapes are drawn. The setColor() method is used to set the color value of the Graphics object first to one color and then another. Each shape is drawn in a different color. The result is shown in Figure 4.3.

Simple Shading

There are some limited built-in shading methods in the Color class. They can, usually, be used to create a Color object that is slightly darker or lighter than the one you already have. This is intended for use in applications such as making stand-out and sunk-in boxes (like with push-buttons and such in a graphical user interface).

The Code

```
import java.awt.*;
import java.awt.event.*;
```

```
class ShowShading extends Frame {
    public static void main(String arg[]) {
        new ShowShading();
    }
    ShowShading() {
        super("ShowShading");
        addWindowListener(new WindowAdapter() {
            public void windowClosing(WindowEvent e)
                { System.exit(0); } } );
        setSize(250,200);
        show();
    }
    public void paint(Graphics g) {
        Color getDarker = Color.white;
        Color getBrighter = Color.darkGray;
        for(int i=0; i<5; i++) {
            g.setColor(getDarker);
            g.fillRect(i * 50,0,50,100);
            g.setColor(getBrighter);
            g.fillRect(i * 50,100,50,100);
            getDarker = getDarker.darker();
            getBrighter = getBrighter.brighter();
        }
    }
}
```

The Commentary

This example paints a sequence of squares in different colors moving across from left to right. The output is shown in Figure 4.4. The top row is a sequence of squares with the colors getting progressively darker and the bottom row getting progressively lighter. This is done by creating a pair of starting Color objects (one light and one dark) and then calling

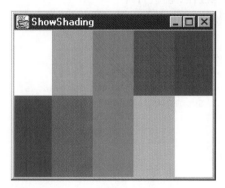

Figure 4.4   Simple shading.

the methods darker() and brighter() to create new a new Color object to be used in drawing the next square.

As you can see, there are only about five steps to go between the extremes of white and black. Almost all colors can be made darker or lighter, but there are exceptions. You cannot make a brighter shade of white. You can make neither a darker nor brighter shade of black.

UNDOING DARKER() WITH BRIGHTER()

If you make a Color object brighter with brighter(), can you expect to undo what you did with darker()? Not necessarily. Due to rounding errors, brighter() and darker() aren't always the inverses of one another.

A Color Gradient

It is possible to set a Graphics2D object to paint by shading one color from another across a distance. That is, it will start with one color at one point and, by slowly changing the color with each pixel painted, it will fade the color from into another. The shading can be defined to fade horizontally, vertically, or any angle in between. This example, and the next few examples, will show how this is done. We start with a very simple example that draws a shaded rectangle.

The Code

```
import java.awt.*;
import java.awt.event.*;
import java.awt.geom.*;
class GradientFill extends Frame {
        public static void main(String arg[]) {
                new GradientFill();
        }
        GradientFill() {
                super("GradientFill");
                addWindowListener(new WindowAdapter() {
                        public void windowClosing(WindowEvent e)
                                { System.exit(0); } } );
                setSize(400,200);
                show();
        }
```

```
public void paint(Graphics g) {
        Graphics2D g2 = (Graphics2D)g;
        GradientPaint gp;
        Rectangle2D rect = new Rectangle2D.Float();
        rect.setRect(50f,50f,300f,100f);
        gp = new GradientPaint(50f,100f,Color.blue,
                        350f,100f,Color.yellow);
        g2.setPaint(gp);
        g2.fill(rect);
    }
}
```

The Commentary

This is a very simple example of gradient shading. The shaded rectangle produced by this example is shown in Figure 4.5. The blue portion of the rectangle, shown in the darker color on the left, slowly fades into the lighter yellow to the right.

The paint() method creates a GradientPaint object. The constructor requires six arguments to define the beginning and ending points of the gradient and the starting and ending colors. The first two arguments are the (x,y) coordinates of the beginning color, which is blue, and the next two arguments are the (x,y) coordinates of the ending color, which is yellow. The setPaint() method is called to tell the Graphics2D object that it is to use the gradient instead of the Color (normally set by setColor()) to do all painting. Once this is done, it is a simple matter of calling any of the graphics methods you like, such as the fill() method used in this example.

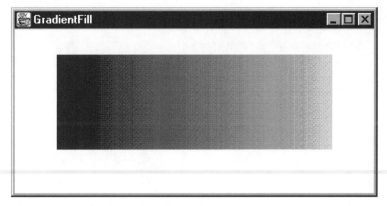

Figure 4.5   A horizontal gradient fill.

The gradient shading is not done pixel by pixel. Rather, it is done with tiling. That is, the GradientPaint object determines the incremental distance—the number of pixels, if you prefer—that can be traversed before any color change will take place. The Graphics2D object, during its painting process, retrieves again and again small rectangular *tiles* of color settings that it uses to fill the entire area. Once all the tiles are set to the specified color, the overall effect is that of a smooth gradient from one color to another.

A Diagonal Color Gradient

This example is the same as the previous one, except that the color gradient is diagonal instead of straight across.

The Code

```
import java.awt.*;
import java.awt.event.*;
import java.awt.geom.*;
class GradientFill2 extends Frame {
    public static void main(String arg[]) {
        new GradientFill2();
    }
    GradientFill2() {
        super("GradientFill2");
        addWindowListener(new WindowAdapter() {
            public void windowClosing(WindowEvent e)
                { System.exit(0); } } );
        setSize(400,400);
        show();
    }
    public void paint(Graphics g) {
        Graphics2D g2 = (Graphics2D)g;
        GradientPaint gp;
        Rectangle2D rect = new Rectangle2D.Float();
        rect.setRect(50f,50f,300f,300f);
        gp = new GradientPaint(50f,50f,Color.blue,350f,350f,Color.yel-
low);
        g2.setPaint(gp);
        g2.fill(rect);
    }
}
```

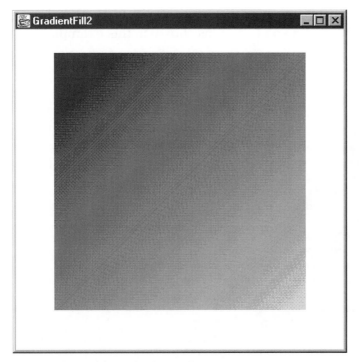

Figure 4.6   A diagonal color gradient.

The Commentary

In this example the points defining the color gradient are at opposite corners of the rectangle—one is the upper left and the other is the lower right.

The rule defining where the gradient occurs is simple enough, but it's hard to explain. The color gradient runs along a line from point A (in the upper left of the rectangle) to point B (in the lower right). Each pixel along that line is shaded between the two colors according the proximity of the pixel to the two end points. Now, make the line very wide—so wide that it takes up the entire window—so all the pixels in the window will be shaded, causing the gradient from one point to another. The output is shown in Figure 4.6.

The Acyclical Color Gradient

A color gradient is defined as occurring on the plane between a pair of points. If there is fill beyond the boundaries of this plane, one of two things can happen. The color that was defined at the end of the gradient can be continued as a solid color, as shown in this example.

The Code

```
import java.awt.*;
import java.awt.event.*;
import java.awt.geom.*;
class AcyclicGradient extends Frame {
    GeneralPath indicator = new GeneralPath();
    public static void main(String arg[]) {
        new AcyclicGradient();
    }
    AcyclicGradient() {
        super("AcyclicGradient");
        addWindowListener(new WindowAdapter() {
            public void windowClosing(WindowEvent e)
                { System.exit(0); } } );
        indicator.moveTo(0f,0f);
        indicator.lineTo(4f,10f);
        indicator.lineTo(-4f,10f);
        indicator.closePath();
        setSize(700,250);
        show();
    }
    public void paint(Graphics g) {
        Graphics2D grect = (Graphics2D)g.create();
        Graphics2D gind = (Graphics2D)g;
        AffineTransform at = new AffineTransform();
        GradientPaint gp;
        Rectangle2D rect = new Rectangle2D.Float(0f,0f,600f,30f);

        // Gradient at full width
        at.setToTranslation(50f,30f);
        grect.setTransform(at);
        gp = new GradientPaint(0f,30f,Color.blue,
                600f,30f,Color.yellow);
        grect.setPaint(gp);
        grect.fill(rect);
        at.setToTranslation(50f,60f);
        gind.setTransform(at);
        gind.fill(indicator);
        at.setToTranslation(650f,60f);
        gind.setTransform(at);
        gind.fill(indicator);

        // Gradient at one-third and two-thirds
        at.setToTranslation(50f,90f);
```

```
        grect.setTransform(at);
        gp = new GradientPaint(200f,90f,Color.blue,
                400f,90f,Color.yellow);
        grect.setPaint(gp);
        grect.fill(rect);
        at.setToTranslation(250f,120f);
        gind.setTransform(at);
        gind.fill(indicator);
        at.setToTranslation(450f,120f);
        gind.setTransform(at);
        gind.fill(indicator);

        // Gradient at two points in the center
        at.setToTranslation(50f,150f);
        grect.setTransform(at);
        gp = new GradientPaint(280f,90f,Color.blue,
                320f,90f,Color.yellow);
        grect.setPaint(gp);
        grect.fill(rect);
        at.setToTranslation(330f,180f);
        gind.setTransform(at);
        gind.fill(indicator);
        at.setToTranslation(370f,180f);
        gind.setTransform(at);
        gind.fill(indicator);
    }
}
```

The Commentary

This example (see Figure 4.7) shows the result of moving the gradient points when the default condition of acyclical gradient is used. The top bar is a rectangle drawn with the gradient points at its extreme left and right ends (as shown by the triangular indicators directly beneath it). The second bar is drawn with the gradient points dividing the bar in thirds, and the bar on the bottom is filled with the gradient points close together at the center.

With the first bar, whether or not the gradient is acyclical doesn't matter because there are no regions filled that are not between the points. The middle bar shows the fact that the fill is acyclic because the filled regions to the left and right of the gradient points are shown as solid colors (blue on the left and yellow on the right) and the color gradient is limited to the area between the two points. The bottom bar is a more extreme version with the gradient limited to a very small range in the center and the rest of the area being filled with solid color.

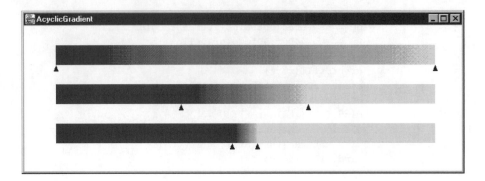

Figure 4.7 An acyclic gradient.

A Cyclical Color Gradient

This example is identical to the previous one, except the gradient is defined as being cyclical.

The Code

The code for this program (on the accompanying CD-ROM as CyclicGradient.java and CyclicGradient.class) is identical to that of the previous example, with the exception of the arguments in this line:

```
gp = new GradientPaint(280f,90f,Color.blue,
              320f,90f,Color.yellow,true);
```

The Commentary

This example is identical to the previous example, except for one thing. The GradientPaint constructor with one extra argument—the Boolean value that determines the cyclical nature of the object—is set to true, causing a cyclical algorithm to be used.

As you can see in Figure 4.8 the bars are drawn with color gradients that extend beyond the defined gradient points. That is, at the gradient points, the gradient reverses itself and cycles back to the original color. This cyclical algorithm results in a gradient fill everywhere, regardless of whether a point is between the two defined gradient points.

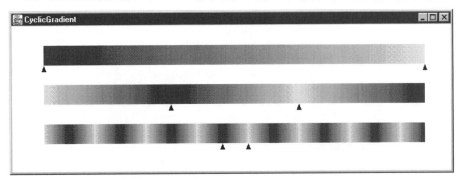

Figure 4.8   A cyclical gradient fill.

Filling with an Image

This is an example of filling an area with a texture. The texture is supplied by a BufferedImage object which, in this example, is constructed from an Image loaded from the disk. A BufferedImage object can be created by line drawing and/or texturing, just the same as any other 2D object.

The Code

```java
import java.awt.*;
import java.awt.event.*;
import java.awt.geom.*;
import java.awt.image.*;
class ImageFill extends Frame {
        Image fillImage;
        Area area;
        public static void main(String arg[]) {
                new ImageFill();
        }
        ImageFill() {
                super("ImageFill");
                addWindowListener(new WindowAdapter() {
                        public void windowClosing(WindowEvent e)
                                { System.exit(0); } } );
                fillImage = getToolkit().getImage("fill.gif");
                MediaTracker mt = new MediaTracker(this);
                mt.addImage(fillImage,1);
                try {
                        mt.waitForAll();
                } catch(Exception e) {
                        System.out.println(e);
                        System.exit(1);
```

```
            }
            area = new Area(new Ellipse2D.Float(50f,50f,200f,200f));
            area.add(new Area(new
Rectangle2D.Float(50f,50f,100f,100f)));
            area.add(new Area(new
Rectangle2D.Float(150f,150f,100f,100f)));
            setSize(300,300);
            show();
        }
        public void paint(Graphics g) {
            Graphics2D g2 = (Graphics2D)g;
            BufferedImage bi = new BufferedImage(36,36,
                        BufferedImage.TYPE_INT_RGB);
            Graphics2D ig = bi.createGraphics();
            ig.drawImage(fillImage,0,0,this);
            Rectangle2D r = new Rectangle2D.Float();
            r.setRect(0f,0f,36f,36f);
            TexturePaint tp = new TexturePaint(bi,r);
            g2.setPaint(tp);
            g2.fill(area);
        }
    }
```

The Commentary

The constructor creates an Image by loading a graphic file into RAM. The graphic is shown in Figure 4.9. The MediaTracker is used to cause the application to wait until the graphic file is completely loaded. Next, the constructor creates an area to be filled. It does this by adding together a pair of rectangles and a circle.

The paint() method creates a BufferedImage object that is the same size as the loaded image, 36×36. A Graphics2D object that can draw to the BufferedImage is used to draw the image into it. A TexturePaint() object, which must be supplied with a rectangle for its internal work area, is constructed and set, by calling setPaint(), into the Graphics2D object used to draw the display. The fill() method then uses the

Figure 4.9   The image used to fill the area.

BufferedImage as the fill area, and tiles it repeatedly in the area. Figure 4.10 shows the textured fill in place.

Figure 4.10   A textured fill into an area.

CHAPTER 5

Positioning and Rotating in Two Dimensions

J ava programs position their graphics on a display, usually a raster screen. Fortunately for programmers, it's easy to think of a raster screen as a two-dimensional coordinate plane. The first thing we learned about when we began to translate mathematical expressions into graphs was the two-dimensional coordinate plane.

In this chapter, you'll learn about placing Java graphics on the display. You'll learn how to put a graphical element in a particular position and find out how to rotate that element into various orientations. The examples here all position an arrow in different ways.

Pay close attention to the examples in this chapter. The same set of positioning procedures can be used to place images and text—something we'll get to soon.

SimpleLine

This is the simplest of the line-drawing graphic programs. It draws seven straight lines to form an arrow. The coordinates of the arrow are in Figure 5.1, and the output from the program is in Figure 5.2.

The Code

```java
import java.awt.*;
import java.awt.event.*;
class SimpleLine extends Frame {
    private static int x[] = { 0, 10, 5, 5, -5, -5, -10, 0 };
    private static int y[] = { -15, 5, 5, 15, 15, 5, 5, -15 };

    public static void main(String arg[]) {
        new SimpleLine();
    }
    SimpleLine() {
        super("SimpleLine");
        enableEvents(AWTEvent.WINDOW_EVENT_MASK);
        setSize(60,90);
        for(int i=0; i<x.length; i++) {
            x[i] += 30;
            y[i] += 45;
        }
        show();
    }
    public void processWindowEvent(WindowEvent event) {
        if(event.getID() == WindowEvent.WINDOW_CLOSING)
            System.exit(0);
    }
    public void paint(Graphics g) {
        for(int i=1; i<x.length; i++)
            g.drawLine(x[i-1],y[i-1],x[i],y[i]);
    }
}
```

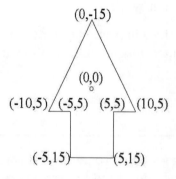

Figure 5.1 The arrow.

Figure 5.2 SimpleLine.

The Commentary

The arrays x and y contain the line segment definitions required to draw the arrow, as initialized right after the class declaration. The coordinates define an arrow that is contained in a rectangle centered on the origin (0,0). The arrow is a total of 20 pixels wide and 30 pixels tall.

The SimpleLine() constructor moves all the points to another location in the window by adding 30 to all x coordinates and 45 to all y coordinates with the following lines of code:

```
for(int i=0; i<x.length; i++) {
    x[i] += 30;
    y[i] += 45;
```

Why is that necessary? Read on....

THE COORDINATE PLANE

The coordinate plane in which SimpleLine (as well as most other programs in this book) draws is a frame—that's the class's entire graphical universe. The origin of the plane—point (0,0)—is at the upper-left corner of the frame, with x coordinates increasing from left to right and y coordinates increasing from top to bottom.

In this particular case, adding 30 to all x coordinates and 45 to all y coordinates puts the arrow where it's visible. If we didn't do this translation, the arrow would be jammed into the upper-left corner where very little of it would be within the frame. Furthermore, had we not done the translation, even the part in the frame wouldn't be visible since the origin of a frame is in the absolute upper-left corner, above the title bar. The arrow would have been outside the frame and behind the title bar.

The paint() method, overloading the method from the superclass, loops through the array and draws a line between each adjacent point in the array, using the drawLine() method.

The call to enableEvents() and the method processWindowEvent() allow the user to use the mouse to close the application.

SimpleLine2

This program illustrates a use of Java2D's AffineTransform class, which you can use to translate a figure from one place to another on a coordinate plane.

SimpleLine2 is very much like SimpleLine—the output is identical, in fact. However, it takes a different approach to getting the job done. This one uses the AffineTransform class to move the arrow from the upper-left corner to the location where it is to be displayed. The values that define the points' coordinates are the same as in SimpleLine except here they are doubles instead of ints (integers), since the AffineTransform class requires doubles.

The Code

```
import java.awt.*;
import java.awt.event.*;
import java.awt.geom.*;
class SimpleLine2 extends Frame {
    private double p[] = {
                0.0,-15.0,
                10.0,5.0,
                5.0,5.0,
                5.0,15.0,
                -5.0,15.0,
                -5.0,5.0,
                -10.0,5.0,
                0.0,-15.0 };
    private AffineTransform at;

    public static void main(String arg[]) {
        new SimpleLine2();
    }
    SimpleLine2() {
        super("Simple Line Drawing");
        enableEvents(AWTEvent.WINDOW_EVENT_MASK);
        setSize(60,90);
        at = new AffineTransform();
        at.setToTranslation(30.0,45.0);
        at.transform(p,0,p,0,8);
        show();
```

```
        }
        public void processWindowEvent(WindowEvent event) {
            if(event.getID() == WindowEvent.WINDOW_CLOSING)
                System.exit(0);
        }
        public void paint(Graphics g) {
            for(int i=3; i<16; i+=2)
                g.drawLine((int)p[i-3],(int)p[i-2],
                    (int)p[i-1],(int)p[i]);
        }
    }
```

The Commentary

The AffineTransform class, here instantiated as at, is used to map points from one location to another. It uses the transform matrix model you learned about in Chapter 3.

In this example, the AffineTransform object is created without arguments. This creates an identity transform—that is, one that will output the same point values that are input to it (effectively moving the figure nowhere). The setToTranslation() method is called to set the transform to one that will move the points:

```
at.setToTranslation(30.0,45.0);
```

In this example, the transform adds 30.0 to the x value and 45.0 to the y value (which is down and to the right), exactly as we did manually in the previous example.

The transform() method then applies the newly altered AffineTransform to the array of points and everything is moved to the new positions. The drawLine() method then draws segments, just as before. Again, the call to enableEvents() and the method processWindowEvent() serve only to allow the user to close the application with the mouse.

As a convenience, the points describing the figure are all kept in a single array. Notice how the paint() method uses the points in the array p[]. Having the whole thing in a single array, with the first and last points being the same, allows the whole figure to be drawn in one simple loop. A line is drawn between the first and second points, then the second and third, then the third and fourth, and so on. The points are in (x,y) pairs in the array. Notice how the index starts at 3 and is increased by two each time through the loop. Each line segment is drawn between $(x1,y1)$ and $(x2,y2)$ where $(x1,y1)$ is found at (p[index-3],p[index-2]) and $(x2,y2)$ is found at (p[index-1],p[index]).

The output of this program looks just like the output of SimpleLine, shown in Figure 5.2.

MoveDownRight

This example alters the paint() method to paint several copies of the arrow in several different locations.

The Code

```
import java.awt.*;
import java.awt.event.*;
import java.awt.geom.*;
class MoveDownRight extends Frame {
    private double p[] = {
                0.0,-15.0,
                10.0,5.0,
                5.0,5.0,
                5.0,15.0,
                -5.0,15.0,
                -5.0,5.0,
                -10.0,5.0,
                0.0,-15.0 };

    public static void main(String arg[]) {
        new MoveDownRight();
    }
    MoveDownRight() {
        super("Move Down Right");
        enableEvents(AWTEvent.WINDOW_EVENT_MASK);
        setSize(110,140);
        show();
    }
    public void processWindowEvent(WindowEvent event) {
        if(event.getID() == WindowEvent.WINDOW_CLOSING)
            System.exit(0);
    }
    public void paint(Graphics g) {
        double pa[] = new double[16];
        AffineTransform at = new AffineTransform();
        at.setToTranslation(30.0,45.0);
        at.transform(p,0,pa,0,8);
        at.setToTranslation(8.0,8.0);
```

```
        for(int k=0; k<5; k++) {
            for(int i=3; i<16; i+=2)
                g.drawLine((int)pa[i-3],(int)pa[i-2],(int)pa[i-
1],(int)pa[i]);
            at.transform(pa,0,pa,0,8);
        }
    }
}
```

The Commentary

This class looks much like SimpleLine2, with some key alterations to the paint() method that overrides that of the superclass.

This class's paint() method creates an AffineTransform, at, and an empty array of doubles, pa. Immediately after at is set to scoot everything over 30.0 and down 45.0, its transform() method is used to translate the points defined in p into new points, stored in pa.

The transform then gets reset with the following line:

```
at.setToTranslation(8..0,8.0);
```

In this incarnation, at is used to move the points to generate four of the five copies of the arrow. In the loop, the arrow is drawn once, then at is applied to move the points 8 pixels to the right and 8 pixels down. The loop repeats this process until five copies of the arrow have been painted in the frame. The original data is left unmodified so the paint() method can be called as many times as necessary to redraw the window.

The call to enableEvents() and the method processWindowEvent() allow the user to close the application with the mouse.

The results of MoveDownRight appear in Figure 5.3.

Figure 5.3   Five copies of the arrow.

Tilt

Tilt displays two copies of the arrow. One is shown straight up and the other is tilted at 22.5 degrees (π / 8 radians). This example demonstrates how to use an AffineTransform to rotate an image and how to combine multiple transform operations into a single operation.

The Code

```java
import java.awt.*;
import java.awt.event.*;
import java.awt.geom.*;
class Tilt extends Frame {
    private double p[] = {
                0.0,-15.0,
                10.0,5.0,
                5.0,5.0,
                5.0,15.0,
                -5.0,15.0,
                -5.0,5.0,
                -10.0,5.0,
                0.0,-15.0 };

    public static void main(String arg[]) {
        new Tilt();
    }
    Tilt() {
        super("Tilt");
        enableEvents(AWTEvent.WINDOW_EVENT_MASK);
        setSize(60,90);
        show();
    }
    public void processWindowEvent(WindowEvent event) {
        if(event.getID() == WindowEvent.WINDOW_CLOSING)
            System.exit(0);
    }
    public void paint(Graphics g) {
        double pa[] = new double[16];
        AffineTransform at = new AffineTransform();
        at.setToTranslation(50.0,45.0);
        at.transform(p,0,pa,0,8);
        for(int i=3; i<16; i+=2)
            g.drawLine((int)pa[i-3],(int)pa[i-2],
                    (int)pa[i-1],(int)pa[i]);
```

```
                  at.setToRotation(Math.PI / 8.0);
                  at.translate(50.0,45.0);
                  at.transform(p,0,pa,0,8);
                  for(int i=3;  i<16;  i+=2)
                        g.drawLine((int)pa[i-3],(int)pa[i-2],
                            (int)pa[i-1],(int)pa[i]);
            }
      }
```

The Commentary

Again, all the action takes place in the paint() method. As before, an empty array of doubles, pa, and a new AffineTransform object, at, get created. The shift assigned to at is a little different here—50.0 pixels across and 45.0 pixels down—but the mechanism is identical to the ones you used in earlier classes. The method then uses at to fill pa with translated versions of the points in p, and proceeds to draw the segments in pa with a for loop.

Note that p contains the same values it has always contained. This fact is important to what happens next.

The at.setToRotation(π / 8.0) method then defines at as a rotation of 22.5 degrees clockwise (π / 8 radians), or a sixteenth of a turn.

PAY ATTENTION TO "SET"

Any AffineTransform method that begins with "set" clears all other properties of the AffineTransform. The method setToRotation() in this class clears all other behaviors of at, namely its inherent ability to shift points 50.0 pixels across and 45.0 pixels down. The line

```
at.translate(50.0,45.0);
```

puts that shift back into at. Since we use the translate() method, not setTranslation, the rotation capability remains intact.

Clearly, this is inefficient program design. We wrote Tilt this way to illustrate this concept and for no other reason.

After at is defined to shift points down, to the right, and with a rotation, the points in p get transformed with at and stored in pa. Another loop paints the new arrow segments.

The results appear in Figure 5.4.

Figure 5.4 The Tilted arrow.

THE SEQUENCE OF EVENTS

In Tilt, the transform was instructed to do the rotation first and the translation was added later. But, by the results, it is obvious that the translation actually occurred first and the rotation occurred second. If the rotation had occurred first, the arrow would have spun about its center (at the origin), and then the spun arrow would have been translated to the same coordinates as the upright arrow.

For the arrow to wind up where it did, the rotation must have occurred after the arrow was moved away from the origin.

Take a look at the next exercise for a way around this sequence.

Spin

This example is very much like the previous one. Here, however, the arrow gets rotated around its own center, rather than around the frame's origin.

The Code

```
import java.awt.*;
import java.awt.event.*;
import java.awt.geom.*;
class Spin extends Frame {
    private double p[] = {
            0.0,-15.0,
            10.0,5.0,
            5.0,5.0,
            5.0,15.0,
            -5.0,15.0,
            -5.0,5.0,
            -10.0,5.0,
            0.0,-15.0 };
```

```java
public static void main(String arg[]) {
    new Spin();
}
Spin() {
    super("Spin");
    enableEvents(AWTEvent.WINDOW_EVENT_MASK);
    setSize(60,90);
    show();
}
public void processWindowEvent(WindowEvent event) {
    if(event.getID() == WindowEvent.WINDOW_CLOSING)
        System.exit(0);
}
public void paint(Graphics g) {
    double pa[] = new double[16];
    AffineTransform at = new AffineTransform();
    at.setToTranslation(50.0,60.0);
    at.transform(p,0,pa,0,8);
    for(int i=3; i<16; i+=2)
        g.drawLine((int)pa[i-3],(int)pa[i-2],
            (int)pa[i-1],(int)pa[i]);
    at.rotate(Math.PI / 4.0);
    at.transform(p,0,pa,0,8);
    for(int i=3; i<16; i+=2)
        g.drawLine((int)pa[i-3],(int)pa[i-2],
            (int)pa[i-1],(int)pa[i]);
}
}
```

The Commentary

Once more, all the action is found in the paint() method. First, pa gets populated with the contents of p, except shifted down and to the right with the aid of at. Then, the first for loop paints the segments that make up the arrow.

After the first copy of the arrow is painted, a rotation is added to at—$\pi/4$, specifically. Then, the transform() method takes the contents of p, translates them (including the rotation), and puts the results into pa (displacing the points that defined the arrow that was painted first). Another for loop then paints the newly defined segments that make up the spun arrow.

The only difference between this class and Tilt is that the arrow is rotated around its center instead of being rotated around the origin of the frame, then moved back to the middle of the frame.

The output is shown in Figure 5.5.

Figure 5.5   The spun arrow.

Circularity

This program demonstrates the rotation of a collection of points about the origin.

The Code

```java
import java.awt.*;
import java.awt.event.*;
import java.awt.geom.*;
class Circularity extends Frame {
    private double p[] = {
                0.0,-15.0,
                10.0,5.0,
                5.0,5.0,
                5.0,15.0,
                -5.0,15.0,
                -5.0,5.0,
                -10.0,5.0,
                0.0,-15.0 };

    public static void main(String arg[]) {
        new Circularity();
    }
    Circularity() {
        super("Circularity");
        enableEvents(AWTEvent.WINDOW_EVENT_MASK);
        setSize(200,200);
        show();
    }
    public void processWindowEvent(WindowEvent event) {
        if(event.getID() == WindowEvent.WINDOW_CLOSING)
            System.exit(0);
    }
    public void paint(Graphics g) {
        double pa[] = new double[16];
        AffineTransform at = new AffineTransform();
        at.setToTranslation(0.0,150.0);
```

```
at.rotate(Math.PI / 2.0);
at.transform(p,0,pa,0,8);
at.setToRotation(-(Math.PI / 8.0));
for(int k=0; k<5; k++) {
    for(int i=3; i<16; i+=2)
        g.drawLine((int)pa[i-3],(int)pa[i-2],
            (int)pa[i-1],(int)pa[i]);
    at.transform(pa,0,pa,0,8);
}
}
}
```

The Commentary

The paint() method does its work in two stages. First, at is set to translate the arrow's points 150 pixels straight down from the origin. Then, at is set to turn the arrow (actually, to reposition its component points, but the effect is to turn the arrow) by π / 2, or a quarter-turn clockwise. The array pa then gets populated with the points in p, after they're run through at. These initial values in pa generate the horizontal arrow pointing to the right, the first one painted in the loop—but not before at is altered. Using the setToRotation() method (which, as you'll recall, wipes out the downward shift previously stored in at), the transform is set to rotate the arrow −π / 8 radians, or a sixteenth turn counterclockwise.

In the second stage of the method's operation, the for loop generates the first arrow, as noted earlier. Then, in the loop, the points in pa get run through at, which converts them into a representation of an arrow turned counterclockwise a sixteenth turn. The loop repeats the process of painting the arrow, then turning it until five arrows have been generated.

The results appear in Figure 5.6. Note that the center of the circling arrows here is the origin—the upper-left corner of the frame. You'll learn how to center the circle on another point in the next exercise.

Circularity2

There are times when you want to circulate around some point other than the origin, like the output shown in Figure 5.7. This program shows how to accomplish that.

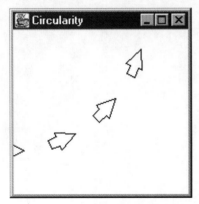

Figure 5.6 Circulating the arrow around the origin.

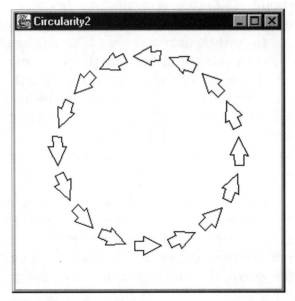

Figure 5.7 Rotation around a point other than the origin.

The Code

```
import java.awt.*;
import java.awt.event.*;
import java.awt.geom.*;
```

```
class Circularity2 extends Frame {
    private double p[] = {
                0.0,-15.0,
                10.0,5.0,
                5.0,5.0,
                5.0,15.0,
                -5.0,15.0,
                -5.0,5.0,
                -10.0,5.0,
                0.0,-15.0 };

    public static void main(String arg[]) {
        new Circularity2();
    }
    Circularity2() {
        super("Circularity2");
        enableEvents(AWTEvent.WINDOW_EVENT_MASK);
        setSize(300,300);
        show();
    }
    public void processWindowEvent(WindowEvent event) {
        if(event.getID() == WindowEvent.WINDOW_CLOSING)
            System.exit(0);
    }
    public void paint(Graphics g) {
        double pa[] = new double[16];
        AffineTransform at = new AffineTransform();
        at.setToTranslation(150.0,250.0);
        at.rotate(Math.PI / 2.0);
        at.transform(p,0,pa,0,8);
        at.setToRotation(-(Math.PI / 8.0),150.0,150.0);
        for(int k=0; k<16; k++) {
            for(int i=3; i<16; i+=2)
                g.drawLine((int)pa[i-3],(int)pa[i-2],(int)pa[i-
1],(int)pa[i]);
            at.transform(pa,0,pa,0,8);
        }
    }
}
```

The Commentary

As you saw in the previous examples, things normally rotate around the
origin. However, if you add a couple of arguments to either rotate() or
setToRotation(), you can specify another center for the rotation. Circu-
larity2 rotates the arrow around the center of a square window.

This program translates the points of the arrow 250 pixels to the right and 150 pixels down, relative to the origin. Then, the arrow is turned to point to the right. In a for loop, it's painted, turned a sixteenth turn counterclockwise and painted again, until 16 arrows have been generated.

The key difference between this program and the previous class, Circularity, is the following line:

```
at.setToRotation(-(Math.PI / 8.0),150.0,150.0);
```

Note that the frame is 300 pixels square (defined in the setSize() statement). Therefore, 150.0,150.0) is the exact center of the frame. That's the center of rotation used by at in this program. That method call tells at to use (150.0,150.0) as the center of rotation.

CircularPlacement

Here we rotate the arrow about a center point, but don't turn the arrow itself. To do this, it is necessary to apply the rotation only to the location of the object, not all the points of the object. Once the location of the object has been determined, this point is used as a translation on the points defining the object.

The Code

```java
import java.awt.*;
import java.awt.event.*;
import java.awt.geom.*;
class CircularPlacement extends Frame {
    private double p[] = {
                0.0,-15.0,
                10.0,5.0,
                5.0,5.0,
                5.0,15.0,
                -5.0,15.0,
                -5.0,5.0,
                -10.0,5.0,
                0.0,-15.0 };

    public static void main(String arg[]) {
        new CircularPlacement();
    }
    CircularPlacement() {
        super("CircularPlacement");
```

```
          enableEvents(AWTEvent.WINDOW_EVENT_MASK);
          setSize(300,300);
          show();
    }
    public void processWindowEvent(WindowEvent event) {
          if(event.getID() == WindowEvent.WINDOW_CLOSING)
              System.exit(0);
    }
    public void paint(Graphics g) {
          double pa[] = new double[16];
          double pt[] = { 150.0, 250.0 };
          AffineTransform at = new AffineTransform();
          AffineTransform atPoint = new AffineTransform();
          atPoint.setToRotation(-(Math.PI / 8.0),150.0,150.0);
          for(int k=0; k<16; k++) {
              at.setToTranslation(pt[0],pt[1]);
              at.transform(p,0,pa,0,8);
              for(int i=3; i<16; i+=2)
                  g.drawLine((int)pa[i-3],(int)pa[i-2],
                      (int)pa[i-1],(int)pa[i]);
              atPoint.transform(pt,0,pt,0,1);
          }
    }
}
```

The Commentary

The paint() method uses two AffineTransform objects, at and atPoint. There's also an array of doubles (pa) that contains the points that define the arrow, and a two-element array of doubles (pt) that defines the point where the arrow is to be painted. Before the loops start looping, things look like this:

- The point contained in pt is (150.0,250.0)
- atPoint is set to rotate points $-\pi/8$ radians, or a sixteenth turn counterclockwise, around point (150.0,150.0), the center of the frame

Then, the loops begin. First, at is set to translate points so that, when painted, they look as if the origin is at the point contained in pt. Then, at translates the contents of p into pa. A nested loop paints the seven segments of the arrow. Finally, atPoint alters the point in pt (rotating it around (150.0,150.0) by a sixteenth turn counterclockwise, you'll recall) and the loop repeats until all 16 arrows have been painted.

The output is shown in Figure 5.8.

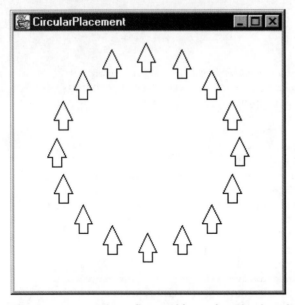

Figure 5.8 Rotating a figure without changing its orientation.

ScaleUp

This will resize the arrow. This program draws several versions of the arrow, each slightly larger than the previous one.

The Code

```
import java.awt.*;
import java.awt.event.*;
import java.awt.geom.*;
class ScaleUp extends Frame {
    private double p[] = {
              0.0,-15.0,
              10.0,5.0,
              5.0,5.0,
              5.0,15.0,
              -5.0,15.0,
              -5.0,5.0,
              -10.0,5.0,
              0.0,-15.0 };

    public static void main(String arg[]) {
```

```
            new ScaleUp();
    }
    ScaleUp() {
        super("ScaleUp");
        enableEvents(AWTEvent.WINDOW_EVENT_MASK);
        setSize(200,200);
        show();
    }
    public void processWindowEvent(WindowEvent event) {
        if(event.getID() == WindowEvent.WINDOW_CLOSING)
            System.exit(0);
    }
    public void paint(Graphics g) {
        double pa[] = new double[16];
        AffineTransform at = new AffineTransform();
        at.setToTranslation(50.0,50.0);
        at.transform(p,0,pa,0,8);
        at.setToScale(1.1,1.1);
        for(int k=0; k<10; k++) {
            for(int i=3; i<16; i+=2)
                g.drawLine((int)pa[i-3],(int)pa[i-2],
                            (int)pa[i-1],(int)pa[i]);
            at.transform(pa,0,pa,0,8);
        }
    }
}
```

The Commentary

There's only one affine transform in this class, at. It's first used to scoot the points that define the arrow 50 pixels down and right from the origin, putting the translated points in the array pa.

After that initial procedure, at is reset with this statement:

```
at.setToScale(1.1,1.1);
```

That line resets at so it does nothing but make a figure 110 percent of its original size (put another way, it multiplies the figure's size by 1.1).

The loop paints the segments of the arrow contained in pa, then runs pa through at. The loop repeats until it has drawn 10 copies of the arrow, each 10 percent bigger than the previous one.

You will notice in Figure 5.9 that the position of the arrow changes with each scaling, also. This is because the part of the information that included the array of points is the offset of the center of the drawing from

Figure 5.9   Expanding the size of a drawing.

the origin of the window, and this distance information also gets scaled, causing the arrow to move farther away from the origin with each scale transformation.

ScaleUp2

This is an example of scaling the size of a drawing independently of its position.

The Code

```
import java.awt.*;
import java.awt.event.*;
import java.awt.geom.*;
class ScaleUp2 extends Frame {
    private double p[] = {
                0.0,-15.0,
                10.0,5.0,
                5.0,5.0,
                5.0,15.0,
                -5.0,15.0,
                -5.0,5.0,
                -10.0,5.0,
                0.0,-15.0 };

    public static void main(String arg[]) {
        new ScaleUp2();
    }
    ScaleUp2() {
```

```
        super("ScaleUp2");
        enableEvents(AWTEvent.WINDOW_EVENT_MASK);
        setSize(400,150);
        show();
    }
    public void processWindowEvent(WindowEvent event) {
        if(event.getID() == WindowEvent.WINDOW_CLOSING)
            System.exit(0);
    }
    public void paint(Graphics g) {
        double pa[] = new double[16];
        AffineTransform at = new AffineTransform();
        double x = 40.0;
        double y = 75.0;
        double scale = 1.0;
        for(int k=0; k<15; k++) {
            at.setToTranslation(x,y);
            at.scale(scale,scale);
            at.transform(p,0,pa,0,8);
            for(int i=3; i<16; i+=2)
                g.drawLine((int)pa[i-3],(int)pa[i-2],
                           (int)pa[i-1],(int)pa[i]);
            x += 20.0;
            scale += 0.1;
        }
    }
}
```

The Commentary

This program gives you the ability to control scaling and position independently of one another. The x and y components of the point used in the affine transform are stored in separate variables, as is the scale factor.

In the loop, at is set to alter things to look as if (x,y) were the origin. It's then also set to scale things up by the percentage contained in scale. A nested loop paints the seven segments of the arrow; then x is increased by 20.0 and scale is upped by 0.1 before the loop repeats. These alterations to x and scale guarantee that the next instance of the arrow will be 10 percent larger and 20.0 pixels to the right of the previous instance.

This is one way to handle several figures that you need to move about independently. You can have them all defined at the origin, do any work you need to do with them there, and then use affine transforms move each one to the location where it should be drawn.

The output of this program appears in Figure 5.10.

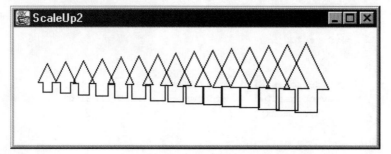

Figure 5.10   Controlling size and position independently.

ScaleDownTurn

To wrap things up, here is an example that does a few things at once. This program displays 15 arrows horizontally across the window—each one is scaled and rotated differently than the one on its left. In turn, each one gets smaller and is rotated through a larger angle.

The Code

```
import java.awt.*;
import java.awt.event.*;
import java.awt.geom.*;
class ScaleDownTurn extends Frame {
    private double p[] = {
            0.0,-15.0,
            10.0,5.0,
            5.0,5.0,
            5.0,15.0,
            -5.0,15.0,
            -5.0,5.0,
            -10.0,5.0,
            0.0,-15.0 };

    public static void main(String arg[]) {
        new ScaleDownTurn();
    }
    ScaleDownTurn() {
        super("ScaleDownTurn");
        enableEvents(AWTEvent.WINDOW_EVENT_MASK);
        setSize(400,150);
        show();
    }
    public void processWindowEvent(WindowEvent event) {
```

```
                    if(event.getID() == WindowEvent.WINDOW_CLOSING)
                        System.exit(0);
            }
        public void paint(Graphics g) {
                double pa[] = new double[16];
                AffineTransform at = new AffineTransform();
                double y = 75.0;
                double x = 40.0;
                double scale = 1.0;
                double rotate = 0.0;
                for(int k=0; k<15; k++) {
                    at.setToTranslation(x,y);
                    at.scale(scale,scale);
                    at.rotate(rotate);
                    at.transform(p,0,pa,0,8);
                    for(int i=3; i<16; i+=2)
                        g.drawLine((int)pa[i-3],(int)pa[i-2],
                                    (int)pa[i-1],(int)pa[i]);
                    x += 20.0;
                    scale *= 0.9;
                    rotate += Math.PI / 8.0;
                }
            }
        }
    }
```

The Commentary

This program includes independent variables for x, y, scale factor, and rotation.

In the loop, the program attaches the various altering variables to at, then applies at to the contents of p as they're moved into pa. A nested loop then paints the arrow's segments, and three of the altering variables are, ahem, altered. This way, you get a line of 16 arrows, in which the arrows get smaller from right to left, each arrow turned a sixteenth turn counterclockwise relative to the one before it.

The output is shown in Figure 5.11.

ScaleDownTurn2

Up until now the transformations have been performed by reading from one array of points and writing the transformed points to another array. This can be quite handy if you have a complicated drawing composed of several parts and you need to transform each one separately. But it has its

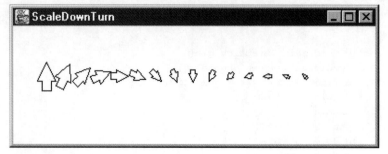

Figure 5.11   Srinking and rotating.

drawbacks. For one thing, you can't transform anything for which you do not have the coordinate points—for example, fonts or images from a file.

This example does the same the previous one does, but the transformation is performed automatically at the time it is drawn. (See Figure 5.12.)

The Code

```
import java.awt.*;
import java.awt.event.*;
import java.awt.geom.*;
class ScaleDownTurn2 extends Frame {
    private double p[] = {
                0.0,-15.0,
                10.0,5.0,
                5.0,5.0,
                5.0,15.0,
                -5.0,15.0,
                -5.0,5.0,
                -10.0,5.0,
                0.0,-15.0 };

    public static void main(String arg[]) {
        new ScaleDownTurn2();
    }
    ScaleDownTurn2() {
        super("ScaleDownTurn2");
        enableEvents(AWTEvent.WINDOW_EVENT_MASK);
        setSize(400,150);
        show();
    }
    public void processWindowEvent(WindowEvent event) {
        if(event.getID() == WindowEvent.WINDOW_CLOSING)
            System.exit(0);
    }
```

```
public void paint(Graphics g) {
    Graphics2D g2 = (Graphics2D)g;
    AffineTransform at = new AffineTransform();
    double y = 75.0;
    double x = 40.0;
    double scale = 1.0;
    double rotate = 0.0;
    for(int k=0; k<15; k++) {
        at.setToTranslation(x,y);
        at.scale(scale,scale);
        at.rotate(rotate);
        g2.setTransform(at);
        for(int i=3; i<16; i+=2)
            g2.drawLine((int)p[i-3],(int)p[i-2],
                        (int)p[i-1],(int)p[i]);
        x += 20.0;
        scale *= 0.9;
        rotate += Math.PI / 8.0;
    }
}
}
```

The Commentary

Just as in the previous example, this program includes independent variables for x, y, scale factor and rotation. In fact, the only differences between this program and the previous one is that a Graphics2D object is used to both transform and draw the figure.

The paint() method expects a Graphics object, and it is happy with what it gets. However, what it really gets is a Graphics2D object, which—because Graphics is a superclass of Graphics2D—can be used as if it were a Graphics object. To be able to access the Graphics2D methods, it is necessary to cast it, telling the compiler that you know the truth.

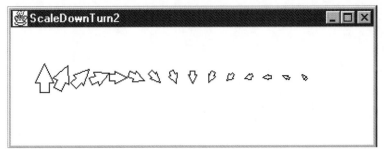

Figure 5.12 Transforming inside Graphics2D.

The execution loop, doing the drawing, works just like the previous example, except the points are not transformed into another array. Instead, the AffineTransform object is attached to the Graphics2D object through the setTransform() method. This transform can be set again and again for a Graphics2D object—to set the transform, it simply replaces the previous one. Notice that although the same AffineTransform object is used every time, it is still necessary to set it because Graphics2D keeps a copy, not the original.

CHAPTER 6

Line Drawing

T his chapter is all about drawing lines. In these pages, you'll learn about the various modifications you can make to lines and shapes that are defined and rendered with the BasicStroke object.

The BasicStroke object allows you to define how lines terminate (with either a squared-off end or a rounded end), how lines join (whether points are snipped off or not), and how wide lines are. In these examples, you'll find out how to add all those adornments to your lines. Further, you'll find out how to make dashed lines—and not just dashed lines in which transparent and opaque segments of equal length alternate, either. You'll find out how to make irregular dashed lines that can be made to fit your specific needs.

The Basic Line Drawings

This class shows how to draw the four line-drawn shapes that are used in the rest of this chapter's examples—a square, a triangle, a circle, and a sort of asterisk comprising a series of lines with a common center point—all with plain, solid lines. The point of this exercise is to clarify how to draw the basic shapes so we can focus on different line styles in upcoming examples.

The Code

```
import java.awt.*;
import java.awt.geom.*;
class LineDrawings {
    static Shape shapeArray[];
    static {
        shapeArray = new Shape[7];
        shapeArray[0] = new Rectangle2D.Float(50f,50f,200f,200f);
        shapeArray[1] = new Ellipse2D.Float(50f,300f,200f,200f);
        GeneralPath triangle = new GeneralPath();
        triangle.moveTo(300f,50f);
        triangle.lineTo(300f,250f);
        triangle.lineTo(500f,250f);
        triangle.closePath();
        shapeArray[2] = (Shape)triangle;
        shapeArray[3] = new Line2D.Float(300f,400f,500f,400f);
        shapeArray[4] = new Line2D.Float(300f,300f,500f,500f);
        shapeArray[5] = new Line2D.Float(400f,300f,400f,500f);
        shapeArray[6] = new Line2D.Float(500f,300f,300f,500f);
    }
    static public Shape[] getShapeArray() {
        return(shapeArray);
    }
}
```

The Commentary

Wait, you say! There are only four shapes, and yet you have created an array containing seven elements!

Yes, we have. The trick is that the four lines that make up the asterisk are separate entries in the array, so shapeArray holds the square, the triangle, the circle, and the four lines of the star—seven elements in all. Here's how it breaks down:

- The square, shapeArray[0], created as a Rectangle2D object
- The circle, shapeArray[1], created as an Ellipse2D object
- The triangle, shapeArray[2], created as a GeneralPath object and defined by the moveTo(), lineTo(), and closePath() statements
- The four asterisk parts, shapeArray[3] through shapeArray[7], created as Line2D objects

Every member of the class is static. The array is constructed using a static initializer and is accessed through getShapeArray(). All the remaining examples in this chapter employ that method.

Note that this class doesn't generate any output—it's just referred to by other classes that *do* generate output.

The Default Stroke

This example draws the shapes with LineDrawings objects set to use the default Stroke object, which, by default, draws lines exactly one pixel thick.

The Code

```
import java.awt.*;
import java.awt.event.*;
import java.awt.geom.*;
class DefaultStroke extends Frame {
    Shape shapeArray[];
    public static void main(String arg[]) {
        new DefaultStroke();
    }
    DefaultStroke() {
        super("DefaultStroke");
        addWindowListener(new WindowAdapter() {
            public void windowClosing(WindowEvent e)
                { System.exit(0); } } );
        setSize(550,550);
        shapeArray = LineDrawings.getShapeArray();
        show();
    }
    public void paint(Graphics g) {
        Graphics2D g2 = (Graphics2D)g;
        for(int i=0; i<shapeArray.length; i++)
            g2.draw(shapeArray[i]);
    }
}
```

The Commentary

This application loads the array of shapes defined in LineDrawings, which you learned about in the previous example, into shapeArray. The paint() method then loops through the shapes in shapeArray, rendering them all with the Graphics2D.draw() method. Graphics2D, by default, uses the BasicStroke line style, which is 1.0 pixels wide, has a

CAP_SQUARE end cap, a JOIN_MITER miter, a miter limit of 10.0, and no dashing. Figure 6.1 shows the output of DefaultStroke.class.

Wide Lines Rounded Off

This example draws the seven elements of the shape array with broad lines that have their corners rounded off.

The Code

```
import java.awt.*;
import java.awt.event.*;
import java.awt.geom.*;
class WideRounded extends Frame {
    Shape shapeArray[];
    public static void main(String arg[]) {
        new WideRounded();
    }
    WideRounded() {
        super("WideRounded");
        addWindowListener(new WindowAdapter() {
            public void windowClosing(WindowEvent e)
                { System.exit(0); } } );
        setSize(550,550);
        shapeArray = LineDrawings.getShapeArray();
        show();
    }
    public void paint(Graphics g) {
        Graphics2D g2 = (Graphics2D)g;
        BasicStroke bs = new BasicStroke(20f,BasicStroke.CAP_ROUND,
                BasicStroke.JOIN_ROUND);
        g2.setStroke(bs);
        for(int i=0; i<shapeArray.length; i++)
            g2.draw(shapeArray[i]);
    }
}
```

The Commentary

There are two particularly interesting lines of code in this program. The first is as follows:

```
BasicStroke  bs  =  new  BasicStroke(20f,BasicStroke.CAP_ROUND,
BasicStroke.JOIN_ROUND);
```

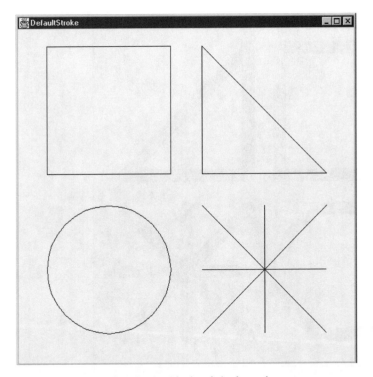

Figure 6.1 Line drawings with the default stroke.

This line creates a BasicStroke object—bs—and sets it to define a stroke of 20.0 pixels in width. It also attaches an end cap attribute—BasicStroke .CAP_ROUND—that dictates that the ends of lines should be rounded. Further, that statement defines a join attribute—BasicStroke.JOIN_ROUND— that mandates curved outside edges on intersecting lines.

The next interesting line of code is as follows:

```
g2.setStroke(bs);
```

That statement attaches the attributes of bs to g2, which ultimately is used to draw the seven elements of shapeArray. The output appears in Figure 6.2.

The Corners Are Mitered and the Ends Are Squared

In this example, the joined lines are mitered and free ends of lines are tapered to a point.

Figure 6.2   Rounded corners and rounded line endings.

The Code

```
import java.awt.*;
import java.awt.event.*;
import java.awt.geom.*;
class WideMiterSquare extends Frame {
    Shape shapeArray[];
    public static void main(String arg[]) {
        new WideMiterSquare();
    }
    WideMiterSquare() {
        super("WideMiterSquare");
        addWindowListener(new WindowAdapter() {
            public void windowClosing(WindowEvent e)
                { System.exit(0); } } );
        setSize(550,550);
        shapeArray = LineDrawings.getShapeArray();
        show();
    }
    public void paint(Graphics g) {
        Graphics2D g2 = (Graphics2D)g;
```

```
        BasicStroke bs = new BasicStroke(20f,BasicStroke.CAP_SQUARE,
                BasicStroke.JOIN_MITER);
        g2.setStroke(bs);
        for(int i=0; i<shapeArray.length; i++)
            g2.draw(shapeArray[i]);
    }
}
```

The Commentary

The key line in this program looks much like the key line in the previous program:

```
BasicStroke  bs  =  new  BasicStroke(20f,BasicStroke.CAP_SQUARE,
BasicStroke.JOIN_MITER);
```

Here, the cap style is set to CAP_SQUARE and the join style is set to JOIN_MITER. The results of this code appear in Figure 6.3.

Figure 6.3 Mitered joins and capped ends.

Wide Lines with Bevelled Corners and Butted Line Endings

In this program, the ends of the lines are simply squared off. Where lines join, the joints are beveled rather than left pointed.

The Code

```
import java.awt.*;
import java.awt.event.*;
import java.awt.geom.*;
class WideBevelButt extends Frame {
    Shape shapeArray[];
    public static void main(String arg[]) {
        new WideBevelButt();
    }
    WideBevelButt() {
        super("WideBevelButt");
        addWindowListener(new WindowAdapter() {
            public void windowClosing(WindowEvent e)
                { System.exit(0); } } );
        setSize(550,550);
        shapeArray = LineDrawings.getShapeArray();
        show();
    }
    public void paint(Graphics g) {
        Graphics2D g2 = (Graphics2D)g;
        BasicStroke bs = new BasicStroke(20f,BasicStroke.CAP_BUTT,
                BasicStroke.JOIN_BEVEL);
        g2.setStroke(bs);
        for(int i=0; i<shapeArray.length; i++)
            g2.draw(shapeArray[i]);
    }
}
```

The Commentary

The key, once again, is the following line:

```
BasicStroke  bs  =  new  BasicStroke(20f,BasicStroke.CAP_BUTT,
BasicStroke.JOIN_BEVEL);
```

The attribute BasicStroke.CAP_BUTT defines the free line ends as squared off, and BasicStroke.JOIN_BEVEL sets the join style to bevel.

Figure 6.4 Bevelled corners and flat-butted lines.

The ends of the lines, as demonstrated by the figure in the lower right, are snipped off flat. Take a look at Figure 6.4 to see what we're talking about.

Dashed Lines

It's possible to render lines as a series of dashes, rather than as solid strokes. This example shows how to set up a dash list to draw a dashed line.

The Code

```
import java.awt.*;
import java.awt.event.*;
import java.awt.geom.*;
class DashLines extends Frame {
    float dashPattern1[] = {40f,40f};
    float dashPattern2[] = {40f,20f};
    float dashPattern3[] = {40f,30f,20f,10f};
```

```
public static void main(String arg[]) {
    new DashLines();
}
DashLines() {
    super("DashLines");
    addWindowListener(new WindowAdapter() {
        public void windowClosing(WindowEvent e)
            { System.exit(0); } } );
    setSize(500,250);
    show();
}
public void paint(Graphics g) {
    Graphics2D g2 = (Graphics2D)g;
    g2.setStroke(new BasicStroke(10f,BasicStroke.CAP_BUTT,
            BasicStroke.JOIN_BEVEL,10f,dashPattern1,0f));
    g2.drawLine(50,50,450,50);
    g2.setStroke(new BasicStroke(10f,BasicStroke.CAP_BUTT,
            BasicStroke.JOIN_BEVEL,10f,dashPattern2,0f));
    g2.drawLine(50,100,450,100);
    g2.setStroke(new BasicStroke(10f,BasicStroke.CAP_BUTT,
            BasicStroke.JOIN_BEVEL,10f,dashPattern3,0f));
    g2.drawLine(50,150,450,150);
    g2.setStroke(new BasicStroke(10f,BasicStroke.CAP_BUTT,
            BasicStroke.JOIN_BEVEL,10f,dashPattern3,70f));
    g2.drawLine(50,200,450,200);
}
}
```

The Commentary

This application introduces a special array of float values called a *dash pattern*. A dash pattern is a numerical definition of the alternating patches of opacity and transparency that form a dashed line. The first number in the array is a count of the number of pixels where the line will be opaque. The second number is the number of pixels where the line is to be transparent.

Dash pattern arrays can have more than two numbers in them, though. Such longer-than-necessary arrays are how you create unusual dashed lines, such as those that have one long opaque dash, then a short transparent space, then a short opaque dash, then a long transparent space, and then a really long opaque dash.

In a dash pattern array, all even-numbered elements (including zero) define the length of opaque segments in pixels. All odd-numbered elements define the length of transparent segments in pixels. Therefore, the array [20.0,5.0,30.0,5.0,50.0] defines a pattern of increasingly long opaque dashes, separated by transparent spaces of 5.0 pixels. As a line is being drawn with a dash pattern and Java gets to the end of the array, it just circles back around to the beginning and starts over.

This example defines three dash arrays. To wit:

```
float dashPattern1[] = {40f,40f};
float dashPattern2[] = {40f,20f};
float dashPattern3[] = {40f,30f,20f,10f};
```

The first pattern is an evenly spaced on-and-off sequence, with opaque dashes and transparent spaces each 40 pixels long. The second pattern is opaque for 40 pixels and then transparent for 20 pixels. The third pattern is on for 40, off for 30, back on for another 20, and off again for 10 more.

The dash patterns are attached to Graphics2D objects for eventual rendering with statements like this:

```
g2.setStroke(new BasicStroke(10f,BasicStroke.CAP_BUTT,
            BasicStroke.JOIN_BEVEL,10f,dashPattern1,0f));
```

As you can see in Figure 6.5, the top line, based on dashPattern1, is an evenly spaced collection of dashes and spaces. In the second line, drawn from the second pattern, the dashes are twice as long as the spaces. In the third line, there are two differently sized spaces and two differently sized dashes.

The bottom line is the same as the third line, except that it starts in a different place. This is done by placing a nonzero value in the last argument of the constructor call to BasicStroke. This last number is the number of pixels to offset into the array before starting. In the example the number is 70. This means that, whenever a line is drawn, it will skip past the first

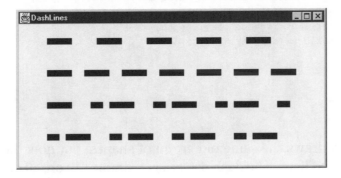

Figure 6.5 Some dashed lines.

40 pixels of opaqueness, and past the 30 pixels of transparency, and start
with the first pixel of the 20 pixels of opaqueness. This example was set
to start at the beginning of one of the segments, but it could just as well
have started in the middle of one.

Drawing Figures with Dashes: Part I

There are some things to consider when drawing anything but straight,
simple lines with dashes. This example explores these challenges.

The Code

```java
import java.awt.*;
import java.awt.event.*;
import java.awt.geom.*;
class DashOne extends Frame {
    Shape shapeArray[];
    float dashPattern[] = {40f,40f};
    public static void main(String arg[]) {
        new DashOne();
    }
    DashOne() {
        super("DashOne");
        addWindowListener(new WindowAdapter() {
            public void windowClosing(WindowEvent e)
                { System.exit(0); } } );
        setSize(550,550);
        shapeArray = LineDrawings.getShapeArray();
        show();
    }
    public void paint(Graphics g) {
        Graphics2D g2 = (Graphics2D)g;
        BasicStroke bs = new BasicStroke(20f,BasicStroke.CAP_BUTT,
                BasicStroke.JOIN_BEVEL,10f,dashPattern,0f);
        g2.setStroke(bs);
        for(int i=0; i<shapeArray.length; i++)
            g2.draw(shapeArray[i]);
    }
}
```

The Commentary

This application draws the same old group of shapes, but now they are
drawn with dashed lines. The dash pattern is a simple "40 on, 40 off" pattern stored in dashPattern.

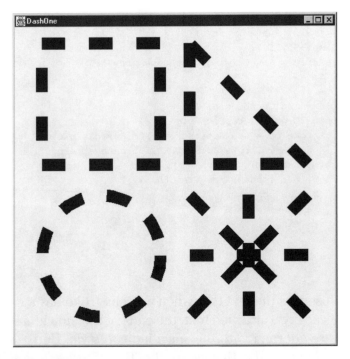

Figure 6.6 Figures drawn with dashed lines.

As you can see in Figure 6.6, none of the figures come out even. To make things work the way you like, you will need to figure the dimensions of your figures and adjust the dash array appropriately.

Drawing Figures with Dashes: Part II

The lines have been set to CAP_ROUND to show the results of drawing a dashed line with round end caps.

The Code

```
import java.awt.*;
import java.awt.event.*;
import java.awt.geom.*;
class DashTwo extends Frame {
    Shape shapeArray[];
    float dashPattern[] = {40f,40f};
    public static void main(String arg[]) {
        new DashTwo();
    }
    DashTwo() {
        super("DashTwo");
        addWindowListener(new WindowAdapter() {
```

```
                    public void windowClosing(WindowEvent e)
                         { System.exit(0); } } );
            setSize(550,550);
            shapeArray = LineDrawings.getShapeArray();
            show();
        }
        public void paint(Graphics g) {
            Graphics2D g2 = (Graphics2D)g;
            BasicStroke bs = new BasicStroke(20f,BasicStroke.CAP_ROUND,
                    BasicStroke.JOIN_ROUND,10f,dashPattern,0f);
            g2.setStroke(bs);
            for(int i=0; i<shapeArray.length; i++)
                g2.draw(shapeArray[i]);
        }
    }
```

The Commentary

This program illustrates the fact that when a BasicStroke has a dash pattern as well as a cap style attached to it, the ends of the individual opaque dash segments are adorned with the specified cap style. Here, the dash segments have round ends, thanks to the BasicStroke.CAP_ROUND attribute in the object-creation statement. Figure 6.7 illustrates this fact.

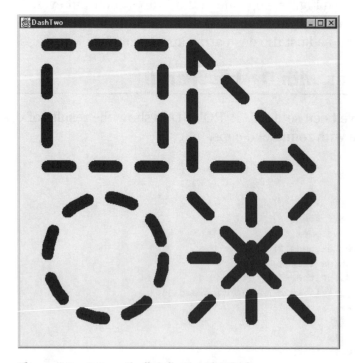

Figure 6.7   Automatically adjusting the dashes.

CHAPTER 7

Making Shapes and Fitting Curves

This chapter explains the capabilities of creating and rendering shapes and curves using Java2D. The chapter begins with simple examples and goes from one example to another demonstrating different aspects of the capabilities.

Building a Rectangle with GeneralPath

This program creates a GeneralPath object that contains the definition of a rectangle, and then uses the fill() method to draw the rectangle to the window.

The Code

```
import java.awt.*;
import java.awt.event.*;
import java.awt.geom.*;
class SimpleRectangle extends Frame {
        public static void main(String arg[]) {
                new SimpleRectangle();
        }
        SimpleRectangle() {
```

```
                    super("SimpleRectangle");
                    addWindowListener(new WindowAdapter() {
                            public void windowClosing(WindowEvent e)
                                    { System.exit(0); } } );
                    setSize(240,70);
                    show();
            }
      public void paint(Graphics g) {
                    Graphics2D g2 = (Graphics2D)g;
                    GeneralPath gp = rectangleShape();
                    g2.fill(gp);
            }

      private GeneralPath rectangleShape() {
                    GeneralPath gp =
                            new GeneralPath(GeneralPath.WIND_EVEN_ODD);
                    gp.moveTo(30.0f,30.0f);
                    gp.lineTo(210.0f,30.0f);
                    gp.lineTo(210.0f,60.0f);
                    gp.lineTo(30.0f,60.0f);
                    gp.closePath();
                    return(gp);
            }
      }
```

The Commentary

The GeneralPath class contains a list of graphical instructions that will be followed by the Graphics2D object in rendering the figure. In this example the moveTo() method is used to set the starting position a polygon (in this case, a rectangle). The lineTo() method calls are used to define three sides of the rectangle. The closePath() method is used to define a line from the last point back to the beginning, thus defining the fourth side of the rectangle.

The fill() method of the Graphics2D object is called with the General-Path (which implements the Shape interface—the argument required by the fill() method) to do the actual drawing of the figure.

Notice that the Graphics object supplied as the argument to the paint() method can be cast directly to a Graphics2D object. This is because the Graphics2D class is derived from the Graphics class, and Java 1.2 creates Graphics2D objects.

The output is shown in Figure 7.1.

Figure 7.1 The simple rectangle.

Transforming with Graphics2D

This program shows how to use the Graphics2D object's built-in affine transform capability to move a polygon wherever you like. This example also demonstrates the capability of the figure to be a polygon.

The Code

```
import java.awt.*;
import java.awt.event.*;
import java.awt.geom.*;
class SimpleArrow extends Frame {
        public static void main(String arg[]) {
                new SimpleArrow();
        }
        SimpleArrow() {
                super("SimpleArrow");
                addWindowListener(new WindowAdapter() {
                        public void windowClosing(WindowEvent e)
                                { System.exit(0); } } );
                setSize(200,200);
                show();
        }
        public void paint(Graphics g) {
                Graphics2D g2 = (Graphics2D)g;
                AffineTransform at = new AffineTransform();
                at.setToTranslation(90.0,90.0);
                at.scale(2.0,2.0);
                g2.setTransform(at);
                GeneralPath gp = getArrow();
                g2.fill(gp);
        }
        private GeneralPath getArrow() {
                GeneralPath gp =
                        new GeneralPath(GeneralPath.WIND_EVEN_ODD);
                gp.moveTo(0.0f,-15.0f);
                gp.lineTo(10.0f,5.0f);
                gp.lineTo(5.0f,5.0f);
```

```
                              gp.lineTo(5.0f,15.0f);
                              gp.lineTo(-5.0f,15.0f);
                              gp.lineTo(-5.0f,5.0f);
                              gp.lineTo(-10.0f,5.0f);
                              gp.closePath();
                              return(gp);
                 }
        }
```

The Commentary

The Graphics2D class uses an AffineTransform on the figures it draws. The default is the identity transform—the one that makes no changes whatsoever to the location of any of the points. This example uses a transform to move an arrow—the same arrow you worked with in Chapter 5—from the origin out to the middle of the window and to scale the arrow to a larger size.

All the interesting stuff goes on in the paint() method here. After an AffineTransform is created and set, it is attached to g2, the Graphics2D object. Then, gp is defined as the arrow (more on that in a second), and this line appears:

```
g2.fill(gp);
```

That's the method that instructs the g2 to take what's in gp, apply the AffineTransform associated with g2, and render it as a filled shape.

As before, the moveTo() and lineTo() methods define a shape—this time, it's an arrow (the f characters in those statements are a shorthand way of deliberate typing—they denote floats).

This program's output appears in Figure 7.2.

Figure 7.2   A scaled and translated arrow.

Scaling Lines

This example shows the result of scaling a line drawing of a General-Path. It uses the same arrow as in the previous example and draws it three times at three different levels of scaling. The results may not be what you would have expected—the thickness of the lines themselves is also scaled.

The Code

```
import java.awt.*;
import java.awt.event.*;
import java.awt.geom.*;
class LineScaling extends Frame {
        public static void main(String arg[]) {
                new LineScaling();
        }
        LineScaling() {
                super("LineScaling");
                addWindowListener(new WindowAdapter() {
                        public void windowClosing(WindowEvent e)
                                { System.exit(0); } } );
                setSize(200,220);
                show();
        }
        public void paint(Graphics g) {
                Graphics2D g2 = (Graphics2D)g;
                GeneralPath gp = getArrow();
                AffineTransform at = new AffineTransform();
                at.setToTranslation(30.0,50.0);
                g2.setTransform(at);
                g2.draw(gp);
                at.setToTranslation(60.0,80.0);
                at.scale(2.0,2.0);
                g2.setTransform(at);
                g2.draw(gp);
                at.setToTranslation(110.0,140.0);
                at.scale(4.0,4.0);
                g2.setTransform(at);
                g2.draw(gp);
        }
        private GeneralPath getArrow() {
                GeneralPath gp =
                        new GeneralPath(GeneralPath.WIND_EVEN_ODD);
                gp.moveTo(0.0f,-15.0f);
                gp.lineTo(10.0f,5.0f);
```

```
                    gp.lineTo(5.0f,5.0f);
                    gp.lineTo(5.0f,15.0f);
                    gp.lineTo(-5.0f,15.0f);
                    gp.lineTo(-5.0f,5.0f);
                    gp.lineTo(-10.0f,5.0f);
                    gp.closePath();
                    return(gp);
            }
        }
```

The arrow is drawn three times. The drawing, shown in the upper left in
Figure 7.3, is not scaled. The second, in the center, has its size doubled,
and the third has its size quadrupled. Notice also that the thickness of
the lines is also doubled and quadrupled.

Dynamic ZigZag

The sides of a shape can cross over themselves. This program defines a
zigzag shape—sort of like the decoration on a jockey's uniform—that
crosses back over itself. Part of the figure is filled; part of it is merely an
outline. This program illustrates the difference between draw() and fill()
and shows how the winding rule applies under Java2D.

The Code

```
import java.awt.*;
import java.awt.event.*;
import java.awt.geom.*;
class ZigZag extends Frame {
        public static void main(String arg[]) {
                new ZigZag();
        }
        ZigZag() {
                super("ZigZag");
                addWindowListener(new WindowAdapter() {
                        public void windowClosing(WindowEvent e)
                                { System.exit(0); } } );
                setSize(325,315);
                show();
        }
        public void paint(Graphics g) {
                Graphics2D g2 = (Graphics2D)g;
                GeneralPath gp = getZigZag();
                AffineTransform at = new AffineTransform();
```

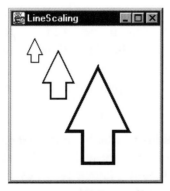

Figure 7.3 A scaled arrow.

```
            at.setToTranslation(30.0,40.0);
            g2.setTransform(at);
            g2.draw(gp);
            at.setToTranslation(30.0,170.0);
            g2.setTransform(at);
            g2.fill(gp);
    }
    private GeneralPath getZigZag() {
            GeneralPath gp =
                    new GeneralPath(GeneralPath.WIND_EVEN_ODD);
            gp.moveTo(0.0f,0.0f);
            gp.lineTo(80.0f,120.0f);
            gp.lineTo(160.0f,0.0f);
            gp.lineTo(240.0f,120.0f);
            gp.lineTo(240.0f,0.0f);
            gp.lineTo(160.0f,120.0f);
            gp.lineTo(80.0f,0.0f);
            gp.lineTo(0.0f,120.0f);
            gp.closePath();
            return(gp);
    }
}
```

The Commentary

As in the previous example, this program creates a Graphics2D object called g2, defines an AffineTransform called at and attaches at to g2, which then renders the figure contained in gp. This process occurs twice in this program.

The difference between the two instances of the zigzag is in the way they're rendered, seen in Figure 7.4. The first instance is painted with draw(), which yields a set of hollow diamonds. The other instance (in addition to having had a different affine transform applied) is painted with draw(). That method causes filled shapes to be painted to the screen.

WHY SETTRANSFORM()?

Even though the same AffineTransform object is used for both transformation definitions here, it is necessary to call setTransform() again because the Graphics2D object makes its own internal copy of the rules—the AffineTransform is simply used to contain the set of transformations to be passed in as the argument.

The other interesting line in this program is the following:

```
GeneralPath gp = new GeneralPath(GeneralPath.WIND_EVEN_ODD);
```

The Winding Rule

The winding rule deals with how to fill the regions created when an outline overlaps itself in such a way that some portion of its interior obscures some other portion of its interior. This program illustrates what happens when you create and fill such a region under Java2D.

Figure 7.4 The draw() method versus the fill() method.

The Code

```
import java.awt.*;
import java.awt.event.*;
import java.awt.geom.*;
class Winding extends Frame {
        public static void main(String arg[]) {
                new Winding();
        }
        Winding() {
                super("Winding");
                addWindowListener(new WindowAdapter() {
                        public void windowClosing(WindowEvent e)
                                { System.exit(0); } } );
                setSize(325,420);
                show();
        }
        public void paint(Graphics g) {
                Graphics2D g2 = (Graphics2D)g;
                GeneralPath gp;
                gp = getWinding(GeneralPath.WIND_EVEN_ODD);
                AffineTransform at = new AffineTransform();
                at.setToTranslation(30.0,60.0);
                g2.setTransform(at);
                g2.draw(gp);
                at.setToTranslation(30.0,180.0);
                g2.setTransform(at);
                g2.fill(gp);
                gp = getWinding(GeneralPath.WIND_NON_ZERO);
                at.setToTranslation(30.0,300.0);
                g2.setTransform(at);
                g2.fill(gp);
        }
        private GeneralPath getWinding(int rule) {
                GeneralPath gp = new GeneralPath(rule);
                gp.moveTo(0.0f,40.0f);
                gp.lineTo(180.0f,40.0f);
                gp.lineTo(180.0f,20.0f);
                gp.lineTo(120.0f,20.0f);
                gp.lineTo(120.0f,80.0f);
                gp.lineTo(60.0f,80.0f);
                gp.lineTo(60.0f,0.0f);
                gp.lineTo(240.0f,0.0f);
                gp.lineTo(240.0f,60.0f);
                gp.lineTo(0.0f,60.0f);
                gp.closePath();
                return(gp);
        }
}
```

The Commentary

Straightforward enough: this program draws two instances of the irregular shape. The upper one is left unfilled, while the lower one is filled, applying the winding rule thanks to the WIND_EVEN_ODD argument in the object declaration. But what is the winding rule, and what's it doing here?

The rule goes like this: If you draw a shape that "covers" a region an odd number of times, the region will be filled. If you draw it an even number of times, it will not.

Consider it this way: If you shine an imaginary beam directly into the screen and it passes through an odd number of "layers" covering a particular region, the region will be filled. If the imaginary light goes through an even number of "layers," the region will not be filled.

The number 1 is odd, so therefore simple, nonoverlapping polygons will always be filled. This program causes one region of overlap. Note that the region is not painted by fill() and is left white in the lower example.

The output is shown in Figure 7.5. The figure is outlined at the top of the window, it is filled with WIND_EVEN_ODD in the middle, and filled with WIND_NON_ZERO at the bottom. Notice that with the even/odd fill, the figure is not filled where it crosses over the top of itself (thus enclosing the area an even number of times). In the bottom figure, drawn with the nonzero rule, the entire region enclosed by the figure is filled except the little square in the center, which, even though it is landlocked, it is not inside the figure.

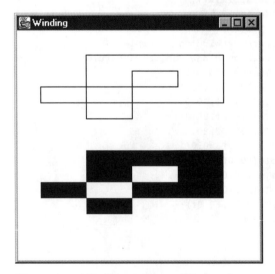

Figure 7.5 Winding and the unfilled region.

Arcs

The Arcs2D.Float class is a shape that can be used to draw an incomplete circle or ellipse. If you wish to draw a complete circle or ellipse, you can do it with Arcs2D.Float, but it will almost always be easier to use the Ellipse class instead.

The Code

```java
import java.awt.*;
import java.awt.event.*;
import java.awt.geom.*;
class Arcs extends Frame {
        public static void main(String arg[]) {
                new Arcs();
        }
        Arcs() {
                super("Arcs");
                addWindowListener(new WindowAdapter() {
                        public void windowClosing(WindowEvent e)
                                { System.exit(0); } } );
                setSize(350,330);
                show();
        }
        public void paint(Graphics g) {
                Graphics2D g2 = (Graphics2D)g;
                Arc2D chord = getArcChord();
                Arc2D open = getArcOpen();
                Arc2D pie = getArcPie();
                AffineTransform at = new AffineTransform();

                // First row
                at.setToTranslation(10.0,30.0);
                g2.setTransform(at);
                g2.draw(pie);
                at.setToTranslation(120.0,30.0);
                g2.setTransform(at);
                g2.draw(open);
                at.setToTranslation(230.0,30.0);
                g2.setTransform(at);
                g2.draw(chord);

                // Second row
                at.setToTranslation(10.0,60.0);
                g2.setTransform(at);
                pie.setAngleExtent(-135.0);
                g2.draw(pie);
```

```
        at.setToTranslation(120.0,60.0);
        g2.setTransform(at);
        open.setAngleExtent(-135.0);
        g2.draw(open);
        at.setToTranslation(230.0,60.0);
        g2.setTransform(at);
        chord.setAngleExtent(-135.0);
        g2.draw(chord);

        // Third row
        at.setToTranslation(10.0,190.0);
        g2.setTransform(at);
        pie.setAngleStart(45.0);
        pie.setAngleExtent(270.0);
        g2.draw(pie);
        at.setToTranslation(120.0,190.0);
        g2.setTransform(at);
        open.setAngleStart(45.0);
        open.setAngleExtent(270.0);
        g2.draw(open);
        at.setToTranslation(230.0,190.0);
        g2.setTransform(at);
        chord.setAngleStart(45.0);
        chord.setAngleExtent(270.0);
        g2.draw(chord);
    }
    private Arc2D getArcPie() {
        Arc2D.Float arc = new Arc2D.Float(
                    0.0f,0.0f,
                    100.0f,100.0f,
                    0.0f,45.0f,
                    Arc2D.PIE);
        return(arc);
    }
    private Arc2D getArcChord() {
        Arc2D.Float arc = new Arc2D.Float(
                    0.0f,0.0f,
                    100.0f,100.0f,
                    0.0f,45.0f,
                    Arc2D.CHORD);
        return(arc);
    }
    private Arc2D getArcOpen() {
        Arc2D.Float arc = new Arc2D.Float(
                    0.0f,0.0f,
                    100.0f,100.0f,
                    0.0f,45.0f,
                    Arc2D.OPEN);
        return(arc);
    }
}
```

The Commentary

When you create an Arc2D.Float object, you specify the starting angle and the sweep of the arc in degrees. At zero degrees, it points off to the right. Positive angles increase counter-clockwise. That is, an angle of positive 45 degrees will point up to the right, and an angle of negative 45 degrees will point down to the right.

An arc is described by two angles; one is the start of the arc and the other is number of degrees of rotation to arrive at the ending angle. That is, the empirical termination angle is determined by adding the value of the ending angle to the value of the starting angle.

An arc is a circle with an open section in it. There are three ways the Arc2D class will handle the gap: It can leave it open, it can draw a straight line—a chord—to connect the two ends, or it can draw a pair of lines back to the center, forming a pie.

In this example, there are three rows of arcs. The first row shows three ways of having an arc subtend an acute angle, the second one is an obtuse angle, and the third one is an almost complete circle. Each of the three columns shows the different ways in which the ends of the arc can be terminated. The first column uses a chord, the second leaves it open, and the third column draws a pair of lines from the ends of the arc back to the center of the circle of which the arcs are a part. In every case, the positioning of the drawn arcs is done with an AffineTransform applied to the Graphics2D object. The output of this program appears in Figure 7.6.

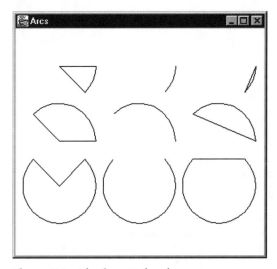

Figure 7.6 The forms taken by an arc.

Figure 7.7 The forms taken by a filled arc.

Figure 7.7 shows the output from the program named ArcFills.java, which appears only on the CD-ROM. The source code of this program identical to Arcs.java, except that all the draw() methods have been replaced with calls to fill(). As you can see, the default for fill(), when there is no specified form of closure for the arc, is the chord.

Scaling an Arc Another Way

There is more than one way to scale an arc.

The Code

```
import java.awt.*;
import java.awt.event.*;
import java.awt.geom.*;
class ArcScale extends Frame {
        public static void main(String arg[]) {
                new ArcScale();
        }
        ArcScale() {
                super("ArcScale");
                addWindowListener(new WindowAdapter() {
                        public void windowClosing(WindowEvent e)
```

```
                                 { System.exit(0); } } );
            setSize(500,300);
            show();
    }
    public void paint(Graphics g) {
            Graphics2D g2 = (Graphics2D)g;
            Arc2D.Float arc = new Arc2D.Float(
                        0.0f,0.0f,
                        100.0f,100.0f,
                        45.0f,-270.0f,
                        Arc2D.PIE);
            AffineTransform at = new AffineTransform();

            // First row
            at.setToTranslation(20.0,30.0);
            g2.setTransform(at);
            g2.fill(arc);
            at.setToTranslation(140.0,30.0);
            at.scale(0.5,1.0);
            g2.setTransform(at);
            g2.fill(arc);
            at.setToTranslation(210.0,30.0);
            at.scale(1.0,0.5);
            g2.setTransform(at);
            g2.fill(arc);
            at.setToTranslation(320.0,30.0);
            at.scale(1.25,1.25);
            g2.setTransform(at);
            g2.fill(arc);

            // Second row
            at.setToTranslation(20.0,160.0);
            g2.setTransform(at);
            g2.fill(arc);
            at.setToTranslation(140.0,160.0);
            g2.setTransform(at);
            arc.setFrame(0.0,0.0,50.0,100.0);
            g2.fill(arc);
            at.setToTranslation(210.0,160.0);
            g2.setTransform(at);
            arc.setFrame(0.0,0.0,100.0,50.0);
            g2.fill(arc);
            at.setToTranslation(320.0,160.0);
            g2.setTransform(at);
            arc.setFrame(0.0,0.0,125.0,125.0);
            g2.fill(arc);
    }
}
```

Figure 7.8 There is more than one way to scale an arc.

The Commentary

When you create an arc object, you specify the starting angle of the arc, the angle that the arc will include in its sweep, and the height and width of the rectangle into which the entire oval (of which the arc is a part) is to fit. Once they are set, there are methods available—setBounds() is used here—in the Arc2D class to modify the values. Beyond the values that are defined inside an Arc2D object, you can also use a transform to modify the height and width as you draw the arcs.

In this example, the first row shows arcs that were scaled by using an AffineTransform and the second row shows arcs scaled by adjusting the bound setting inside the arc object itself. The results are the same—which method you prefer depends on your application.

The output of ArcScale appears in Figure 7.8.

Variations on Scaling

There is one difference in the two scaling methods presented in the previous example. This example shows how they differ.

The Code

```
import java.awt.*;
import java.awt.event.*;
import java.awt.geom.*;
```

```
class ArcScaleDraw extends Frame {
        public static void main(String arg[]) {
                new ArcScaleDraw();
        }
        ArcScaleDraw() {
                super("ArcScaleDraw");
                addWindowListener(new WindowAdapter() {
                        public void windowClosing(WindowEvent e)
                                { System.exit(0); } } );
                setSize(500,300);
                show();
        }
        public void paint(Graphics g) {
                Graphics2D g2 = (Graphics2D)g;
                Arc2D.Float arc = new Arc2D.Float(
                                0.0f,0.0f,
                                100.0f,100.0f,
                                45.0f,-270.0f,
                                Arc2D.PIE);
                AffineTransform at = new AffineTransform();

                // First row
                at.setToTranslation(20.0,30.0);
                g2.setTransform(at);
                g2.draw(arc);
                at.setToTranslation(140.0,30.0);
                at.scale(0.5,1.0);
                g2.setTransform(at);
                g2.draw(arc);
                at.setToTranslation(210.0,30.0);
                at.scale(1.0,0.5);
                g2.setTransform(at);
                g2.draw(arc);
                at.setToTranslation(320.0,30.0);
                at.scale(1.25,1.25);
                g2.setTransform(at);
                g2.draw(arc);

                // Second row
                at.setToTranslation(20.0,160.0);
                g2.setTransform(at);
                g2.draw(arc);
                g2.draw(arc.getBounds());
                at.setToTranslation(140.0,160.0);
                g2.setTransform(at);
                arc.setFrame(0.0,0.0,50.0,100.0);
                g2.draw(arc);
                g2.draw(arc.getBounds());
                at.setToTranslation(210.0,160.0);
                g2.setTransform(at);
                arc.setFrame(0.0,0.0,100.0,50.0);
                g2.draw(arc);
                g2.draw(arc.getBounds());
```

```
at.setToTranslation(320.0,160.0);
g2.setTransform(at);
arc.setFrame(0.0,0.0,125.0,125.0);
g2.draw(arc);
g2.draw(arc.getBounds());
    }
}
```

The Commentary

If you draw instead of fill scaled shapes, the lines take on a slightly different appearance because using the scale() method of the AffineTransform also scales the thickness of the lines. Figure 7.3 shows an example of lines being made thicker through scaling a figure to a larger size. The opposite is also true—if you use scaling to reduce the size of a figure, the thickness of the lines is also reduced. There is, however, a safety limit—the lines can't be thinner than one pixel. This prevents the lines from disappearing. In ArcScaleDraw, shown in Figure 7.9, the lines before scaling have a thickness of one pixel and some of the dimensions are scaled to half size, but the thickness of the lines is not reduced. The program ArcScaleDraw is identical to ArcScale except that all the fill()method calls are replaced by draw() method calls, and the bounding boxes of the lower row of figures is also drawn.

There is also an indication of the bounding box. The figures are placed on the window by the position of the upper-left corner of the bounding box. The bounding box of a shape is the smallest box possible that completely contains the shape. For consistency, it also contains parts of the shape that would be present if they were not trimmed off.

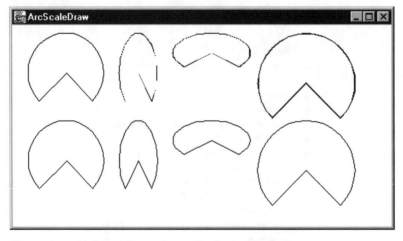

Figure 7.9   Scaling a figure also scales its outline.

Ellipse

In Java2D, the ellipse is a simplified form of an arc. It always has its ending angle 360 degrees from its start, so it never has an opening. A circle is a special case—it is an ellipse where the height and width are equal. Just like the arc, you can specify the height and width, and you can use a transform to modify its shape.

Because an ellipse is defined in terms of its bounding rectangle, it can, like the arc, be reshaped only in the vertical or horizontal directions. However, an AffineTransform can be used to rotate the ellipse so its eccentricity appears in any direction you wish. This program, EllipseAround, displays an ellipse in several positions as it rotates around its origin.

The Code

```
import java.awt.*;
import java.awt.event.*;
import java.awt.geom.*;
class EllipseAround extends Frame {
        public static void main(String arg[]) {
                new EllipseAround();
        }
        EllipseAround() {
                super("EllipseAround");
                addWindowListener(new WindowAdapter() {
                        public void windowClosing(WindowEvent e)
                                { System.exit(0); } } );
                setSize(300,290);
                show();
        }
        public void paint(Graphics g) {
                Graphics2D g2 = (Graphics2D)g;
                Ellipse2D.Float ellipse = new Ellipse2D.Float(
                        0.0f,0.0f,50.0f,100.0f);
                AffineTransform at = new AffineTransform();
                double angle = 0.0;
                for(int i=0; i<16; i++) {
                        at.setToTranslation(150.0,150.0);
                        at.rotate(angle);
                        g2.setTransform(at);
                        g2.draw(ellipse);
                        angle += Math.PI / 8;
                }
        }
}
```

The Commentary

This program generates 16 ellipses, identical except for their positions. Each ellipse is contained in a rectangle that is 50 pixels long by 100 pixels wide. This program creates a Graphics2D object called g2 and an Ellipse2D.Float object called ellipse. Then, an AffineTransform object gets created and the loop begins.

The origin of an ellipse is the upper-left-hand corner of its bounding rectangle. The first ellipse drawn, the one where the angle is 0.0, is the one at the bottom of the circle standing on its end. Then, each iteration of the loop scoots the ellipse $\pi/8$, or one-sixteenth of a circle, clockwise.

The output of the program appears in Figure 7.10.

Figure 7.10 Rotating ellipses.

Quadratic Curves

The QuadCurve2D class is capable of defining a regular symmetric curve that turns in one direction only. If you need an asymmetric curve, or one that can turn back on itself, see the following section on cubic curves. This program demonstrates quadratic curves.

The Code

```
import java.awt.*;
import java.awt.event.*;
import java.awt.geom.*;
class QuadCurve extends Frame {
        public static void main(String arg[]) {
                new QuadCurve();
        }
        QuadCurve() {
                super("QuadCurve");
                addWindowListener(new WindowAdapter() {
                        public void windowClosing(WindowEvent e)
                                { System.exit(0); } } );
                setSize(300,110);
                show();
        }
        public void paint(Graphics g) {
                Graphics2D g2 = (Graphics2D)g;
                float x1, y1;
                float xctl, yctl;
                float x2, y2;
                QuadCurve2D.Float curve;

                // First curve
                x1 = 10.0f; y1 = 30.0f;
                xctl = 60.0f; yctl = 30.0f;
                x2 = 60.0f; y2 = 80.0f;
                curve = new QuadCurve2D.Float(
                        x1,y1,xctl,yctl,x2,y2);
                g2.fill(dot(x1,y1));
                g2.fill(dot(x2,y2));
                g2.draw(dot(xctl,yctl));
                g2.draw(curve);

                // Second curve
                x1 = 110.0f; y1 = 30.0f;
                xctl = 90.0f; yctl = 60.0f;
                x2 = 110.0f; y2 = 90.0f;
                curve = new QuadCurve2D.Float(
                        x1,y1,xctl,yctl,x2,y2);
                g2.fill(dot(x1,y1));
                g2.fill(dot(x2,y2));
                g2.draw(dot(xctl,yctl));
                g2.draw(curve);

                // Third curve
                x1 = 150.0f; y1 = 30.0f;
                xctl = 180.0f; yctl = 60.0f;
                x2 = 150.0f; y2 = 90.0f;
```

```
                            curve = new QuadCurve2D.Float(
                                    x1,y1,xctl,yctl,x2,y2);
                            g2.fill(dot(x1,y1));
                            g2.fill(dot(x2,y2));
                            g2.draw(dot(xctl,yctl));
                            g2.draw(curve);

                            // Fourth curve
                            x1 = 210.0f; y1 = 30.0f;
                            xctl = 230.0f; yctl = 90.0f;
                            x2 = 250.0f; y2 = 30.0f;
                            curve = new QuadCurve2D.Float(
                                    x1,y1,xctl,yctl,x2,y2);
                            g2.fill(dot(x1,y1));
                            g2.fill(dot(x2,y2));
                            g2.draw(dot(xctl,yctl));
                            g2.draw(curve);
                    }
            private Shape dot(float x,float y) {
                    return(new Rectangle2D.Float(x - 3.0f,y -
    3.0f,6.0f,6.0f));
                    }
            }
```

The Commentary

The basic idea behind quadratic curves is that any curve can be defined by two endpoints and two intersecting lines. They most often are used to put rounded corners on a rectangle or to put a rounded end on a couple of parallel lines. They can, however, be used to make a curved connection on any two straight lines that, if extended, would cross one another. To make the curved connection, you simply define the point on each line where you would like the curve to begin, and also specify the point at which the two lines would cross if they continued in a straight line.

The program QuadCurve is an example of four pairs of points being joined by a curved line. So you can see what is being done, the two endpoints are shown as black boxes and the point at which the straight lines would cross—the control point—is shown as a small square. In the code, the endpoints are called x1 and x2, the control points are called xctl, and the curves are defined by successive definitions of a QuadCurve2D.Float object, called curve.

The curves start toward the control point but never reach it. The algorithm makes a smooth curve to connect the two points. The output produced by QuadCurve is shown in Figure 7.11.

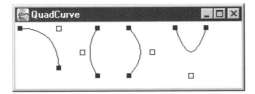

Figure 7.11 Symmetric quadratic curves.

Drawing Asymmetrical Quadratic Curves

The curves are not always symmetric. By placing the control point in a nonsymmetric location—that is, in a location other than one equidistant from the two control points—the curve itself is drawn asymmetrically.

The Code

```
import java.awt.*;
import java.awt.event.*;
import java.awt.geom.*;
class QuadCurve2 extends Frame {
        public static void main(String arg[]) {
                new QuadCurve2();
        }
        QuadCurve2() {
                super("QuadCurve2");
                addWindowListener(new WindowAdapter() {
                        public void windowClosing(WindowEvent e)
                                { System.exit(0); } } );
                setSize(300,110);
                show();
        }
        public void paint(Graphics g) {
                Graphics2D g2 = (Graphics2D)g;
                float x1, y1;
                float xctl, yctl;
                float x2, y2;
                QuadCurve2D.Float curve;

                // First curve
                x1 = 10.0f; y1 = 30.0f;
                xctl = 30.0f; yctl = 30.0f;
                x2 = 60.0f; y2 = 80.0f;
                curve = new QuadCurve2D.Float(
                        x1,y1,xctl,yctl,x2,y2);
                g2.fill(dot(x1,y1));
```

```
                g2.fill(dot(x2,y2));
                g2.draw(dot(xctl,yctl));
                g2.draw(curve);

                // Second curve
                x1 = 110.0f; y1 = 30.0f;
                xctl = 90.0f; yctl = 100.0f;
                x2 = 110.0f; y2 = 90.0f;
                curve = new QuadCurve2D.Float(
                        x1,y1,xctl,yctl,x2,y2);
                g2.fill(dot(x1,y1));
                g2.fill(dot(x2,y2));
                g2.draw(dot(xctl,yctl));
                g2.draw(curve);

                // Third curve
                x1 = 150.0f; y1 = 30.0f;
                xctl = 180.0f; yctl = 30.0f;
                x2 = 150.0f; y2 = 90.0f;
                curve = new QuadCurve2D.Float(
                        x1,y1,xctl,yctl,x2,y2);
                g2.fill(dot(x1,y1));
                g2.fill(dot(x2,y2));
                g2.draw(dot(xctl,yctl));
                g2.draw(curve);

                // Fourth curve
                x1 = 210.0f; y1 = 30.0f;
                xctl = 280.0f; yctl = 90.0f;
                x2 = 250.0f; y2 = 30.0f;
                curve = new QuadCurve2D.Float(
                        x1,y1,xctl,yctl,x2,y2);
                g2.fill(dot(x1,y1));
                g2.fill(dot(x2,y2));
                g2.draw(dot(xctl,yctl));
                g2.draw(curve);
        }
        private Shape dot(float x,float y) {
                return(new Rectangle2D.Float(x - 3.0f,y -
   3.0f,6.0f,6.0f));
        }
   }
```

The Commentary

This program matches the one that precedes it, except for the fact that each curve's control point is not equidistant from the curve's two endpoints. The quadratic curves are skewed as a result. The output from QuadCurve2 appears in Figure 7.12.

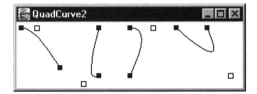

Figure 7.12 Asymmetric quadratic curves.

Symmetric Cubic Curves

A CubicCurve2D shape can be used whenever you wish to connect two points with a curved line. The curve will either be single or double as needed. A single curve turns only in one direction, a double will curve in two directions—an S-curve.

The Code

```
import java.awt.*;
import java.awt.event.*;
import java.awt.geom.*;
class CubicCurve extends Frame {
        public static void main(String arg[]) {
                new CubicCurve();
        }
        CubicCurve() {
                super("CubicCurve");
                addWindowListener(new WindowAdapter() {
                        public void windowClosing(WindowEvent e)
                                { System.exit(0); } } );
                setSize(300,100);
                show();
        }
        public void paint(Graphics g) {
                Graphics2D g2 = (Graphics2D)g;
                float x1, y1;
                float x1ctl, y1ctl;
                float x2ctl, y2ctl;
                float x2, y2;
                CubicCurve2D.Float curve;

                // First curve
                x1 = 20.0f; y1 = 40.0f;
                x1ctl = 30.0f; y1ctl = 40.0f;
```

```
            x2ctl = 60.0f; y2ctl = 70.0f;
            x2 = 60.0f; y2 = 80.0f;
            curve = new CubicCurve2D.Float(
                    x1,y1,x1ctl,y1ctl,
                    x2ctl,y2ctl,x2,y2);
            controlLine(g2,x1,y1,x1ctl,y1ctl);
            controlLine(g2,x2,y2,x2ctl,y2ctl);
            g2.draw(curve);

            // Second curve
            x1 = 90.0f; y1 = 40.0f;
            x1ctl = 110.0f; y1ctl = 40.0f;
            x2ctl = 130.0f; y2ctl = 60.0f;
            x2 = 130.0f; y2 = 80.0f;
            curve = new CubicCurve2D.Float(
                    x1,y1,x1ctl,y1ctl,
                    x2ctl,y2ctl,x2,y2);
            controlLine(g2,x1,y1,x1ctl,y1ctl);
            controlLine(g2,x2,y2,x2ctl,y2ctl);
            g2.draw(curve);


            // Third curve
            x1 = 160.0f; y1 = 40.0f;
            x1ctl = 190.0f; y1ctl = 40.0f;
            x2ctl = 200.0f; y2ctl = 50.0f;
            x2 = 200.0f; y2 = 80.0f;
            curve = new CubicCurve2D.Float(
                    x1,y1,x1ctl,y1ctl,
                    x2ctl,y2ctl,x2,y2);
            controlLine(g2,x1,y1,x1ctl,y1ctl);
            controlLine(g2,x2,y2,x2ctl,y2ctl);
            g2.draw(curve);

            // Fourth curve
            x1 = 230.0f; y1 = 40.0f;
            x1ctl = 240.0f; y1ctl = 40.0f;
            x2ctl = 270.0f; y2ctl = 50.0f;
            x2 = 270.0f; y2 = 80.0f;
            curve = new CubicCurve2D.Float(
                    x1,y1,x1ctl,y1ctl,
                    x2ctl,y2ctl,x2,y2);
            controlLine(g2,x1,y1,x1ctl,y1ctl);
            controlLine(g2,x2,y2,x2ctl,y2ctl);
            g2.draw(curve);
        }
    private void controlLine(Graphics2D g2,
                float x1,float y1,float x2,float y2) {
            g2.fill(new Rectangle2D.Float(x1 - 3.0f,y1 -
3.0f,6.0f,6.0f));
            g2.drawLine((int)x1,(int)y1,(int)x2,(int)y2);
```

```
        }
    }
```

The Commentary

You define a cubic curve by giving it a pair of endpoints and assigning each endpoint a control point. The purpose of the endpoints is obvious—the curve must begin and end somewhere. The control points are used to tell the CubicCurve2D class how you want the curve to be drawn. That is, the control points determine in which direction the curve will depart from the endpoints, how sharply should the curve bend, and whether the curve should be eccentric or symmetric. This program draws four curves, connecting lines that meet at a 90 degree angle.

The syntax involved in creating the curves involves only creating new instances of the CubicCurve2D.Float class, then using the draw() method of a Graphics2D object to actually paint the curves.

The output from the program CubicCurve.java is shown in Figure 7.13. So you can better visualize what is going on, the endpoints are drawn as dots with a straight line from each endpoint to its associated control point.

As you can see in Figure 7.13, each of these curves join to points using very similar curves. In fact, in all four cases, the pair of points have the same physical relationship to one another, but the curves joining them are different. The further a control point is from its endpoint, the sharper the curve bends in its middle. The first three figures are completely symmetric—that is, the two control points are the same distance from each of their endpoints, causing the curve to be symmetric.

Asymmetrical Cubic Curves

In this example, the cubic curves have one control point further from its companion endpoint, causing an asymmetry, so one end makes a shallower curve than the other.

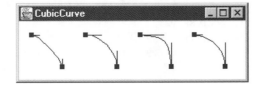

Figure 7.13   Four like curves with varying magnitude.

The Code

```java
import java.awt.*;
import java.awt.event.*;
import java.awt.geom.*;
class CubicCurve2 extends Frame {
        public static void main(String arg[]) {
                new CubicCurve2();
        }
        CubicCurve2() {
                super("CubicCurve2");
                addWindowListener(new WindowAdapter() {
                        public void windowClosing(WindowEvent e)
                                { System.exit(0); } } );
                setSize(300,110);
                show();
        }
        public void paint(Graphics g) {
                Graphics2D g2 = (Graphics2D)g;
                float x1, y1;
                float x1ctl, y1ctl;
                float x2ctl, y2ctl;
                float x2, y2;
                CubicCurve2D.Float curve;

                // First curve
                x1 = 30.0f; y1 = 40.0f;
                x1ctl = 50.0f; y1ctl = 30.0f;
                x2ctl = 50.0f; y2ctl = 100.0f;
                x2 = 30.0f; y2 = 90.0f;
                curve = new CubicCurve2D.Float(
                        x1,y1,x1ctl,y1ctl,
                        x2ctl,y2ctl,x2,y2);
                controlLine(g2,x1,y1,x1ctl,y1ctl);
                controlLine(g2,x2,y2,x2ctl,y2ctl);
                g2.draw(curve);

                // Second curve
                x1 = 90.0f; y1 = 40.0f;
                x1ctl = 110.0f; y1ctl = 50.0f;
                x2ctl = 110.0f; y2ctl = 80.0f;
                x2 = 90.0f; y2 = 90.0f;
                curve = new CubicCurve2D.Float(
                        x1,y1,x1ctl,y1ctl,
                        x2ctl,y2ctl,x2,y2);
                controlLine(g2,x1,y1,x1ctl,y1ctl);
                controlLine(g2,x2,y2,x2ctl,y2ctl);
                g2.draw(curve);

                // Third curve
```

```
                     x1 = 150.0f; y1 = 40.0f;
                     x1ctl = 170.0f; y1ctl = 40.0f;
                     x2ctl = 170.0f; y2ctl = 70.0f;
                     x2 = 150.0f; y2 = 90.0f;
                     curve = new CubicCurve2D.Float(
                             x1,y1,x1ctl,y1ctl,
                             x2ctl,y2ctl,x2,y2);
                     controlLine(g2,x1,y1,x1ctl,y1ctl);
                     controlLine(g2,x2,y2,x2ctl,y2ctl);
                     g2.draw(curve);

                     // Fourth curve
                     x1 = 210.0f; y1 = 40.0f;
                     x1ctl = 240.0f; y1ctl = 40.0f;
                     x2ctl = 280.0f; y2ctl = 80.0f;
                     x2 = 250.0f; y2 = 80.0f;
                     curve = new CubicCurve2D.Float(
                             x1,y1,x1ctl,y1ctl,
                             x2ctl,y2ctl,x2,y2);
                     controlLine(g2,x1,y1,x1ctl,y1ctl);
                     controlLine(g2,x2,y2,x2ctl,y2ctl);
                     g2.draw(curve);
          }
          private void controlLine(Graphics2D g2,
                      float x1,float y1,float x2,float y2) {
                     g2.fill(new Rectangle2D.Float(x1 - 3.0f,y1 -
   3.0f,6.0f,6.0f));
                     g2.drawLine((int)x1,(int)y1,(int)x2,(int)y2);
          }
   }
```

The Commentary

The output from CubicCurve2.java is shown in Figure 7.14. This example demonstrates that control points can be used to connect any two points as long as the connection can be made with a curve that does not have to bend in two directions.

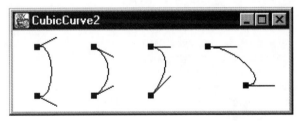

Figure 7.14   Four curves with varying angles.

A Double Cubic Curve

In the previous examples you could extend the lines from the endpoints through their control points and find a place where the two would intersect. This means that the line only had to curve in one direction to make a connection from one to another. However, the curve is cubic and has the ability to make a double curve—an S-curve—to make its connection. This program shows how to make S-curves with the CubicCurve.Float class.

The Code

```java
import java.awt.*;
import java.awt.event.*;
import java.awt.geom.*;
class CubicCurve3 extends Frame {
        public static void main(String arg[]) {
                new CubicCurve3();
        }
        CubicCurve3() {
                super("CubicCurve3");
                addWindowListener(new WindowAdapter() {
                        public void windowClosing(WindowEvent e)
                                { System.exit(0); } } );
                setSize(300,110);
                show();
        }
        public void paint(Graphics g) {
                Graphics2D g2 = (Graphics2D)g;
                float x1, y1;
                float x1ctl, y1ctl;
                float x2ctl, y2ctl;
                float x2, y2;
                CubicCurve2D.Float curve;

                // First curve
                x1 = 30.0f; y1 = 40.0f;
                x1ctl = 50.0f; y1ctl = 30.0f;
                x2ctl = 10.0f; y2ctl = 100.0f;
                x2 = 30.0f; y2 = 90.0f;
                curve = new CubicCurve2D.Float(
                        x1,y1,x1ctl,y1ctl,
                        x2ctl,y2ctl,x2,y2);
                controlLine(g2,x1,y1,x1ctl,y1ctl);
                controlLine(g2,x2,y2,x2ctl,y2ctl);
                g2.draw(curve);

                // Second curve
```

```
x1 = 90.0f;  y1 = 40.0f;
x1ctl = 110.0f;  y1ctl = 50.0f;
x2ctl = 70.0f;  y2ctl = 80.0f;
x2 = 90.0f;  y2 = 90.0f;
curve = new CubicCurve2D.Float(
        x1,y1,x1ctl,y1ctl,
        x2ctl,y2ctl,x2,y2);
controlLine(g2,x1,y1,x1ctl,y1ctl);
controlLine(g2,x2,y2,x2ctl,y2ctl);
g2.draw(curve);


// Third curve
x1 = 150.0f;  y1 = 40.0f;
x1ctl = 170.0f;  y1ctl = 40.0f;
x2ctl = 130.0f;  y2ctl = 70.0f;
x2 = 150.0f;  y2 = 90.0f;
curve = new CubicCurve2D.Float(
        x1,y1,x1ctl,y1ctl,
        x2ctl,y2ctl,x2,y2);
controlLine(g2,x1,y1,x1ctl,y1ctl);
controlLine(g2,x2,y2,x2ctl,y2ctl);
g2.draw(curve);

// Fourth curve
x1 = 210.0f;  y1 = 40.0f;
x1ctl = 240.0f;  y1ctl = 40.0f;
x2ctl = 220.0f;  y2ctl = 80.0f;
x2 = 250.0f;  y2 = 80.0f;
curve = new CubicCurve2D.Float(
        x1,y1,x1ctl,y1ctl,
        x2ctl,y2ctl,x2,y2);
controlLine(g2,x1,y1,x1ctl,y1ctl);
controlLine(g2,x2,y2,x2ctl,y2ctl);
g2.draw(curve);
}
private void controlLine(Graphics2D g2,
            float x1,float y1,float x2,float y2) {
        g2.fill(new Rectangle2D.Float(x1 - 3.0f,y1 -
3.0f,6.0f,6.0f));
        g2.drawLine((int)x1,(int)y1,(int)x2,(int)y2);
    }
}
```

The Commentary

The output from CubicCurve3 appears in Figure 7.15. As you can see, the same rules of direction and magnitude apply for a double curve as for a single one.

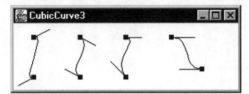

Figure 7.15   Curving that requires bending in both directions.

Drawing Square-Cornered Rectangles

The most commonly drawn shapes, other than straight lines, are squares and rectangles. To simplify the task, the Java2D API includes a pair of pre-defined rectangles—one with square corners and one with rounded corners. This example program, SquareRect, shows how simple it is to create rectangular outlines and filled rectangular areas with square corners.

The Code

```java
import java.awt.*;
import java.awt.event.*;
import java.awt.geom.*;
class SquareRect extends Frame {
        public static void main(String arg[]) {
                new SquareRect();
        }
        SquareRect() {
                super("SquareRect");
                addWindowListener(new WindowAdapter() {
                        public void windowClosing(WindowEvent e)
                                { System.exit(0); } } );
                setSize(220,220);
                show();
        }
        public void paint(Graphics g) {
                Graphics2D g2 = (Graphics2D)g;
                Rectangle2D rect = new Rectangle2D.Float();
                rect.setRect(10f,30f,80f,40f);
                g2.draw(rect);
                rect.setRect(100f,30f,60f,60f);
                g2.draw(rect);
                rect.setRect(170f,30f,40f,80f);
                g2.draw(rect);
                rect.setRect(10f,130f,80f,40f);
                g2.fill(rect);
                rect.setRect(100f,130f,60f,60f);
                g2.fill(rect);
```

```
        rect.setRect(170f,130f,40f,80f);
        g2.fill(rect);
    }
}
```

The Commentary

This program creates and draws six rectangles—three hollow and three filled. The process of creating a square-cornered rectangle involves declaring a new instance of the Rectangle2D.Float object, then using the setRect() method to locate the rectangle in space. Here's one such procedure:

```
Rectangle2D rect = new Rectangle2D.Float();
rect.setRect(10f,30f,80f,40f);
```

Hollow rectangles are actually written to the screen with the draw() method:

```
g2.draw(rect);
```

Alternately, filled rectangles are drawn with the fill() method:

```
g2.fill(rect);
```

The output is shown in Figure 7.16.

Drawing Round-Cornered Rectangles

The program RoundRect is very much like the previous example, except that there are "roundness" values supplied for each rectangle that define the softness of the rectangles' corners.

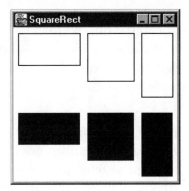

Figure 7.16 Square-cornered rectangles.

The Code

```
import java.awt.*;
import java.awt.event.*;
import java.awt.geom.*;
class RoundRect extends Frame {
    public static void main(String arg[]) {
        new RoundRect();
    }
    RoundRect() {
        super("RoundRect");
        addWindowListener(new WindowAdapter() {
            public void windowClosing(WindowEvent e)
                { System.exit(0); } } );
        setSize(440,440);
        show();
    }
    public void paint(Graphics g) {
        Graphics2D g2 = (Graphics2D)g;
        RoundRectangle2D rect = new RoundRectangle2D.Float();
        rect.setRoundRect(20f,60f,160f,80f,20f,20f);
        g2.draw(rect);
        rect.setRoundRect(200f,60f,120f,120f,24f,24f);
        g2.draw(rect);
        rect.setRoundRect(340f,60f,80f,160f,20f,44f);
        g2.draw(rect);
        rect.setRoundRect(20f,260f,160f,80f,20f,20f);
        g2.fill(rect);
        rect.setRoundRect(200f,260f,120f,120f,28f,28f);
        g2.fill(rect);
        rect.setRoundRect(340f,260f,80f,160f,20f,44f);
        g2.fill(rect);
    }
}
```

The Commentary

Note that when the rectangles are located with setRect()—they're instances of the RoundRectangle2D.Float class, by the way—there are six floats in the arguments, as opposed to the four that defined the square rectangles. The extra two floats dictate the degree to which the corners are broken.

There are two roundness numbers—the first for horizontal and the second for vertical. In each case, the roundness specifications are the number of pixels back from the corner (the point at which the lines would intersect, were they continued) where the curvature will start. The corners are curved exactly like the quadratic curves described earlier with an implied control point at the imaginary rectangle corner and the two roundness values defining the endpoints of the curve. The output appears in Figure 7.17.

Using a GenPath Object to Append Shapes

It is possible to combine a number of Shape objects into a single GeneralPath object (which itself is a Shape object). A Shape object is one that implements the Shape interface. The classes that do this, either directly or through inheritance, are:

- Arc2D
- CubicCurve2D
- Ellipse2D
- GeneralPath
- Line2D

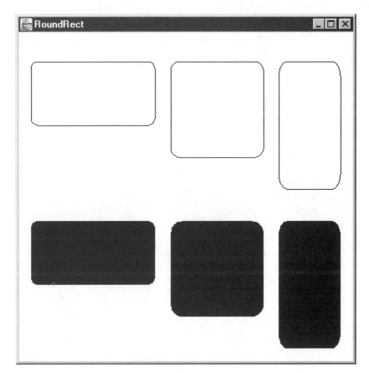

Figure 7.17 Rounded rectangles.

- Polygon
- QuadCurve2D
- Rectangle
- Rectangle2D
- RectangularShape
- RoundRectangle2D

This means that an object of any of these classes can be used as an argument in the attach() method of a GeneralPath object. The following program shows how this works.

The output of the program is shown in Figure 7.18.

The Code

```
import java.awt.*;
import java.awt.event.*;
import java.awt.geom.*;
class Combine extends Frame {
        GeneralPath part1;
        GeneralPath part2;
        GeneralPath part3;
        public static void main(String arg[]) {
                new Combine();
        }
        Combine() {
                super("Combine");
                addWindowListener(new WindowAdapter() {
                        public void windowClosing(WindowEvent e)
                                { System.exit(0); } } );
                setSize(300,500);
                makeParts();
                show();
        }
        private void makeParts() {
                part1 = new GeneralPath(
                                GeneralPath.WIND_EVEN_ODD);
                part1.moveTo(25f,100f);
                part1.lineTo(50f,25f);
                part1.lineTo(75f,100f);

                part2 = new GeneralPath(
                                GeneralPath.WIND_EVEN_ODD);
                part2.moveTo(100f,25f);
                part2.lineTo(100f,100f);
```

```
                    part3 = new GeneralPath(
                                 GeneralPath.WIND_EVEN_ODD);
                    part3.moveTo(125f,25f);
                    part3.lineTo(150f,100f);
                    part3.lineTo(175f,25f);
            }

        public void paint(Graphics g) {
                    Graphics2D g2 = (Graphics2D)g;
                    AffineTransform at = new AffineTransform();
                    // Top row
                    at.setToTranslation(25f,50f);
                    g2.setTransform(at);
                    g2.draw(part1);
                    g2.draw(part2);
                    g2.draw(part3);
                    // Middle row
                    GeneralPath unconnected = new GeneralPath(
                                 GeneralPath.WIND_EVEN_ODD);
                    unconnected.append(part1,false);
                    unconnected.append(part2,false);
                    unconnected.append(part3,false);
                    at.setToTranslation(25f,175f);
                    g2.setTransform(at);
                    g2.draw(unconnected);
                    // Bottom row
                    GeneralPath connected = new GeneralPath(
                                 GeneralPath.WIND_EVEN_ODD);
                    connected.append(part1,true);
                    connected.append(part2,true);
                    connected.append(part3,true);
                    at.setToTranslation(25f,300f);
                    g2.setTransform(at);
                    g2.draw(connected);
            }
    }
```

The Commentary

The program defines three simple shapes as the GeneralPath object part1, part2, and part3. The three parts are then displayed separately, and are also combined into a GeneralPath object and displayed again as a single Shape.

The three parts are displayed three times. The first row shows how the three of them look when displayed separately—each one requiting its own draw() method call. The second row shows how they are displayed as a single unit after being combined into the GeneralPath object named

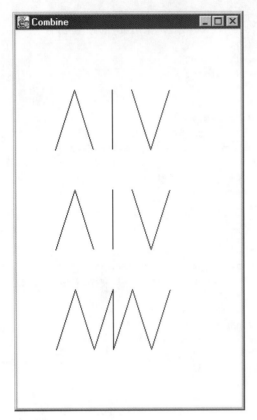

Figure 7.18 Combining three line segments into one.

unconnected. The drawings themselves remain at the same locations but the program uses an AffineTransform on the Graphics2D object to move them to separate locations in the frame.

False Arguments

Note that the append() method calls use false as their second arguments to add the three parts to unconnected—this instructs the GeneralPath not to draw a line from the end of the previous figure to the beginning of the next one. This causes the three figures to have no connections to one another and to show up as three disjointed figures just as they were when they were drawn separately.

The third row is a display of the GeneralPath object called connected. This third row shows the results of connecting the end of one drawing with the beginning of another by specify true as the second argument on the append() method calls. Notice that even though true was specified for the first of the three, there is no line drawn to its beginning because there was no information already inside the GeneralPath object, so there was no previously defined point from which to draw a line.

Connecting Shapes

The program GeneralShape shows how you can connect different types of Shapes and use drawing methods to create an irregular shape.

The Code

```
import java.awt.*;
import java.awt.event.*;
import java.awt.geom.*;
class GeneralShape extends Frame {
        GeneralPath widget;
        public static void main(String arg[]) {
                new GeneralShape();
        }
        GeneralShape() {
                super("GeneralShape");
                addWindowListener(new WindowAdapter() {
                        public void windowClosing(WindowEvent e)
                                { System.exit(0); } } );
                setSize(300,320);
                widget = makeWidget();
                show();
        }
        private GeneralPath makeWidget() {
                GeneralPath w = new GeneralPath(
                        GeneralPath.WIND_EVEN_ODD);
                // Top left corner
                w.moveTo(110f,100f);
                w.lineTo(110f,120f);
                w.lineTo(150f,120f);
                // Top connecting curve
                CubicCurve2D cc1 = new CubicCurve2D.Float(
                        150f,120f,
                        170f,120f,
                        230f,100f,
                        250f,100f);
                w.append(cc1,true);
                // Oval on right
                w.curveTo(270f,80f,
                        270f,140f,
```

```
                            250f,120f);
                    // Bottom connecting curve
                    CubicCurve2D cc2 = new CubicCurve2D.Float(
                            250f,120f,
                            230f,120f,
                            170f,300f,
                            110f,300f);
                    w.append(cc2,true);
                    // Half circle at left
                    Arc2D arc = new Arc2D.Float(10f,100f,
                            200f,200f,
                            270f,-135f,
                            Arc2D.OPEN);
                    w.append(arc,true);
                    // Draw a straight line to close figure
                    w.closePath();
                    return(w);
            }

            public void paint(Graphics g) {
                    Graphics2D g2 = (Graphics2D)g;
                    g2.draw(widget);
            }
    }
```

The Commentary

The program first constructs a GeneralPath object by calling the makeWidget() method. The shape of the widget is made up of different shapes all joined together end to end.

First, the makeWidget() method draws a 90-degree angle by drawing two straight lines. This creates the corner at the top of the shape as shown in Figure 7.19.

Second, a CubicCurve2D object is created and then appended, by a call to the append() method, to the previously drawn straight lines. The ending coordinates of the line match the beginning coordinates of a curve, and true is specified on the call to the append() method so the two link up cleanly. If the points were not at the same location, the append() method would simply draw a straight line to connect them.

Third, the oval on the right is drawn by using the curveTo() method of GeneralPath—the result of doing this is the same as the previous operation of creating a cubic curve separately and appending it.

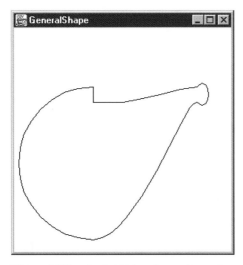

Figure 7.19 An irregular shape drawn by combining different shapes.

Fourth, another cubic curve is appended to draw the line of the figure from the oval down and to the bottom center.

Fifth, the figure is enclosed on the left by appending an arc circling clockwise from the bottom leaving only a small gap at the upper left of the figure. Notice that the arc starts at 270 degrees (straight down) and rotates clockwise (negative degrees) to wind up at the upper left of the figure.

Finally, the closePath() method is called to instruct GeneralPath to close the figure (drawing a straight line if necessary to do so). A line is drawn from the end of the last segment (the arc) to the beginning of the first segment (the straight line).

The output of this program appears in Figure 7.19.

Using an Area Object To Combine Shapes

This example uses an Area object to create new shapes by combining existing shapes. The combinations are made in different ways.

The Code

```
import java.awt.*;
import java.awt.event.*;
```

```
import java.awt.geom.*;
public class AreaManipulate extends Frame {
        Area box;
        Area ellipse;
        public static void main(String arg[]) {
                new AreaManipulate();
        }
        AreaManipulate() {
                super("AreaManipulate");
                addWindowListener(new WindowAdapter() {
                        public void windowClosing(WindowEvent e)
                                { System.exit(0); } } );
                setSize(460,400);
                show();
        }
        private void makeParts() {
                Rectangle2D b = new Rectangle2D.Float(50f,0f,100f,40f);
                box = new Area(b);
                Ellipse2D e = new Ellipse2D.Float(0f,10f,200f,20f);
                ellipse = new Area(e);
        }

        public void paint(Graphics g) {
                Graphics2D g2 = (Graphics2D)g;
                AffineTransform at = new AffineTransform();
                // Top center. Separate figures.
                makeParts();
                at.setToTranslation(110f,50f);
                g2.setTransform(at);
                g2.draw(box);
                g2.draw(ellipse);
                // Area add().
                makeParts();
                box.add(ellipse);
                at.setToTranslation(10f,100f);
                g2.setTransform(at);
                g2.draw(box);
                at.setToTranslation(220f,100f);
                g2.setTransform(at);
                g2.fill(box);
                // Area exclusiveOr().
                makeParts();
                box.exclusiveOr(ellipse);
                at.setToTranslation(10f,150f);
                g2.setTransform(at);
                g2.draw(box);
                at.setToTranslation(220f,150f);
                g2.setTransform(at);
                g2.fill(box);
                // Area intersect().
                makeParts();
                box.intersect(ellipse);
```

```
                g2.setTransform(at);
                at.setToTranslation(10f,200f);
                g2.draw(box);
                at.setToTranslation(220f,200f);
                g2.setTransform(at);
                g2.fill(box);
                // Area subtract().
                makeParts();
                box.subtract(ellipse);
                at.setToTranslation(10f,250f);
                g2.setTransform(at);
                g2.draw(box);
                at.setToTranslation(220f,250f);
                g2.setTransform(at);
                g2.fill(box);
                // Area subtract().
                makeParts();
                ellipse.subtract(box);
                at.setToTranslation(10f,300f);
                g2.setTransform(at);
                g2.draw(ellipse);
                at.setToTranslation(220f,300f);
                g2.setTransform(at);
                g2.fill(ellipse);
        }
    }
```

The Commentary

This example uses several different methods of combining a rectangle and an ellipse, and then renders the results of each with both a fill and drawing action. The output is shown in Figure 7.20.

The method makeParts() is used to create two objects—a rectangle and an ellipse. This is done by first creating Rectangle2D and Ellipse2D objects and using the appropriate Area constructor to create an Area instance for each of them. This gives us two Area objects that can be combined. The makeParts() method is called repeatedly to create new fundamental objects that we combine in different ways.

The paint() method does all the work. It begins by displaying, at the top center, the two separate Areas, one on top of the other. The paint() method goes on to combine these two Areas, the box and the ellipse, in different ways. Any number of areas can be combined into one—this example combines simple pairs to demonstrate the results of different combining methods.

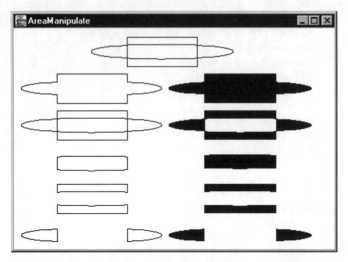

Figure 7.20 Combining shapes with an area object.

Using the add() method to combine two Areas results in an Area from the outer perimeter of the shapes being combined. The topmost pair (drawn on the left and filled on the right) demonstrate the results. As you can see, the result is an outline tracing with all interior lines eliminated.

The next row of the display shows the results of combining the figures using the exclusiveOr() method. This results in a figure that includes all the areas included by one figure or the other, but not by both. Although the drawing of the outline looks like the outline of both the original figures, when the figure is filled it shows that it is really four figures that meet only at the points at which the original outlines crossed.

The next row shows the results of using the intersect() method. As you can see, it is sort of the opposite—the complement, if you prefer—of the exclusiveOr() method. It includes only the regions that are inside both figures.

The two bottom rows use the subtract() method to combine areas. Whenever one shape is subtracted from another, the entire area of the subtracted shape is removed. If it happens to overlap a part of the shape being subtracted from, that part is removed also. The next-to-last row is the result of subtracting the ellipse from the box, and the last row is the box being subtracted from the ellipse.

Please note that AreaManipulate worked properly in Java 2 betas, but not in the final version of Java 2 (in that version, the program fills the shapes, but won't draw them). JavaSoft knows about this problem and may have fixed it by the time you run this program.

CHAPTER 8

Fitting Text

The terms defined in this chapter are used to describe text in Java. A *string* is a collection of characters that make up the body of the text. These characters are kept in a String object in Java. A String object is basically an array of 16-bit Unicode characters, and a string is an array of a fixed number of these characters.

A *glyph* is the drawing of a Unicode character. The same character can have a number of different glyphs to represent it—that is, a character can be drawn in different ways. Also, there are glyphs that represent more than one Unicode character. These character pairs are called *ligatures* and are often used to combine the first two letters of words, such as the "fi" in "finger" and the "Æ" in "Aesop." This means that there is not always a one-to-one correspondence between the characters and the glyphs.

A *font* is a collection of glyphs that all have a common style. That is, all the glyphs of any particular font will look like they all go together to form a set. The words you are reading right now are all from the same font and so they have same sort of appearance—they all come from a set of glyphs designed together.

A single font can have multiple *faces*. The faces of a font will differ in specific ways, such as heavy, medium, oblique, and regular. The basic

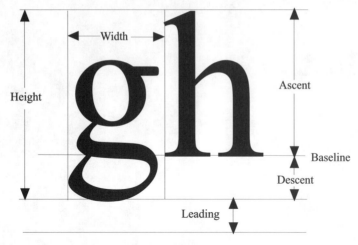

Figure 8.1 The dimensions of a glyph.

appearance of the font is the same, but each glyph has been modified to have a slightly different appearance, while still being recognizable as a member of the same font. A font *family* is the collection of all the font faces for a particular font.

The dimensions of a glyph have some specific names, as shown in Figure 8.1. The height is the sum of the ascent and the descent from the baseline. The width of a glyph—sometimes called the *advance* because it is the number of pixels to advance to display the next character—includes the space on one side of the glyph.

All the Font Families

There are a number of font families distributed as a part of Java. Inside a program, a font family is identified by its name. If a program requests a font family that does not exist, Java silently supplies the program with one that does exist. This program shows how you can list all the font family names that should be resident on your system.

The Code

```
import java.awt.*;
public class ListAllFontFamilies {
    public static void main(String[] arg) {
        GraphicsEnvironment gi =
            GraphicsEnvironment.getLocalGraphicsEnvironment();
```

```
        String[] name = gi.getAvailableFontFamilyNames();
        for(int i=0; i<name.length; i++) {
            Font pl = new Font(name[i],Font.PLAIN,12);
            Font bo = new Font(name[i],Font.BOLD,12);
            Font it = new Font(name[i],Font.ITALIC,12);
            Font bi = new Font(name[i],Font.BOLD | Font.ITALIC,12);
            System.out.println(name[i]);
            System.out.println("      plain[family=" + pl.getFamily()
                + ",font=" + pl.getFontName() + "]");
            System.out.println("     italic[family=" + it.getFamily()
                + ",font=" + it.getFontName() + "]");
            System.out.println("       bold[family=" + bo.getFamily()
                + ",font=" + bo.getFontName() + "]");
            System.out.println("  bold/ital[family=" + bi.getFamily()
                + ",font=" + bi.getFontName() + "]");
            System.out.println();
        }
        System.exit(0);
    }
}
```

The Commentary

The default GraphicsEnvironment object is retrieved and its method get-LocalGraphcisEnvironment() is used to retrieve the array of names of font families. This array is then used in a loop to create four different fonts from each of the font families. The family name and actual font names are printed for each of them. Most of the printed entries have consistent names and look something like these:

```
Allegro BT
      plain[family=Allegro BT,font=Allegro BT]
     italic[family=Allegro BT,font=Allegro BT]
       bold[family=Allegro BT,font=Allegro BT]
  bold/ital[family=Allegro BT,font=Allegro BT]

AmerType Md BT
      plain[family=AmerType Md BT,font=American Typewriter Medium BT]
     italic[family=AmerType Md BT,font=American Typewriter Medium BT]
       bold[family=AmerType Md BT,font=American Typewriter Medium BT]
  bold/ital[family=AmerType Md BT,font=American Typewriter Medium BT]

Arial
      plain[family=Arial,font=Arial]
     italic[family=Arial,font=Arial]
       bold[family=Arial,font=Arial]
  bold/ital[family=Arial,font=Arial]
```

Different implementations of Java will have different lists of font families. The version we used to generate this list contained a total of 72 font families. And there are some special cases that show up—it might be best to consider the name supplied to the constructor of the Font class as a hint because some internal decisions are made when the exact font you ask for is not available. For example, using the Default name can cause different fonts to be returned for different styles:

```
Default
      plain[family=Arial,font=Arial]
     italic[family=sansserif.italic,font=sansserif.italic]
       bold[family=sansserif.bold,font=sansserif.bold]
  bold/ital[family=sansserif.bolditalic,font=sansserif.bolditalic]
```

For some, there can be a translation from one font family name to another to satisfy a request. For example, the Dialog font has a different family for each style:

```
Dialog
      plain[family=dialog,font=dialog]
     italic[family=dialog.italic,font=dialog.italic]
       bold[family=dialog.bold,font=dialog.bold]
  bold/ital[family=dialog.bolditalic,font=dialog.bolditalic]
```

If you request a font with a style that cannot be produced by that family, the constructor may translate the request to another family. This way, if a program requests some special style in a font family, the resulting text will at least look different. For example, if a request is made to a family that only has one style, the request results in another family being chosen, like this:

```
dialog.bold
      plain[family=dialog.bold,font=dialog.bold]
     italic[family=Arial,font=Arial Negreta]
       bold[family=Arial,font=Arial Negreta]
  bold/ital[family=Arial,font=Arial Negreta]

dialog.bolditalic
      plain[family=dialog.bolditalic,font=dialog.bolditalic]
     italic[family=Arial,font=Arial Negreta cursiva]
       bold[family=Arial,font=Arial Negreta cursiva]
  bold/ital[family=Arial,font=Arial Negreta cursiva]

dialog.italic
      plain[family=dialog.italic,font=dialog.italic]
     italic[family=Arial,font=Arial Cursiva]
```

```
      bold[family=Arial,font=Arial Cursiva]
 bold/ital[family=Arial,font=Arial Cursiva]
```

All the Fonts

There is another way to get the names of the fonts. The default Graphics-Environment object produces an array of Font objects—one for each font defined in the system.

The Code

```
import java.awt.*;
public class ListAllFonts {
    public static void main(String[] arg) {
        GraphicsEnvironment gi =
            GraphicsEnvironment.getLocalGraphicsEnvironment();
        Font[] font = gi.getAllFonts();
        for(int i=0; i<font.length; i++) {
            System.out.println(font[i].getFontName());
        }
        System.exit(0);
    }
}
```

The Commentary

The array of Font objects returned from getAllFonts() includesevery font defined in the system. These Font objects are not directly usable because they have their points sizes set to 1. The actual font list could vary from one platform to another. Table 8.1 is a typical list.

Table 8.1 The Complete List of Fonts

Allegro BT	Oz Handicraft BT
American Typewriter Medium BT	Poster Bodoni BT
Arial	Serifa BT
Arial Black	Serifa Bold BT
Arial Cursiva	Serifa Italic BT
Arial Negreta	Serifa Thin BT
Arial Negreta cursiva	Shelley Allegro BT
Avant Garde Book BT	Souvenir Demi BT *Continues*

Table 8.1   The Complete List of Fonts *(Continued)*

Avant Garde Book Oblique BT	Souvenir Demi Italic BT
Avant Garde Medium BT	Souvenir Light BT
Avant Garde Medium Oblique BT	Souvenir Light Italic BT
Bank Gothic Medium BT	Staccato 222 BT
Benguiat Bold BT	Swiss 911 Extra Compressed BT
Bernhard Fashion BT	Symbol
Bernhard Modern Bold BT	Tahoma
Bernhard Modern Bold Italic BT	Times New Roman
Bremen Bold BT	Times New Roman Negreta
Charlesworth Bold	Times New Roman Negreta cursiva
Comic Sans MS	Times New Roman cursiva
Comic Sans MS Bold	Typo Upright BT
CommonBullets	Verdana
Copperplate Gothic Bold BT	Verdana Cursiva
Courier New	Verdana Negreta
Courier New Cursiva	Verdana Negreta cursiva
Courier New Negreta	Wingdings
Courier New Negreta cursiva	Zapf Elliptical 711 BT
Dauphin	Zapf Elliptical 711 Bold BT
Futura Black BT	Zapf Elliptical 711 Bold Italic BT
Futura Bold BT	Zapf Elliptical 711 Italic BT
Futura Bold Italic BT	Zurich Black Extended BT
Futura Extra Black BT	Zurich Extended BT
Futura Light BT	dialog
Futura Light Italic BT	dialog.bold
Goudy Handtooled BT	dialog.bolditalic
Goudy Old Style BT	dialog.italic
Goudy Old Style Bold BT	dialoginput
Goudy Old Style Bold Italic BT	dialoginput.bold
Goudy Old Style Italic BT	dialoginput.bolditalic
Humanist 521 BT	dialoginput.italic
Humanist 521 Bold BT	monospaced
Humanist 521 Bold Italic BT	monospaced.bold

Table 8.1 *Continued*

Humanist 521 Italic BT	monospaced.bolditalic
Impact	monospaced.italic
Kabel Book BT	sansserif
Kabel Ultra BT	sansserif.bold
Lithograph Bold	sansserif.bolditalic
LithographLight	sansserif.italic
Lucida Console	serif
Lucida Sans Unicode	serif.bold
Marlett	serif.bolditalic
OCR-A BT	serif.italic
OCR-B 10 Pitch BT	

Showing All Fonts

This example uses a list of all the fonts to allow the user to display each one with selected attributes.

The Code

```
import java.awt.*;
import java.awt.event.*;
public class FontDemo extends Frame
        implements ActionListener, ItemListener {
    private FontDemoCanvas fontDemoCanvas;
    private Choice fontChoice;
    private Choice pointChoice;
    private Checkbox bold;
    private Checkbox italic;

    private static int MIN_POINTSIZE = 6;
    private static int MAX_POINTSIZE = 72;
    private static int DEFAULT_POINTSIZE = 20;

    private Font[] fontArray;
    private Font font;
    private int fontIndex;
    private int fontStyle;
    private int pointSize;
```

```java
        public static void main(String[] arg) {
            new FontDemo();
        }
        FontDemo() {
            setInitialValues();
            createDialog();
            pack();
            show();
        }
        private void setInitialValues() {
            fontStyle = Font.PLAIN;
            pointSize = DEFAULT_POINTSIZE;
            fontIndex = 0;
            GraphicsEnvironment gi =
                GraphicsEnvironment.getLocalGraphicsEnvironment();
            fontArray = gi.getAllFonts();
            font = fontArray[fontIndex].deriveFont(fontStyle,
(float)pointSize);
        }
        private void createDialog() {
            fontDemoCanvas = new FontDemoCanvas(300,100);
            add("Center",fontDemoCanvas);
            Panel p = new Panel();
            createFontChoice();
            p.add(fontChoice);
            createPointChoice();
            p.add(pointChoice);
            bold = new Checkbox("Bold");
            bold.addItemListener(this);
            p.add(bold);
            italic = new Checkbox("Italic");
            italic.addItemListener(this);
            p.add(italic);
            Button exit = new Button("Exit");
            exit.addActionListener(this);
            p.add(exit);
            add("South",p);
            fontDemoCanvas.setValues(font);
        }
        private void createFontChoice() {
            fontChoice = new Choice();
            fontChoice.addItemListener(this);
            for(int i=0; i<fontArray.length; i++)
                fontChoice.addItem(fontArray[i].getFontName());
        }
        private void createPointChoice() {
            pointChoice = new Choice();
            pointChoice.addItemListener(this);
            for(int i=MIN_POINTSIZE; i<=MAX_POINTSIZE; i++)
                pointChoice.addItem(i + " pt");
            pointChoice.select(DEFAULT_POINTSIZE + " pt");
```

```
                    pointSize = DEFAULT_POINTSIZE;
            }
        public void itemStateChanged(ItemEvent event) {
            if(bold.getState()) {
                if(italic.getState()) {
                    fontStyle = Font.BOLD | Font.ITALIC;
                } else {
                    fontStyle = Font.BOLD;
                }
            } else if(italic.getState()) {
                fontStyle = Font.ITALIC;
            } else {
                fontStyle = Font.PLAIN;
            }
            pointSize = pointChoice.getSelectedIndex();
            pointSize += MIN_POINTSIZE;
            fontIndex = fontChoice.getSelectedIndex();
            font = fontArray[fontIndex].deriveFont(fontStyle,
(float)pointSize);
            fontDemoCanvas.setValues(font);
        }
        public void actionPerformed(ActionEvent event) {
            System.exit(0);
        }
class FontDemoCanvas extends Canvas {
    Font font;
    public FontDemoCanvas(int width,int height) {
        setSize(width,height);
    }
    public void setValues(Font font) {
        this.font = font;
        repaint();
    }
    public void paint(Graphics gc) {
        gc.setFont(font);
        gc.setColor(Color.black);
        gc.drawString(font.getFontName(),5,getSize().height * 2 / 3);
    }
}
}
```

The Commentary

This program displays a dialog window that can be used to select a font and its characteristics. The window is shown in Figure 8.2 with the font selection list displaying a few of the font names. As you select names and options, you will see that some fonts are not affected by the settings while others are.

Figure 8.2 The current selection is monospaced and set to bold.

The method setInitialValues() defines the current values to be displayed—the font and its settings. The static method getAllFonts() of the GraphicsEnvironment class is used to retrieve an array containing one member for each of the available fonts. The default font is taken to be the first member of the fontArray. A FontDemoObject class is created to be used as the component to display the text demonstrating the characteristics of the font.

The Font objects returned from getAllFonts() all have their point sizes set to one, and have the bold and italic styles turned off. However, some fonts are always bold and/or italic, and some are never bold and/or italic—changing the style flags simply has no effect on them. Some fonts will change their appearance, requested by the style settings, by switching to another font in the list. A few will keep the same name but render themselves in a fashion suitable to the settings.

The method createDialog() constructs the display window and sets up the callback method as being itemStateChanged(). This will be the method called each time a registered component changes state—that is to say, changes its value. To create the dialog, the method createFontChoice() is used to instantiate a Choice object that contains a list of all the font names—this is done by getting the names from the array of Font objects in fontArray. The method createPointChoice() is used to build a choice box from which the point size can be selected. The point sizes made available range from MIN_POINTSIZE to MAX_POINTSIZE. The starting point size is set to the DEFAULT_POINTSIZE.

The method itemStateChanged() is called each time the user changes a value displayed in the dialog window. This method looks at the current settings to determine which font is used, and to determine what characteristics it has. This done, a new Font object is created by calling one of the deriveFont() methods of the Font class, and the setValues() method of the FontDemoCanvas object is called to display it. There is more than one of these deriveFont() methods in the Font class—each one takes different arguments, so there is more than one way to derive a new font from an old one.

The class FontDemoCanvas is a Canvas object that is used to display a rectangular area containing the name of the font in the left. The method setValues() is called to supply a new font and to have it displayed. It calls the method repaint()—which schedules a call to paint().

A bug in Java shows up here, though it may have been fixed by the time you read this. If you change a font's bold or italic attribute, it won't show up unless you also change the font's size.

Basics of String Drawing

There are a number of ways to draw strings of characters to a window. This program demonstrates several ways to do it. Consider this program as sort of an overview of the mechanics of getting characters onto the display—the examples following this one give more detail on character manipulation based the techniques shown here.

The Code

```
import java.awt.*;
import java.awt.event.*;
import java.awt.font.*;
import java.awt.geom.*;
import java.text.*;
import java.util.*;
class LayingOutText extends Frame {
    public static void main(String arg[]) {
        new LayingOutText();
    }
    LayingOutText() {
        super("LayingOutText");
        addWindowListener(new WindowAdapter() {
            public void windowClosing(WindowEvent e)
                { System.exit(0); } } );
        add(new LayingOutTextCanvas());
```

```java
            pack();
            show();
    }
    class LayingOutTextCanvas extends Canvas {
        Font font;
        LayingOutTextCanvas() {
            AffineTransform at = new AffineTransform();
            at.setToShear(1.2,0);
            font = new Font("TimesRoman",Font.BOLD,32);
            setSize(350,450);
        }
        public void paint(Graphics g) {
            Graphics2D g2 = (Graphics2D)g;
            g2.setFont(font);
            simpleString(g2,50,50);
            simpleCharArray(g2,50,100);
            simpleTextLayout(g2,50,150);
            outlineTextLayout(g2,50,200);
            simpleAttributedString(g2,50,250);
            mappedAttributedString(g2,50,300);
            simpleGlyphVector(g2,50,350);
            mappedGlyphVector(g2,50,400);
        }
        private void simpleString(Graphics2D g2,int x,int y) {
            g2.drawString("Simple String",x,y);
        }
        private void simpleCharArray(Graphics2D g2,int x,int y) {
            char[] array = { 'C','h','a','r',' ','A','r','r','a','y' };
            g2.drawChars(array,0,10,x,y);
        }
        private void simpleTextLayout(Graphics2D g2,int x,int y) {
            AffineTransform at = new AffineTransform();
            FontRenderContext frc = new FontRenderContext(at,false,false);
            TextLayout tl = new TextLayout("TextLayout",font,frc);
            tl.draw(g2,x,y);
        }
        private void outlineTextLayout(Graphics2D g2,int x,int y) {
            AffineTransform at = new AffineTransform();
            at.setToTranslation(x,y);
            FontRenderContext frc = new FontRenderContext(at,false,false);
            TextLayout tl = new TextLayout("TextLayout outline",font,frc);
            Shape s = tl.getOutline(null);
            g2.draw(s);
        }
        private void simpleAttributedString(Graphics2D g2,int x,int y) {
            AttributedString as =
                    new AttributedString("AttributedString default");
            AttributedCharacterIterator aci = as.getIterator();
            g2.drawString(aci,x,y);
        }
        private void mappedAttributedString(Graphics2D g2,int x,int y) {
            Map map = font.getAttributes();
```

```
                   AttributedString as =
                         new AttributedString("AttributedString Map",map);
                   AttributedCharacterIterator aci = as.getIterator();
                   g2.drawString(aci,x,y);
             }
        private void simpleGlyphVector(Graphics2D g2,int x,int y) {
             AffineTransform at = new AffineTransform();
             FontRenderContext frc = new FontRenderContext(at,false,false);
             GlyphVector gv = font.createGlyphVector(frc,"GlyphVector");
             g2.drawGlyphVector(gv,x,y);
        }
        private void mappedGlyphVector(Graphics2D g2,int x,int y) {
             AffineTransform at = new AffineTransform();
             FontRenderContext frc = new FontRenderContext(at,false,false);
             Map map = font.getAttributes();
             AttributedString as = new AttributedString("Mapped
    GlyphVector",map);
             AttributedCharacterIterator aci = as.getIterator();
             GlyphVector gv = font.createGlyphVector(frc,aci);
             g2.drawGlyphVector(gv,x,y);
        }
    }
    }
```

The Commentary

A Canvas window is opened and various methods are used to display strings of characters. For the most part, the techniques used here aren't anything fancy—the resulting display is straightforward and could have been done in a much simpler way—but this program was designed to demonstrate the basic steps necessary in the creation and use some of the more complicated character graphics.

The paint() method, called by the system to display the dialog, casts the Graphics object into a Graphics2D object and sets the font. Then methods are called for different ways to display a string of characters—each of these methods is passed the Graphics2D object and the x,y location of the string.

The method simpleString() uses the method drawString() in the Graphics2D object to display the contents of a String object.

The method simpleCharArray() creates an array that will hold ten chars and then uses the method drawChars() to display them. The second argument is the starting point in the array. The third argument is the number of characters to display. There is another method, named draw-Bytes(), that uses the same arguments and works the same way as this one, except it uses a byte array instead of a char array.

The method simpleTextLayout() creates a TextLayout object and uses its draw() method—not any of the methods in the Graphics2D object. The TextLayout class has some flexibility in the way strings can be displayed (as shown in the following section), so it needs more information on its constructor. It needs a string of characters, the font and its attributes, and a FontRenderContext. For this example, a default FontRenderContext is created.

The method outlineTextLayout() is the same as the previous example, except it does not draw the string—it draws a Shape that is the outline of the string. An AffineTransform is used as an argument in the creation of the FontRenderContext which, in turn, is used to create the TextLayout. The getOutline() method of TextLayout is used to return the Shape. Normally, the argument to getOutline() is an AffineTransform, but, if one were used here, both it and the internal one would apply to the Shape. In this example a null argument was passed to prevent more than one transform from occurring.

The method simpleAttributedString() creates an AttributedString object, taking the default attribute settings, and retrieves an AttributedCharacterIterator from it. The Graphics2D method drawString() displays the results using its own context—the font is supplied by the AttributedString.

The method mappedAttributedString() is the same as the previous one, except it uses a Map object to set the attributes.

The method simpleGlyphVector() demonstrates the creation of a GlyphVector object and uses the method drawGlyphVector() of Graphics2D. The GlyphVector requires a FontRenderContext object which, in turn, requires an AffineTransform object. The FontRenderContext has two setting, both of which are boolean values: One specifies whether there is to be antialiasing and/or fractional-metrics to smooth the edges of the displayed characters. The GlyphVector object is constructed by the Font object, so it gets its style information from there.

The method mappedGlyphVector() is much like the previous method, except there is a bit more involved in creating the GlyphVector. Instead of getting it directly from a string, the characters are supplied by an AttributedCharacterIterator object which, in turn, is supplied by an AttributedString. Figure 8.3 shows the results of the various approaches, all of which yield similar results.

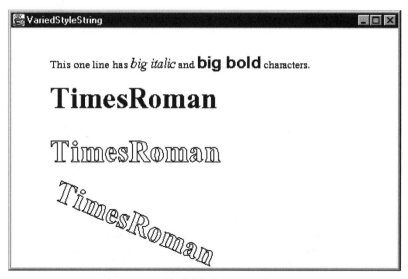

Figure 8.3 The results of different approaches to laying out text.

Basic Operations with TextLayout

The TextLayout class is a very handy tool for doing some specific things with text.

Code

```java
import java.awt.*;
import java.awt.event.*;
import java.awt.geom.*;
import java.awt.font.*;
import java.text.*;
class LayoutTextShow extends Frame {
    public static void main(String arg[]) {
        new LayoutTextShow();
    }
    LayoutTextShow() {
        super("LayoutTextShow");
        addWindowListener(new WindowAdapter() {
            public void windowClosing(WindowEvent e)
                { System.exit(0); } } );
        add(new LayoutTextShowCanvas());
        pack();
        show();
    }
class LayoutTextShowCanvas extends Canvas {
    Font font;
```

```
    LayoutTextShowCanvas() {
        font = new Font("Times New Roman",Font.BOLD,42);
        setSize(350,450);
    }
    public void paint(Graphics g) {
        Graphics2D g2 = (Graphics2D)g;
        g2.setFont(font);
        showBounding(g2,50,50);
        showHighlight(g2,50,100);
        showOutlining(g2,50,150);
        showTiltedLine(g2,50,200);
        showTiltedOutline(g2,50,250);
        showShear(g2,50,400);
    }
    private void showBounding(Graphics2D g2,int x,int y) {
        FontRenderContext frc = g2.getFontRenderContext();
        TextLayout tl = new TextLayout("Bounded Text",font,frc);
        tl.draw(g2,x,y);
        Rectangle2D rect = tl.getBounds();
        rect.setRect(rect.getX() + x,rect.getY() + y,
                rect.getWidth(),rect.getHeight());
        g2.draw(rect);
    }
    private void showHighlight(Graphics2D g2,int x,int y) {
        FontRenderContext frc = g2.getFontRenderContext();
        TextLayout tl = new TextLayout("Highlighting",font,frc);
        Rectangle2D rect = tl.getBounds();
        rect.setRect(rect.getX() + x,rect.getY() + y,
                rect.getWidth(),rect.getHeight());
        g2.setColor(Color.lightGray);
        g2.fill(rect);
        g2.setColor(Color.black);
        tl.draw(g2,x,y);
    }
    private void showOutlining(Graphics2D g2,int x,int y) {
        AffineTransform at = new AffineTransform();
        at.setToTranslation(x,y);
        FontRenderContext frc = g2.getFontRenderContext();
        TextLayout tl = new TextLayout("Outlined Text",font,frc);
        Shape s = tl.getOutline(at);
        g2.setColor(Color.red);
        g2.fill(s);
        g2.setColor(Color.black);
        g2.draw(s);
    }
    private void showTiltedLine(Graphics2D g2,int x,int y) {
        AffineTransform at = new AffineTransform();
        at.rotate(Math.PI / 8.0);
        FontRenderContext frc = new FontRenderContext(at,false,false);
        TextLayout tl = new TextLayout("Tilted Text",font,frc);
        tl.draw(g2,x,y);
```

```
    }
    private void showTiltedOutline(Graphics2D g2,int x,int y) {
        AffineTransform at = new AffineTransform();
        at.setToTranslation(x,y);
        at.rotate(Math.PI / 8.0);
        FontRenderContext frc = new FontRenderContext(at,false,false);
        TextLayout tl = new TextLayout("Tilted Outline",font,frc);
        Shape s = tl.getOutline(null);
        g2.draw(s);
    }
    private void showShear(Graphics2D g2,int x,int y) {
        AffineTransform at = new AffineTransform();
        at.shear(0.5,0.0);
        FontRenderContext frc = new FontRenderContext(at,false,false);
        TextLayout tl = new TextLayout("Sheared text",font,frc);
        tl.draw(g2,x,y);
    }
  }
}
```

Commentary

This program contains a set of methods each displaying one line of text, and each displaying the text in different way. The output from the program is shown in Figure 8.4. There is a bit of flexibility in using TextLayout, and each drawing method in the example takes a slightly different path in getting the text on the display.

The construction of a TextLayout object requires the use of a FontRenderContext. There are two ways of coming up with a FontRenderContext object. It can be retrieved from the Graphics2D object by calling the getFontRenderingContext() method, and it can be instantiated from scratch. This example program demonstrates both ways. It may look, at first, as if it is the same doing it one way as the other. However, the constructor requires an AffineTransform object be supplied to it. When you pull the one from the Graphics2D object it uses the internal AffineTransform object—if you create your own instance, you must supply your own object. So far, so good, but there is a hidden gotcha here. If you use

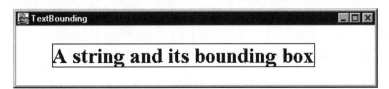

Figure 8.4 Some capabilites of LayoutText.

the draw() method of TextLayout to do the rendering, both AffineTransforms are applied—or, if the same AffineTransform was used in both places, the AffineTransform is applied twice. Knowing this, the double application can be either avoided or used to advantage.

The method showBounding() displays text, and displays its bounding box. The TextLayout class is given the characters of the string and the FontRenderContext object from the Graphics2D object. The TextLayout's draw() method places the text on the display at the desired location. The getBounds() method returns a rectangle of the correct size and shape to exactly contain the text. However, the text was drawn at a location other than the origin, so, to draw the bounding box, it is necessary to add the offset to the rectangle values.

The method showHighlight() is very much like the previous one, except, in this case, the bounding box is used to paint a gray background behind the characters. Notice that the background is filled first, and the glyphs are then drawn on top of it.

The method showOutlining() converts the glyphs in to a Shape object, and then fills in the shape in one color and draws the edges of the shape with another color. By converting the display string into a Shape object, all the manipulation and displaying available for a Shape are also available for text. Notice that the getOutline() method used to make the conversion accepts an AffineTransform. In this example, we used that technique to reposition the output, which allowed us to use the simple forms of draw() and fill(). Here again, take care that you don't get two, or even three, transforms in the process (the Graphics2D, FontRenderContext, and as an argument to the getOutline() method).

The method showTiltedLine() uses the transform to tilt the output by 45 degrees. The AffineTransform defining the rotation is used in the constructor of the FontRenderContext object—it could just as well have been applied to the Graphics2D object with a call to setTransform().

The showTiltedOutline() method creates an AffineTransform to rotate the display, and uses the AffineTransform to create a FontRenderContext object. The text is converted to a shape with a call to the getOutline() method of TextLayout. The getOutline() method is passed a null instead of an AffineTransform that would alter the produced Shape object.

The method showShear() uses an AffineTransform to shear the text in a sort of a reversed italic appearance.

Mixing Text Attributes

It is possible to create a string that contains information on how it should be displayed. The attributes can be inserted to apply to the entire string, or to any part of it.

The Code

```
import java.awt.*;
import java.awt.event.*;
import java.awt.geom.*;
import java.awt.font.*;
import java.text.*;
class MultipleStyles extends Frame {
    public static void main(String arg[]) {
        new MultipleStyles();
    }
    MultipleStyles() {
        super("MultipleStyles");
        addWindowListener(new WindowAdapter() {
            public void windowClosing(WindowEvent e)
                { System.exit(0); } } );
        add(new MultipleStylesCanvas());
        pack();
        show();
    }
class MultipleStylesCanvas extends Canvas {
    MultipleStylesCanvas() {
        setSize(450,350);
    }
    public void paint(Graphics g) {
        Graphics2D g2 = (Graphics2D)g;
        mixedFonts(g2,50,50);
        mixedColors(g2,50,100);
        wordUnderline(g2,50,150);
        wordInversion(g2,50,200);
        wordStrike(g2,50,250);
        expandingText(g2,50,300);
    }
    private void mixedFonts(Graphics2D g2,int x,int y) {
        FontRenderContext frc = g2.getFontRenderContext();
        Font font1 = new Font("Times New Roman",Font.BOLD,32);
        Font font2 = new Font("sansserif",Font.PLAIN,50);
        AttributedString as = new AttributedString("TwoFonts");
        as.addAttribute(TextAttribute.FONT,font1,0,3);
        as.addAttribute(TextAttribute.FONT,font2,3,8);
        AttributedCharacterIterator aci = as.getIterator();
```

```
            g2.drawString(aci,x,y);
        }
        private void mixedColors(Graphics2D g2,int x,int y) {
            FontRenderContext frc = g2.getFontRenderContext();
            Font font = new Font("Courier New Negreta",Font.BOLD,50);
            AttributedString as = new AttributedString("TwoColors");
            as.addAttribute(TextAttribute.FONT,font,0,9);
            as.addAttribute(TextAttribute.FOREGROUND,Color.red,3,9);
            AttributedCharacterIterator aci = as.getIterator();
            g2.drawString(aci,x,y);
        }
        private void wordUnderline(Graphics2D g2,int x,int y) {
            FontRenderContext frc = g2.getFontRenderContext();
            Font font = new Font("Times New Roman",Font.BOLD,40);
            AttributedString as = new AttributedString("Underline one
word");
            as.addAttribute(TextAttribute.FONT,font,0,18);
            as.addAttribute(TextAttribute.UNDERLINE,
                TextAttribute.UNDERLINE_ON,10,13);
            AttributedCharacterIterator aci = as.getIterator();
            g2.drawString(aci,x,y);
        }
        private void wordInversion(Graphics2D g2,int x,int y) {
            FontRenderContext frc = g2.getFontRenderContext();
            Font font = new Font("Times New Roman",Font.BOLD,40);
            AttributedString as = new AttributedString("Invert one word");
            as.addAttribute(TextAttribute.FONT,font,0,15);
            as.addAttribute(TextAttribute.SWAP_COLORS,
                TextAttribute.SWAP_COLORS_ON,0,6);
            AttributedCharacterIterator aci = as.getIterator();
            g2.drawString(aci,x,y);
        }
        private void wordStrike(Graphics2D g2,int x,int y) {
            FontRenderContext frc = g2.getFontRenderContext();
            Font font = new Font("Monospace",Font.BOLD,40);
            AttributedString as = new AttributedString("Strike one word");
            as.addAttribute(TextAttribute.FONT,font,0,15);
            as.addAttribute(TextAttribute.STRIKETHROUGH,
                TextAttribute.STRIKETHROUGH_ON,0,6);
            AttributedCharacterIterator aci = as.getIterator();
            g2.drawString(aci,x,y);
        }
        private void expandingText(Graphics2D g2,int x,int y) {
            FontRenderContext frc = g2.getFontRenderContext();
            AttributedString as = new AttributedString("an expanding text
line");
            for(int i=0; i<22; i++) {
                Font font = new Font("Monospace",Font.BOLD,i+20);
                as.addAttribute(TextAttribute.FONT,font,i,i+1);
            }
            AttributedCharacterIterator aci = as.getIterator();
```

```
            g2.drawString(aci,x,y);
        }
    }
}
```

The Commentary

This program demonstrates some of the capabilities of formatting by an AttributedString. An AttributedString is a string that can be used to assign character-by-character attributes. The available value settings for the attributes are in a class named TextAttribute. The actual attribute settings are done with a call to the addAttribute() method of Attributed-String. The first argument is the type of attribute to be set, the second is an Object that is the value of the setting, and the last two are the beginning and ending indexes of the characters to receive the attribute. Looking at the constants in TextAttribute, the ones declared as TextAttribute are for the first argument and the other values (the type varies from one to the other) are for the value settings.

The method mixedFonts() demonstrates a way to have the font change in the middle of a string. An AttributedString object containing the character string is created, then two fonts are specified—one for the first three characters and one for the balance of the string. To display the string, an AttributedCharacterIterator is returned from the getIterator() method—the Graphics2D drawString() method knows how to display it from the iterator. Figure 8.5 shows how a string's appearance can be adjusted arbitrarily.

- In the method mixedColors() there is only one font, but there are two colors. The font is set for the entire extent of the string, but the color is set for only the last six characters.

- The method wordUnderline() shows that an attribute can be applied to a center portion of the string with no effect on the characters on each side.

Figure 8.5 Altering appearance characteristics mid-string.

- The method wordInversion() performs a simple foreground/background switch of colors. The background is filled to the edge of the bounding box and the glyphs are drawn over it.

- The method wordStrike() shows the technique of displaying a string with a strikethrough.

- The method expandingText() displays a string in which each character is larger thatn the one to its left. This is done by creating a new font—each with its point size incremented by one—for each character in the string.

Drawn Letters

By using the shape of the glyphs from a font, it is possible to draw the characters in something besides solid colors.

The Code

```
import java.awt.*;
import java.awt.event.*;
import java.awt.geom.*;
import java.awt.font.*;
import java.text.*;
class LetterGrid extends Frame {
    public static void main(String arg[]) {
        new LetterGrid();
    }
    LetterGrid() {
        super("LetterGrid");
        addWindowListener(new WindowAdapter() {
            public void windowClosing(WindowEvent e)
                { System.exit(0); } } );
        add(new LetterGridCanvas());
        pack();
        show();
    }
class LetterGridCanvas extends Canvas {
    private int width = 550;
    private int height = 200;
    LetterGridCanvas() {
        setSize(width,height);
        setBackground(Color.lightGray);
    }
```

```
public void paint(Graphics g) {
    Graphics2D g2 = (Graphics2D)g;
    AffineTransform at = new AffineTransform();
    at.setToTranslation(10,160);
    Font font = new Font("Times New Roman",Font.BOLD,180);
    FontRenderContext frc = new FontRenderContext(at,false,false);
    TextLayout tl = new TextLayout("Waffle",font,frc);
    Shape shape = tl.getOutline(null);
    GeneralPath gp = new GeneralPath(shape);
    gp.setWindingRule(GeneralPath.WIND_NON_ZERO);
    g2.clip(gp);
    for(int w=0; w<width; w+= 5) {
        g2.drawLine(w,0,w,height);
    }
    for(int h=0; h<height; h+= 5) {
        g2.drawLine(0,h,width,h);
    }
}
}
}
```

The Commentary

The paint() method proceeds step-by-step to create a clipping region, use it to clip the output window, and then draw the desired pattern. The word "Waffle" is used to create a clip region in a window filled with horizontal and vertical lines, as shown in Figure 8.6.

An AffineTransform is created to position the upper-left corner of the clipping mask. A large font (bold and 180 points) is created—its outline is to become the clipping region. A FontRenderContext is constructed from the AffineTransform. A TextLayout object is then created from a string of characters, the Font, and the FontRenderContext.

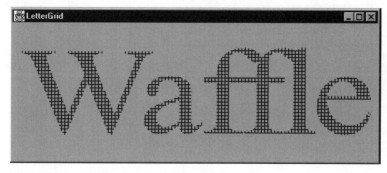

Figure 8.6 Using letters to define clipping regions.

In a Graphics object, a clipping region is specified by a closed shape in the form of a Shape object. A closed shape is one in which the last point joins the first point. One Shape object can actually contain more than one shape—that is, more than one closed figure. This is fortunate because that's what we need to do with the string of glyphs.

Only things inside the clip region—the closed shape—are drawn. For example, if you wanted to render a drawing while making sure there was a margin all around the window, you would need to create a Rectangle of the right size and location, and apply it as a clip region.

The Shape object returned from the getOutline() method of TextLayout would work directly for the clip region, except for one small detail. The winding rule is defaulted to odd/even. This causes overlapping letters to have their overlaps disappear as shown in Figure 8.7. The solution is to create a GeneralShape object, based on the existing Shape, so the method setWindingRule() can be used to change the rule to nonzero.

Once the clip region is defined, drawing can proceed as if it were going to fill the entire window. Only the areas within the clip region are actually filled.

Drawn Letters II

The previous example works, but it has one drawback: It is slow. Every time the window needs to be redrawn, all of the objects have to be created and the entire clipping and masking occurs from scratch. For most graphics operations this doesn't matter because the time can be measured in fractions of seconds. In this case, however, the delay is quite noticeable.

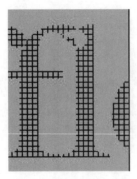

Figure 8.7 Overlapping with odd/even winding.

There is no way to prevent the delay from happening once at the beginning, but, by using an Image object to store the results, the speed is greatly improved whenever the screen must be redrawn.

The Code

```
import java.awt.*;
import java.awt.event.*;
import java.awt.geom.*;
import java.awt.font.*;
import java.text.*;
class LetterGrid2 extends Frame {
    public static void main(String arg[]) {
        new LetterGrid2();
    }
    LetterGrid2() {
        super("LetterGrid2");
        addWindowListener(new WindowAdapter() {
            public void windowClosing(WindowEvent e)
                { System.exit(0); } } );
        add(new LetterGrid2Canvas());
        pack();
        show();
    }
class LetterGrid2Canvas extends Canvas {
    private GeneralPath generalPath;
    private int width = 550;
    private int height = 200;
    private Image image;
    LetterGrid2Canvas() {
        setSize(width,height);
        setBackground(Color.lightGray);
        AffineTransform at = new AffineTransform();
        at.setToTranslation(10,160);
        Font font = new Font("Times New Roman",Font.BOLD,180);
        FontRenderContext frc = new FontRenderContext(at,false,false);
        TextLayout tl = new TextLayout("Waffle",font,frc);
        generalPath = new GeneralPath(tl.getOutline(null));
        generalPath.setWindingRule(GeneralPath.WIND_NON_ZERO);
    }
    public void paint(Graphics g) {
        if(image == null) {
            image = createImage(width,height);
            Graphics2D g2 = (Graphics2D)image.getGraphics();
            g2.clip(generalPath);
            for(int w=0; w<width; w+= 5) {
                g2.drawLine(w,0,w,height);
            }
            for(int h=0; h<height; h+= 5) {
```

```
                    g2.drawLine(0,h,width,h);
            }
        }
        g.drawImage(image,0,0,null);
    }
  }
  }
```

The Commentary

There are two major differences between this version and the previous one.

First, the code creating the Shape—in the form of a GeneralPath object—has been moved into the constructor so it will only execute once.

Second, an Image object is used to store the actual graphics. The first time the paint() method executes, it will discover that the Image is null and follow the steps necessary to create one. The image is clipped and painted the same way the output window was in the previous example. Once the image has been displayed, all the paint() method needs to do to redisplay the window is to call drawImage() to refresh the screen.

The output is the same as the previous example shown in Figure 8.6.

Letters with Pictures

Text can be displayed with pictures in the background and, using the letter outlines for clipping, the letters can be made up from the contents of the pictures. This example loads a single picture and uses it to display text. There are three different displays as shown in Figures 8.8 through 8.10. Clicking the mouse on the displayed window changes it from one to the other.

Figure 8.8 The picture without text.

Figure 8.9 The image with text appearing as a cutout.

Figure 8.10 The image with text made from the picture.

The Code

```
import java.awt.*;
import java.awt.event.*;
import java.awt.geom.*;
import java.awt.font.*;
import java.text.*;
class LetterPicture extends Frame {
    public static void main(String arg[]) {
        new LetterPicture();
    }
    LetterPicture() {
        super("LetterPicture");
        setBackground(Color.black);
        addWindowListener(new WindowAdapter() {
            public void windowClosing(WindowEvent e)
                { System.exit(0); } } );
        add(new LetterPictureCanvas());
        pack();
```

```java
            show();
    }
class LetterPictureCanvas extends Canvas
                implements MouseListener {
    private int width = 548;
    private int height = 187;
    private GeneralPath generalPath;
    private Image image;
    private Image pictureImage;
    private int state = 0;
    LetterPictureCanvas() {
        setSize(width,height);
        addMouseListener(this);
        AffineTransform at = new AffineTransform();
        at.setToTranslation(0,160);
        at.scale(0.6,1.0);
        Font font = new Font("Times New Roman",Font.BOLD,210);
        FontRenderContext frc = new FontRenderContext(at,false,false);
        TextLayout tl = new TextLayout("ALASKA",font,frc);
        generalPath = new GeneralPath(tl.getOutline(null));
        generalPath.setWindingRule(GeneralPath.WIND_NON_ZERO);
        loadPictureImage("alaska.jpg");
    }
    private void loadPictureImage(String name) {
        pictureImage = getToolkit().getImage(name);
        MediaTracker mt = new MediaTracker(this);
        mt.addImage(pictureImage,1);
        try {
            mt.waitForAll();
        } catch(Exception e) {
            System.out.println("Unable to load " + name);
            e.printStackTrace();
            pictureImage = null;
        }
    }

    public void paint(Graphics g) {
        Graphics2D g2 = (Graphics2D)g;
        if(image == null) {
            image = createImage(width,height);
            Graphics2D gi = (Graphics2D)image.getGraphics();
            gi.clip(generalPath);
            gi.drawImage(pictureImage,0,0,null);
        }
        switch(state) {
        case 0:
            g2.drawImage(pictureImage,0,0,null);
            break;
        case 1:
            g2.drawImage(pictureImage,0,0,null);
            g2.fill(generalPath);
            break;
```

```
            case 2:
                g2.drawImage(image,0,0,null);
                break;
        }
    }
    public void mouseClicked(MouseEvent event) {
        if(++state > 2)
            state = 0;
        repaint();
    }
    public void mouseEntered(MouseEvent event) {}
    public void mouseExited(MouseEvent event) {}
    public void mousePressed(MouseEvent event) {}
    public void mouseReleased(MouseEvent event) {}
  }
}
```

The Commentary

The initial setup is about the same as in the previous example—a General-Path object is constructed for holding the shape of the text.

The method loadPicture() loads an image from a disk file. The loading of the image file is initiated by a call to getImage() of the default Toolkit(). An Image object is returned from the call to getImage(), but it doesn't necessarily contain image data itself. The getImage() method starts a separate thread that is involved in loading the image. This asynchronous organization can be handy when you are, say, loading a lot of images but are not going to use them all right away. In this example, we can't do anything until the image is loaded, so a MediaTracker object is created and the loading Image object is added to it. The waitForAll() method will not return until everything in the list (in this case, one Image) has been completely loaded. By the way, the second argument to addImage() is an ID number that enables the MediaTracker to wait for one thing at a time instead of simply doing a waitForAll().

The paint() method, the first time it is called, creates an image by using the GeneralPath (the one holding the outline of the glyphs in the string) as a clipping mask. Once the clipping is set, the loaded image is drawn onto it, and the clipping only allows the picture to be drawn inside the letters. This Image is saved so it can be displayed over and over again.

The paint() method takes one of three actions depending on the value of the "state" variable. If the state is zero, the pictureImage is drawn.

This is the unmodified image that was loaded from disk. If the state is one, the unmodified image is drawn and the character glyphs are drawn on top of it. The character drawing is done with fill() because the General path only holds the outlines of the glyphs. If the state is two, the image that was created from clipping is drawn, allowing the picture to show only in the areas inside the glyphs.

To make the mouse work, the LetterPictureCanvas class implements the MouseListener interface. This interface requires the implementation of mouseClicked(), mouseEntered(), mouseExited(), mousePressed() and mouseReleased(). The calls to all except mouseClicked() are ignored. Each time the mouse is clicked two things happen—the value of "state" changes and a call is made to repaint(). The call to repaint() causes the paint() method to be called and, since the state has changed, the window switches from one picture to another.

Dynamic Resizing

A window can be resized, and text can be stretched and shrunken to fit it. When the size of text is specified by points, the aspect ratio between height and width remain constant, so it is not possible to make the letters fit exactly. Using an AffineTransform, with its scale factors set properly, can make any rectangle fit any other rectangle.

The Code

```
import java.awt.*;
import java.awt.event.*;
import java.awt.geom.*;
import java.awt.font.*;
import java.text.*;
class Resize extends Frame {
   public static void main(String arg[]) {
      new Resize();
   }
   Resize() {
      super("Resize");
      addWindowListener(new WindowAdapter() {
         public void windowClosing(WindowEvent e)
            { System.exit(0); } } );
      add(new ResizeCanvas(200,50));
      pack();
      show();
```

```
        }
    class ResizeCanvas extends Canvas {
        private TextLayout textLayout;
        private AffineTransform affineTransform;
        ResizeCanvas(int width,int height) {
            setSize(width,height);
            Font font = new Font("Arial",Font.PLAIN,40);
            FontRenderContext frc = new FontRenderContext(null,false,false);
            textLayout = new TextLayout("RubberWord",font,frc);
        }
        private void createTransform() {
            Rectangle2D tRect = textLayout.getBounds();
            Rectangle2D wRect = getBounds();
            double xDelta = (wRect.getWidth()-5) / tRect.getWidth();
            double yDelta = (wRect.getHeight()-5) / tRect.getHeight();
            affineTransform = new AffineTransform();
            affineTransform.scale(xDelta,yDelta);
            affineTransform.translate(0,30);
        }
        public void paint(Graphics g) {
            createTransform();
            Shape text = textLayout.getOutline(affineTransform);
            Graphics2D g2 = (Graphics2D)g;
            g2.fill(text);
        }
    }
    }
```

The Commentary

The constructor of ResizeCanvas creates a TextLayout object that contains both a font and a rendering context. The RenderingContext object is constructed without an affine transform (the null argument) and both anti-aliasing and fractional metrics disabled. This TextLayout object is used by the paint() method as the source of the text to be displayed.

The paint() method assumes the window has been resized and recalculates everything. It's first job is to create the affine transform that will size the text to exactly fit the desired rectangle. The getOutline() method of the TextLayout object has the job of producing a Shape object that contains the outline of the text to be rendered—it uses the AffineTransform object to cause the Shape itself to be scaled properly. The fill() method of the Graphics2D object is used to draw the letters. It could just have well have been the draw() method to render the outline of the characters.

The createTransform() method compares the size of the text in the Text-Layout object with the size of the window and creates a transform that will resize the text to fit. This is done by using getBounds() methods to get the bounding rectangle of the characters in TextLayout and the size of the window. The values xDelta and yDelta hold the amount the size will need to change to go from one size to the other—a negative value will shrink the size and a positive value will expand it. The fudge factor of –5 is inserted to allow for a little border. Also, there is an offset of 30 added to the y-axis to allow for the title bar at the top.

Figure 8.11 shows the appearance of the resizeable window in a few of its positions. You can resize the window by dragging any of the four corners or four edges, and the text will follow.

Figure 8.11   Text resizes with the window.

Performing Animation

Animation is the act of showing a series of similar pictures one after another in rapid succession in such a way that to an observer, whose brain can handle only so many new images in a given period of time, the things portrayed in the pictures appear to be moving. Taken literally, animated images appear to come to life—the word derives from the Latin *anima*, meaning "breath" or "soul." Further back, the root comes from the Greek *anemos*, meaning "wind." Animation breathes life into still images.

The process isn't too hard to conceptualize. Recall those flip books you made as a child. You drew slightly different pictures—perhaps a running figure, if you were a better childhood artist than we were, with its legs moving back and forth from one frame to the next. You then used your thumb to flip the pages by in quick succession and your brain, overrun by so much visual input, interpreted what you saw as a moving image. Disney Studios exploited this technique to great effect, creating their animated films one frame at a time—there are 32 frames in one second of motion picture—by photographing slightly different drawings, in sequence, one after another.

Animation of computer graphics works much the same way as the Disney filmmakers' methods by displaying a series of images in rapid succession through a period of time. It's where the images come from that makes for interesting discussion. Yes, it's possible to store bitmapped images in memory and display them sequentially—but that requires a lot of memory. A better way to do things is to program the computer to paint certain pixels and extinguish others as the animation progresses. There are tricks here—for example, say you want an animation that shows a cartoon locomotive moving across a bridge. As the engine moves, the bridge and the surrounding terrain don't change one bit. Why not create a routine that draws the background once, then concerns itself only with updating the image of the locomotive? That's one trick—it's called *clipping*—you'll learn in this chapter, albeit not with an animated locomotive (you'll learn plenty from dots and blocks, and the examples will be less cluttered with image information).

Animation itself is really nothing new in Java2D; it has been with Java from the beginning. In fact, it is probably the one thing that Java is best known for (Java's detractors like to claim that it's a toy language, good for little other than animated applets). We include animation here because no book about Java graphics would be complete without basic instructions in animation.

A Pong Applet

Remember Pong, one of the first widely popular video games? This applet generates part of the game—the bouncing ball. You'll learn a lot about basic animation by decoding the graphics procedures that make the ball appear to move around smoothly and even deform slightly as it hits the walls of its frame.

The Code

```
import java.awt.*;
import java.applet.*;

public class PongApplet extends Applet implements Runnable {
    private int pause = 5;
    private Color backgroundColor = Color.white;
    private Color ballColor = Color.red;
    private Rectangle rectangle;
    private Image image = null;
    private Thread looper;

    private static final int maximumRadius = 20;
```

```
private static final int minimumRadius = 15;
private int x = maximumRadius;
private int y = maximumRadius;
private int xRadius = maximumRadius;
private int yRadius = maximumRadius;
private boolean xMovingRight = true;;
private boolean yMovingDown = true;;

public void init() {
    rectangle = new Rectangle();
}
public void start() {
    if(looper == null) {
        looper = new Thread(this);
        looper.start();
    }
}
public void run() {
    try {
        while(true) {
            repaint();
            Thread.sleep(pause);
        }
    } finally {
        return;
    }
}


public void update(Graphics g) {
    if(looper.isAlive()) {
        if(!rectangle.equals(getBounds()) || (image == null)) {
            rectangle = getBounds();
            image =
createImage(rectangle.width,rectangle.height);
            firstFrame();
        }
        if(nextFrame()) {
            paint(image.getGraphics());
            g.drawImage(image,0,0,null);
        }
    }
}

public void paint(Graphics g) {
    g.setColor(backgroundColor);
    g.fillRect(0,0,rectangle.width,rectangle.height);
    g.setColor(ballColor);
    g.fillOval(x - xRadius,y - yRadius,xRadius * 2,yRadius * 2);
}

private void firstFrame() {
```

```
                if((x + maximumRadius) > rectangle.width)
                    x = rectangle.width - maximumRadius;
                if((y + maximumRadius) > rectangle.height)
                    y = rectangle.height - maximumRadius;
                xRadius = maximumRadius;
                yRadius = maximumRadius;
            }

        private boolean nextFrame() {
            if(xMovingRight) {
                x++;
                if(x > rectangle.width - minimumRadius)
                    xMovingRight = false;
            } else {
                x--;
                if(x < minimumRadius)
                    xMovingRight = true;
            }
            if(yMovingDown) {
                y++;
                if(y > rectangle.height - minimumRadius)
                    yMovingDown = false;
            } else {
                y--;
                if(y < minimumRadius)
                    yMovingDown = true;
            }
            xRadius = Math.min(maximumRadius,Math.min(rectangle.
    width-x,x));
            yRadius = Math.min(maximumRadius,Math.min(rectangle.
    height-y,y));
            return(true);
        }
    }
```

The Commentary

This applet takes the typical form of an animation applet. The class extends Applet and implements Runnable. The Applet class defines the methods necessary to run the applet inside a browser (such as Netscape Navigator or the Appletviewer that is supplied with the JDK). For a browser to run the applet, it must be embedded in an HTML document. You'll find PongApplet.html on the companion CD-ROM, ready to go.

When the applet first loads, the browser calls the init() method. When the browser decides to display the applet window, it calls the start() method to begin the animation. The start() method creates a thread called looper. That thread will continue to run in the background, even while the browser is off doing something else. After looper is started, it calls the run() method. The run() method is the mainline for the thread—the applet will stay in execution until the run() method returns. To do animation, the run() method goes into a continuous loop that times and redraws each new frame.

Each time run() calls repaint(), the browser schedules a high-priority call to the update() method. The update() method checks to see if the thread is active by calling isAlive(). If the thread is active (i.e., if isAlive returns true), a frame is drawn.

In this example, because we are bouncing things off the side, we need to know how big the window is. Once we have the window size, and also have an Image object of that size, and firstFrame() has set up the initial values, a frame can be drawn. The values for the new frame are calculated by nextFrame() and, if it returns true, which would indicate that there is something new about the picture, then a frame is drawn.

The paint() method does not draw the frame directly to the screen. Instead, it draws it to an Image object and then, using drawImage(), it places the entire image to the window at once. This is to defeat the flicker that occurs when a frame is drawn piece-by-piece directly to the display.

The applet is a simple ball bouncing around in a rectangle. The reason the calculations are a little complicated is that the ball squishes just a bit as it hits an edge. To do this it is necessary to keep track of the position of the ball in relation to the sides and adjust its radius accordingly. The applet appears in Figure 9.1.

A Pong Application

The same animation mechanism used for applets in a browser can be used for applications that run in standalone mode, directly with the Java Virtual Machine (JVM). It is a simple matter to derive an animated window from the Canvas class and include it in a window with any other components in the window. This example shows how that can be done with an inner class.

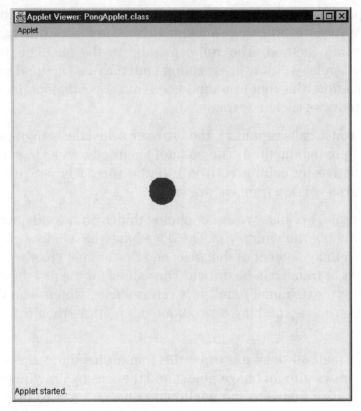

Figure 9.1 An animated applet.

The Code

```
import java.awt.*;
import java.awt.event.*;
class PongApplication extends Frame {
    public static void main(String arg[]) {
        new PongApplication();
    }
    PongApplication() {
        super("PongApplication");
        addWindowListener(new WindowAdapter() {
            public void windowClosing(WindowEvent e)
                { System.exit(0); } } );
        PongPanel pp = new PongPanel();
        add(pp);
        pack();
        show();
    }
class PongPanel extends Canvas implements Runnable {
```

```
private int pause = 5;
private Color backgroundColor = Color.white;
private Color ballColor = Color.red;
private Rectangle rectangle = new Rectangle();
private Image image = null;
private Thread looper;

private final int maximumRadius = 20;
private final int minimumRadius = 15;
private int x = maximumRadius;
private int y = maximumRadius;
private int xRadius = maximumRadius;
private int yRadius = maximumRadius;
private boolean xMovingRight = true;;
private boolean yMovingDown = true;;

PongPanel() {
    setSize(250,150);
    looper = new Thread(this);
    looper.start();
}
public void run() {
    try {
        while(true) {
            repaint();
            Thread.sleep(pause);
        }
    } finally {
        return;
    }
}


public void update(Graphics g) {
    if(looper.isAlive()) {
        if(!rectangle.equals(getBounds()) || (image == null)) {
            rectangle = getBounds();
            image =
createImage(rectangle.width,rectangle.height);
            firstFrame();
        }
        if(nextFrame()) {
            paint(image.getGraphics());
            g.drawImage(image,0,0,null);
        }
    }
}

public void paint(Graphics g) {
    g.setColor(backgroundColor);
    g.fillRect(0,0,rectangle.width,rectangle.height);
    g.setColor(ballColor);
```

```
            g.fillOval(x - xRadius,y - yRadius,xRadius * 2,yRadius * 2);
    }

    private void firstFrame() {
        if((x + maximumRadius) > rectangle.width)
            x = rectangle.width - maximumRadius;
        if((y + maximumRadius) > rectangle.height)
            y = rectangle.height - maximumRadius;
        xRadius = maximumRadius;
        yRadius = maximumRadius;
    }

    private boolean nextFrame() {
        if(xMovingRight) {
            x++;
            if(x > rectangle.width - minimumRadius)
                xMovingRight = false;
        } else {
            x—;
            if(x < minimumRadius)
                xMovingRight = true;
        }
        if(yMovingDown) {
            y++;
            if(y > rectangle.height - minimumRadius)
                yMovingDown = false;
        } else {
            y—;
            if(y < minimumRadius)
                yMovingDown = true;
        }
        xRadius = Math.min(maximumRadius,Math.min(rectangle.
width-x,x));
        yRadius = Math.min(maximumRadius,Math.min(rectangle.
height-y,y));
        return(true);
    }
}
}
```

The Commentary

This is the same program as the applet, except that it has been converted
to an application. This is done by creating, as the animated portion, an
inner class named PongPanel that extends Canvas for drawing and
implements Runnable so it can be executed as a thread.

The actions it performs are the same, but they are in slightly different
places. The PongPanel constructor sets the size of the window, creates a

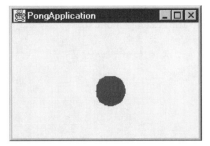

Figure 9.2   An animated application.

new thread, and starts it running. The call to start() in the thread initializes the Java Virtual Machine and causes a call to be made to run(). The PongPanel object will remain in execution until run() returns. The timing of the loop and the process of calculating and drawing the graphic is identical to the processes of the applet in the previous example. Figure 9.2 shows what this looks like.

Electrons

It is possible to keep several things moving at once by keeping track of all their positions, speeds, and directions, and drawing each one independently. This example simulates some electrons orbiting about an imaginary nucleus.

The Code

```
import java.awt.*;
import java.awt.event.*;
class Electrons extends Frame {
    public static void main(String arg[]) {
        new Electrons();
    }
    Electrons() {
        super("Electrons");
        addWindowListener(new WindowAdapter() {
            public void windowClosing(WindowEvent e)
                { System.exit(0); } } );
        ElectronsPanel op = new ElectronsPanel();
        add(op);
        pack();
        show();
```

```
        }
class ElectronsPanel extends Canvas implements Runnable {
    private int pause = 15;
    private Color backgroundColor = Color.lightGray;
    private int elecronCount = 15;
    private Color[] electronColor;
    private boolean ready = false;
    private Image image;
    private Thread looper;
    private Rectangle rectangle;

    private double a[] = new double[elecronCount];
    private double b[] = new double[elecronCount];
    private double sine[] = new double[elecronCount];
    private double cosine[] = new double[elecronCount];
    private double angle[] = new double[elecronCount];
    private int colorIndex[] = new int[elecronCount];
    private int xCenter;
    private int yCenter;

    ElectronsPanel() {
        setSize(400,200);
        electronColor = new Color[4];
        electronColor[0] = Color.blue;
        electronColor[1] = Color.cyan;
        electronColor[2] = Color.magenta;
        electronColor[3] = Color.red;
        rectangle = new Rectangle();
        setBackground(backgroundColor);
        looper = new Thread(this);
        looper.start();
    }
    public void run() {
        try {
            while(true) {
                repaint();
                Thread.sleep(pause);
            }
        } finally {
            return;
        }
    }

    public void update(Graphics g) {
        if(looper.isAlive()) {
            if(!rectangle.equals(getBounds()) || (image == null)) {
                rectangle = getBounds();
                image =
createImage(rectangle.width,rectangle.height);
                firstFrame();
            }
```

```
                    if(nextFrame()) {
                        paint(image.getGraphics());
                        g.drawImage(image,0,0,null);
                    }
            }
        }

        public void paint(Graphics g) {
            g.setColor(backgroundColor);
            g.fillRect(0,0,getSize().width,getSize().height);
            for(int i=0; i<elecronCount; i++) {
                g.setColor(electronColor[colorIndex[i]]);
                int x = (int)(a[i] * cosine[i]);
                int y = (int)(b[i] * sine[i]);
                g.fillOval(x + xCenter,y + yCenter,5,5);
            }
        }

        private void firstFrame() {
            xCenter = rectangle.width / 2;
            yCenter = rectangle.height / 2;
            int index = 0;
            for(int i=0; i<elecronCount; i++) {
                a[i] = Math.random() * rectangle.width / 2;
                b[i] = Math.random() * rectangle.height / 2;
                angle[i] = Math.random() * Math.PI * 2;
                colorIndex[i] = index;
                if(++index >= electronColor.length)
                    index = 0;
            }
        }

        private boolean nextFrame() {
            for(int i=0; i<elecronCount; i++) {
                angle[i] += 5.0 / (a[i] + b[i]);
                cosine[i] = Math.cos(angle[i]);
                sine[i] = Math.sin(angle[i]);
            }
            return(true);
        }
    }
}
```

The Commentary

This program has the same basic structure as the previous one, but it keeps several balls in the air at once. These balls are independent graphics "sprites," each of which runs without regard to the others. In fact, the only differences occur in the paint(), firstFrame(), and nextFrame() methods to do the calculations and the actual drawings.

The paint() method has the job of painting the background and then painting each individual electron. The firstFrame() method uses the size of the rectangle to locate the center of the atom and to construct a random orbit for each electron. The nextFrame() method just moves each electron to the next position in its orbit.

You may have noticed that the nextFrame() method returns a Boolean. This program doesn't use that value, but the program is constructed so that if nextFrame() were to return a false, the display would not be redrawn. This is an efficiency tool that can be used whenever there is no change from one frame to the next. Figure 9.3 shows the electrons orbiting.

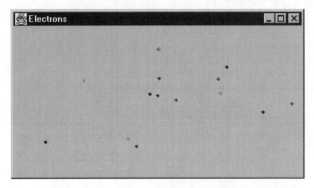

Figure 9.3   Electrons in orbit, demonstrating multiple-sprite animation.

CHAPTER 10

Plotting and Graphing

We writers would like to argue the notion that a picture is worth a thousand words, but there's no doubt that a picture is worth a thousand numbers. A graph can communicate relationships and trends in a way that data tables simply cannot. Graphs communicate information directly into the brain, saving it the trouble of analysis. This fact can be used for evil as well as for good. If a graph-maker creates a graph that exaggerates a relationship—perhaps by using a truncated or magnified scale for the y-axis that makes a slight difference look like a change of one-third—the graph-maker is guilty of bending the truth (or, at least, the graph-maker is guilty of marketing). When you create graphs, you have to be careful that they represent relationships among data accurately. Read Edward Tufte's *The Visual Display of Quantitative Information* for the definitive discussion of how to show numbers in the form of charts, graphs, maps, and other illustrations.

One of the exciting things about Java graphing is that the display capabilities can be combined with the java.net.* classes to create transnetwork monitoring tools. These tools would glean data from some source, perhaps in a remote or dangerous location, then either store it in a file or transmit it across the network. An application or applet would then read the data and display status and trend information in the form of graphs.

The person monitoring the remote or dangerous device would know at a glance what was going on and could make adjustments if they were needed.

This chapter shows you how to create plots and graphs with Java programs. The first example provides you with an excellent utility—a module that reads data from ASCII files. Most graphing programs will have to be able to do that. Then, you'll learn about creating several different kinds of graphs, including various line graphs, bar graphs, scatter plots with trend lines, and pie graphs. You'll be able to adapt these examples to your situation.

Reading Data Files

Any graphing program that is to be at all flexible needs to be able to read data into itself. The data might come from a data stream or—as is the case in the examples in this chapter—from a text file.

Reading data from files into Java programs isn't as easy to do as one would like. You need to construct a clean way to input one token of data (one string, keyword, or number) at a time. We've created a class—Lex—that does that for you. This class reads data from a file so the application can get input in a logical and readable manner. You can use Lex in any program that requires taking data from files.

Lex is used in several of the examples that follow. It is the general workhorse for reading data.

The Code

```
import java.io.*;
public class Lex {
    public static final int EOF = 0;
    public static final int STRING = 1;
    public static final int SYMBOL = 2;
    public static final int NUMBER = 3;

    public static final int UNKNOWN = 1000;

    private DataInputStream in;
    private int tokenType;
    private String token;
    private char character;
```

```java
private boolean eofHit;
private String fileName;
private int lineNumber = 1;

public Lex(String fileName) {
    this.fileName = fileName;
    try {
        FileInputStream fis = new FileInputStream(fileName);
        BufferedInputStream bis = new BufferedInputStream(fis);
        DataInputStream dis = new DataInputStream(bis);
        this.in = dis;
        character = ' ';
        eofHit = false;
    } catch(FileNotFoundException e) {
        System.err.println(e);
        eofHit = true;
    }
}

public int gtkn() {
    token = "";
    while(Character.isWhitespace(character))
        gc();
    if(eofHit)
        return(tokenType = EOF);

    if(Character.isLetter(character) || (character == '_')) {
        while(Character.isLetterOrDigit(character) ||
                (character == '_') ||
                (character == '.'))
            pgc();
        return(tokenType = SYMBOL);
    }
    if(character == '"') {
        gc();
        while(character != '"') {
            if(character == '\\') {
                pgc();
                if(character == '\\') {
                    gc();
                } else {
                    pgc();
                }
            } else {
                pgc();
            }
        }
        gc();
        return(tokenType = STRING);
    }
    if(Character.isDigit(character) || (character == '.') ||
```

```java
                    (character == '-') || (character == '+')) {
                while(!Character.isWhitespace(character))
                    pgc();
                return(tokenType = NUMBER);
            }
        tokenType = UNKNOWN;
        pgc();
        return(tokenType);
    }
    private final void pgc() {
        token += character;
        gc();
    }
    private void gc() {
        if(eofHit) {
            character = '\u0000';
            return;
        }
        try {
            character = (char)in.readByte();
            if(character == '\n')
                ++lineNumber;
        } catch(EOFException e) {
            character = '\u0000';
            eofHit = true;
            try {
                in.close();
            } catch(IOException ex) {
                System.err.println(ex);
            }
        } catch(IOException e) {
            System.err.println(e);
            System.exit(2);
        }
    }
    public String getToken() {
        return(token);
    }
    public int getTokenType() {
        return(tokenType);
    }
    public int getInteger() {
        if(tokenType != NUMBER)
            expected("number");
        return(Integer.parseInt(token));
    }
    public float getFloat() {
        if(tokenType != NUMBER)
            expected("number");
        return(Float.valueOf(token).floatValue());
    }
```

```
    public void expected(String expect) {
        System.err.println("Line " + lineNumber + " of " + fileName);
        System.err.println("Expected " + expect);
        if(eofHit)
            System.err.println("Found EOF");
        else
            System.err.println("Found " + token);
        System.exit(2);
    }
}
```

The Commentary

This is a very simple lexical scanner. It can handle strings, keywords, and numbers.

The constructor takes a file name. The file is opened for input, but nothing else happens until there is a call to the gtkn() method. Each call to gtkn() will read the next token (word, string, or number) from the file and return the constant value that indicates its type. The gtkn() method gets its input by calling gc() to read one character at a time and then, to construct the token character-by-character, calls pc() to save it. The convenient method pgc() simply calls pc() and then gc() to save the current character and immediately get another one.

There are a group of get methods that can be used to access the current token. The method getToken() returns the token strings itself and getTokenType() returns the integer that indicates the current type of token. The methods getInteger() and getFloat() will convert the current numeric token into an integer or float and return it to the caller.

If there is an error—that is, if, for some reason, the caller did not get the expected token, a call to expected() will send information about the current token, and the expected token, to System.err and the process exits immediately. Lex has error detection but no error recovery.

A RAM-Resident Trace

Though the terminology is not universal, the word *trace* is sometimes used to refer to a line drawn or plotted on a graph to represent data. In this case, the class Trace is designed to hold the data points and other information about a trace inside an object and supply the information to a plotting routine in a logical manner as requested.

The Trace class uses Lex to read the descriptive data from a trace file into random-access memory and then to return information about the trace that can be used by the caller to display the data. There is more to a trace than just (x,y) data pairs. Here is an example showing the format of a trace file:

```
tag "The first set"
color 255 0 0
dash 10 5
point 0 20
point 5 28
point 10 39
 . . .
```

A trace file optionally contains a tag, which is the name of the trace. This can be used by the application to display some sort of legend describing the data being displayed. The color, in the form of three RGB values between 0 and 255, inclusive, can be specified. Files also can specify a dash pattern, described in Chapter 6. The data can be any number of pairs of (x,y) points. The class Trace knows how to read and interpret this file format.

The Code

```java
import java.util.*;
import java.awt.*;
import java.awt.geom.*;
public class Trace {
    float[] x = new float[100];
    float[] y = new float[100];
    int size = 100;
    int next = 0;
    String traceTag = "Unnamed";
    int red = 0;
    int green = 0;
    int blue = 0;
    float[] dash = null;
    float[] defaultDash = {10f,0f};
    Trace(String fileName) {
        Lex lex = new Lex(fileName);
        lex.gtkn();
        while(lex.getTokenType() != Lex.EOF) {
            if(lex.getToken().equals("tag")) {
                if(lex.gtkn() != Lex.STRING)
                    lex.expected("quoted string");
                traceTag = lex.getToken();
```

```
                              lex.gtkn();
                  } else if(lex.getToken().equals("color")) {
                        lex.gtkn();
                        red = lex.getInteger();
                        lex.gtkn();
                        green = lex.getInteger();
                        lex.gtkn();
                        blue = lex.getInteger();
                        lex.gtkn();
                  } else if(lex.getToken().equals("dash")) {
                        while(lex.gtkn() == Lex.NUMBER) {
                              float value = lex.getFloat();
                              if(dash == null) {
                                    dash = new float[1];
                                    dash[0] = value;
                              } else {
                                    float[] oldDash = dash;
                                    dash = new float[oldDash.length+1];
                                    for(int i=0; i<oldDash.length; i++)
                                          dash[i] = oldDash[i];
                                    dash[oldDash.length] = value;
                              }
                        }
                  } else if(lex.getToken().equals("point")) {
                        lex.gtkn();
                        float xPoint = lex.getFloat();
                        lex.gtkn();
                        float yPoint = lex.getFloat();
                        addPoint(xPoint,yPoint);
                        lex.gtkn();
                  } else {
                        lex.expected("a keyword");
                  }
            }
            sort();
      }
      void addPoint(float xPoint,float yPoint) {
            if(next >= size) {
                  int sizeNew = size + 100;
                  float[] xNew = new float[sizeNew];
                  float[] yNew = new float[sizeNew];
                  for(int i=0; i<next; i++) {
                        xNew[i] = x[i];
                        yNew[i] = y[i];
                  }
                  x = xNew;
                  y = yNew;
                  size = sizeNew;
            }
            x[next] = xPoint;
            y[next] = yPoint;
```

```
        next++;
    }
    public GeneralPath getGeneralPath() {
        if(next < 2)
            return(null);
        GeneralPath gp = new GeneralPath();
        gp.moveTo(x[0],y[0]);
        for(int i=1; i<next; i++)
            gp.lineTo(x[i],y[i]);
        return(gp);
    }
    public GeneralPath getGeneralPath(float finish) {
        GeneralPath gp = getGeneralPath();
        if(gp != null) {
            gp.lineTo(x[next-1],finish);
            gp.lineTo(x[0],finish);
            gp.closePath();
        }
        return(gp);
    }
    public Color getColor() {
        return(new Color(red,green,blue));
    }
    public BasicStroke getBasicStroke() {
        if(dash == null) {
            return(new BasicStroke(1f,BasicStroke.CAP_SQUARE,
                    BasicStroke.JOIN_MITER,10f,defaultDash,0f));
        } else {
            return(new BasicStroke(1f,BasicStroke.CAP_SQUARE,
                    BasicStroke.JOIN_MITER,10f,dash,0f));
        }
    }
    public int getPointCount() {
        return(next);
    }
    public float x(int index) {
        if(index < next)
            return(x[index]);
        return(0f);
    }
    public float y(int index) {
        if(index < next)
            return(y[index]);
        return(0f);
    }
    void sort() {
        float xHold;
        float yHold;
        int i = 1;
        while(i < next) {
```

```
        if(x[i-1] > x[i]) {
            xHold = x[i-1];
            yHold = y[i-1];
            x[i-1] = x[i];
            y[i-1] = y[i];
            x[i] = xHold;
            y[i] = yHold;
            if(−i < 1)
                i = 2;
        } else {
            i++;
        }
    }
}
}
```

The Commentary

An object of this class is constructed with a filename. It uses the filename to construct a Lex object (about which you read in the previous example) and reads the tokens from it to build its internal data. It uses a while loop to scan the file in search of words that have meaning to it and, when it finds one, it reads the data associated with that word.

If the keyword "tag" is found, the Trace object will take the string contained in the following quotation marks and store it in RAM as the name of the trace, overwriting the default "Unnamed." If it finds the keyword "color," Trace will use the following RGB triplet to overwrite the default black triplet that defines the trace's color. The keyword "dash" will cause Trace to read a series of values to be used to set the dash property of the line to be drawn—the default is a solid line. The "point" keyword, expected to be found a number of times, will add one (x,y) data pair to the array of points.

The point values can arrive in any order because they will be sorted in order for tracing. They must be sorted in order to graph properly. (The mathematical term that describes a sorted list of points is *monotonic*, which is required for a plottable function.) It doesn't really matter whether point values are sorted with the largest first or the smallest first, because the plotting routine will simply put them where they belong. They must be in order so the lines being drawn between them connect the right dots.

If you wish to reverse the order of the sort, you could add a new keyword, say, "decreasing," that would cause the sort routine to work in the opposite direction. In fact, a number of options can easily be added to the data file and to the Trace class, but the number of whistles and bells were kept small to keep the example code readable. For example, along with color, there could be settings for line width as well as settings for line capping and joining, as described in Chapter 6.

There are some get methods that supply information about the trace. The getGeneralPath() method returns an object containing the trace points in a form that can be drawn directly to a Java window, as we do in the following example. The getColor() method returns a Color object of the color of this trace. The getBasicStroke() method returns a BasicStroke object that can be passed on to a Graphics2D object to define the appearance of the line to be drawn.

Multiple Traces in One Window

Using the two utility classes—Lex and Trace—it is not hard to write an application that draws data traces to a display window. The following example draws three traces.

The Code

```
import java.io.*;
import java.awt.*;
import java.awt.geom.*;
import java.awt.event.*;
import java.util.*;
class MultipleTraces extends Frame {
    public static void main(String arg[]) {
        new MultipleTraces();
    }
    MultipleTraces() {
        super("MultipleTraces");
        addWindowListener(new WindowAdapter() {
            public void windowClosing(WindowEvent e)
                { System.exit(0); } } );
        TracePanel tp = new TracePanel();
        tp.addTrace(new Trace("trace1.data"));
        tp.addTrace(new Trace("trace2.data"));
        tp.addTrace(new Trace("trace3.data"));
        add(tp);
        pack();
        show();
    }
```

```
        }

        class TracePanel extends Canvas {
            int pixelWidth = 400;
            int pixelHeight = 400;
            float beginx = 0f;
            float beginy = 100f;
            float endx = 100f;
            float endy = -100;
            Vector traceVector = new Vector();
            TracePanel() {
                setSize(pixelWidth,pixelHeight);
            }
            public void paint(Graphics g) {
                Graphics2D g2 = (Graphics2D)g;
                GeneralPath gp;
                Trace trace;
                float userWidth = endx - beginx;
                float userHeight = endy - beginy;
                float fx = pixelWidth / (endx - beginx);
                float fy = pixelHeight / (endy - beginy);
                float ox = -fx * beginx;
                float oy = -fy * beginy;
                AffineTransform at = new AffineTransform(
                        fx,0f,
                        0f,fy,
                        ox,oy);
                g2.setTransform(at);
                g2.drawLine((int)beginx,0,(int)(endx-beginx),0);
                for(int i=0; i<traceVector.size(); i++) {
                    trace = (Trace)traceVector.elementAt(i);
                    g2.setColor(trace.getColor());
                    g2.setStroke(trace.getBasicStroke());
                    gp = trace.getGeneralPath();
                    if(gp != null)
                        g2.draw(gp);
                }
            }
            public void addTrace(Trace trace) {
                traceVector.addElement(trace);
            }
        }
```

The Commentary

The MultipleTraces constructor creates a TracePanel object to do the drawing. It then loads three trace data files and adds them to the list of traces that are held in the TracePanel. The TracePanel itself, extended from the Canvas class, is added to the Frame of the MultipleTraces object and the methods pack() and show() are called to size the window and display it. This will cause the paint() method of the TracePanel to be called whenever there is a need to display the window.

The TracePanel class, extended from Canvas, contains the constant values used for the sizes and extents of the data. There are two coordinate systems here—one for the pixels in the window (400x400) and one for the extent of the data (100x200). The pixels, in both the x and y directions, range from 0 to 400. The world data (sometimes called the real-world data) goes from 0 to 100 along the x-axis and from 100 to –100 along the y-axis.

Notice that the real-world values along the y-axis range from positive to negative. This is a form of remapping the origin. The pixel values of the window have their origin at the upper-left corner of the window with larger values proceeding down and to the right. We are more accustomed to thinking of data as having its origin in the lower-left corner and increasing up and to the right. The mapping from one to the other is achieved by using the upper-left coordinate system of the pixels as the basis of everything and simply reversing the real-world starting and ending values in the vertical direction. A small quirk, but if you don't fix it here, it will have to be done in some other place, and this seems to be the easiest place to do it.

All the action occurs in the paint() method of TracePanel. In a real-life application, you may want to have the constructor do some of the work and store the values away for later use, but it seemed clearer for purposes of explanation to have them all in one place.

Chapter 3 describes how to create a mapping transform to map data from the real world to the pixel world and, if you are not familiar with it, you may want to refer to that section now. The two factors fx and fy are created from the ratio of the widths—the pixels always start at zero, so there is no need to include them in the expression. Also, expressions creating the offsets ox and oy are simplified by the zero starting of the pixels. There are some very simple-looking calculations that really do some pretty sophisticated work for you inside the AffineTransform. Of course, if you wish to move your graph window out into the window somewhere—that is, move the origin away from the upper-left corner—you will need to put the numbers back in.

Once the transform is created, it is set as the transform for the Graphics2D object that will be used for drawing. You can see the output in Figure 10.1.

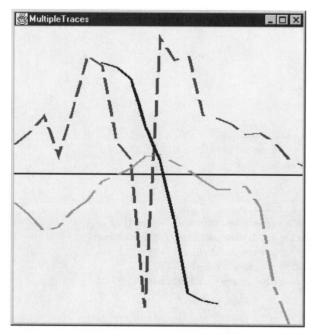

Figure 10.1 Three traces above and below zero.

There is a horizontal line drawn across the window where y is zero. This is done with the line

```
g2.drawLine((int)beginx,0,(int)(endx-beginx),0);
```

Notice that the coordinates are world coordinates, not pixel coordinates. Since we have the transform in place, we must always work with world coordinates because the Graphics2D object will always interpret everything that way.

A loop is executed once for each trace. The color of the trace is passed to the Graphics2D object with a call to setColor(), and the characteristics of the line is set with a call to setStroke() using the BasicStroke object from the Trace itself. Finally, the GeneralPath is retrieved and the trace data is drawn to the display in one simple draw() call.

Filling a Trace

Instead of drawing a line to represent the data, it is possible to fill the area enclosed by two traces, creating a shaded region between them.

The Code

```
import java.io.*;
import java.awt.*;
import java.awt.geom.*;
import java.awt.event.*;
import java.util.*;
class FillTrace extends Frame {
    public static void main(String arg[]) {
        new FillTrace();
    }
    FillTrace() {
        super("FillTrace");
        addWindowListener(new WindowAdapter() {
            public void windowClosing(WindowEvent e)
                { System.exit(0); } } );
        TracePanel tp = new TracePanel();
        tp.addTrace(new Trace("trace1.data"));
        add(tp);
        pack();
        show();
    }
}
class TracePanel extends Canvas {
    int pixelWidth = 400;
    int pixelHeight = 400;
    float beginx = 0f;
    float beginy = 100f;
    float endx = 100f;
    float endy = -100;
    Vector traceVector = new Vector();
    TracePanel() {
        setSize(pixelWidth,pixelHeight);
    }
    public void paint(Graphics g) {
        Graphics2D g2 = (Graphics2D)g;
        GeneralPath gp;
        Trace trace;
        float userWidth = endx - beginx;
        float userHeight = endy - beginy;
        float fx = pixelWidth / (endx - beginx);
        float fy = pixelHeight / (endy - beginy);
        float ox = -fx * beginx;
        float oy = -fy * beginy;
        AffineTransform at = new AffineTransform(
                fx,0f,
                0f,fy,
                ox,oy);
        g2.setTransform(at);
        g2.drawLine((int)beginx,0,(int)(endx-beginx),0);
        for(int i=0; i<traceVector.size(); i++) {
```

```
                trace = (Trace)traceVector.elementAt(i);
                g2.setColor(trace.getColor());
                g2.setStroke(trace.getBasicStroke());
                gp = trace.getGeneralPath(0f);
                if(gp != null)
                    g2.fill(gp);
            }
        }
        public void addTrace(Trace trace) {
            traceVector.addElement(trace);
        }
    }
}
```

The Commentary

The following example is a simplified version of the previous example in that it displays only one trace. It fills in the regions bonded by the trace and the x-axis.

To do this, the GeneralPath representing the trace is generated slightly differently. An argument, the value of the line above and below which it fills, is supplied to the getGeneralPath method of Trace. This causes the GeneralPath to return a version of the trace that encloses a polygon by drawing a straight line at the vertical position specified by the argument. Figure 10.2 shows the results of the fill() method used on this polygon.

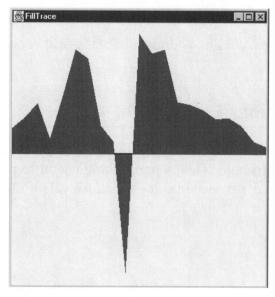

Figure 10.2 Filling above and below zero.

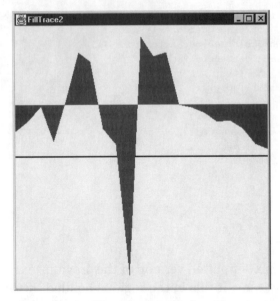

Figure 10.3   Filling above and below 40.

If a different argument value is supplied to the method, the horizontal line will appear in a different position. Figure 10.3 shows the output from FillTrace2, which is exactly the same as FillTrace, except the line of code that creates the polygon is this:

```
gp = trace.getGeneralPath(40f);
```

This means that the horizontal line is drawn, in real-world coordinates, at 40 instead of 0.

Fill Above and Draw Lines Below

It is possible to fill only above (or below) the threshold and draw the line below (or above) the threshold. This is particularly useful to highlight the fact that the values have exceeded some specific level or other.

The Code

```
import java.io.*;
import java.awt.*;
```

```java
import java.awt.geom.*;
import java.awt.event.*;
import java.util.*;
class FillTraceAbove extends Frame {
    public static void main(String arg[]) {
        new FillTraceAbove();
    }
    FillTraceAbove() {
        super("FillTraceAbove");
        addWindowListener(new WindowAdapter() {
            public void windowClosing(WindowEvent e)
                { System.exit(0); } } );
        TracePanel tp = new TracePanel();
        tp.addTrace(new Trace("trace1.data"));
        add(tp);
        pack();
        show();
    }
}
class TracePanel extends Canvas {
    int pixelWidth = 400;
    int pixelHeight = 400;
    float beginx = 0f;
    float beginy = 100f;
    float endx = 100f;
    float endy = -100;
    Vector traceVector = new Vector();
    TracePanel() {
        setSize(pixelWidth,pixelHeight);
    }
    public void paint(Graphics g) {
        Graphics2D g2 = (Graphics2D)g;
        GeneralPath gp;
        Trace trace;
        float userWidth = endx - beginx;
        float userHeight = endy - beginy;
        float fx = pixelWidth / (endx - beginx);
        float fy = pixelHeight / (endy - beginy);
        float ox = -fx * beginx;
        float oy = -fy * beginy;
        float cutoff = 40f;
        AffineTransform at = new AffineTransform(
                fx,0f,
                0f,fy,
                ox,oy);
        g2.setTransform(at);
        for(int i=0; i<traceVector.size(); i++) {
            trace = (Trace)traceVector.elementAt(i);
            g2.setColor(trace.getColor());
            g2.setStroke(trace.getBasicStroke());
            gp = trace.getGeneralPath(cutoff);
```

```
                        if(gp != null) {
                            g2.setClip(makeClip(beginx,beginy,endx,cutoff));
                            g2.fill(gp);
                        }
                        gp = trace.getGeneralPath();
                        if(gp != null) {
                            g2.setClip(makeClip(beginx,cutoff,endx,endy));
                            g2.draw(gp);
                        }
                    }
                }
                private GeneralPath makeClip(float x1,float y1,float x2,float y2) {
                    GeneralPath gp = new GeneralPath();
                    gp.moveTo(x1,y1);
                    gp.lineTo(x2,y1);
                    gp.lineTo(x2,y2);
                    gp.lineTo(x1,y2);
                    gp.closePath();
                    return(gp);
                }
                public void addTrace(Trace trace) {
                    traceVector.addElement(trace);
                }
            }
        }
```

The Commentary

Because there are two different types of things to be drawn, there are two different drawing actions. To draw the filled region, a GeneralPath is acquired by the call to getGeneralPath() in Trace. Supplying the threshold argument causes the returned GeneralPath to be completed as an enclosed region suitable for being filled. It is returned as a completed polygon with a horizontal segment at the point where filling changes to line drawing. The portion of the graph that is to be drawn—that is, the part below the threshold—is a trace instead of an enclosed figure. The figure is clipped to fill only the top portion, and then it is clipped to draw only the bottom portion.

The result is shown in Figure 10.4. The traces are filled in the area above the cutoff line, but it is only drawn below it. This effectively highlights all values that crossed over the threshold.

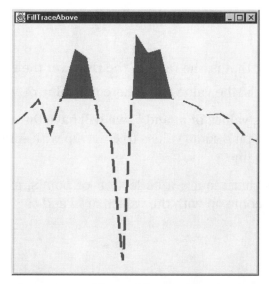

Figure 10.4 Filling and line-drawing simultaneously

Scattergram with Least Squares

There are times when a trace should not be shown as a squiggly line following from one dot to another—that would indicate that all the data points are believed to be absolutely accurate. Frequently, people analyzing data want to derive a general trend from lots of individual data points, each of which is inaccurate to some degree. The strength of the inaccurate data points lies in their quantity. The idea is that, statistically, lots of individual aberrations throughout a population cancel each other out, and truth can be deduced from the population taken as a whole.

A scattergram—or scatter plot—is made by taking a group of points and plotting them. You don't connect the points; rather, you leave them hanging in space, scattered throughout your graph. If the points are not random, there will be a general trend that describes the placement of the points. To identify the trend, you apply a mathematical algorithm to them. This algorithm identifies the slope and y intercept of a trend line, which can then be superimposed on the scattergram. The algorithm used by this program is the most popular one—it's called *least squares*. Here's an explanation.

A line is defined by a pair of points, or by an equation. If we have the equation it is easy to find all the points we need. The slope-intercept form of the equation of a line takes this form:

$$y = m*x+b$$

where

m is the slope of the line; that is, the ratio of the rise over the run

b is the y intercept; that is, the value of x where the value of y is zero

If we can come up with the values of m and b, we will have the equation of a line into which we can plug some values to come up with some end-points to draw our straight line.

There are two equations that require a collection of points, as in the trace, and can be used to come up with the values of m and b:

$$m = \frac{n*sxy - sx*sxy}{n*sxx - sx*sx}$$

where

n is the total number of points

sx is the sum of all values of x

sy is the sum of all values of y

sxx is the sum of all values of x squared

sxy is the sum of all values of x times y

The following program, LeastSquares.class, puts those equations to use in identifying trend lines through the points it plots.

The Code

```
import java.io.*;
import java.awt.*;
import java.awt.geom.*;
import java.awt.event.*;
import java.util.*;
class LeastSquares extends Frame {
    public static void main(String arg[]) {
        new LeastSquares();
    }
    LeastSquares() {
        super("LeastSquares");
        addWindowListener(new WindowAdapter() {
            public void windowClosing(WindowEvent e)
                { System.exit(0); } } );
        TracePanel tp = new TracePanel();
        tp.setTrace(new Trace("trace4.data"));
        add(tp);
```

```
            pack();
            show();
      }
class TracePanel extends Canvas {
      int pixelWidth = 400;
      int pixelHeight = 400;
      float beginx = 0f;
      float beginy = 100f;
      float endx = 100f;
      float endy = 0f;
      int x1;
      int y1;
      int x2;
      int y2;
      Trace trace;
      TracePanel() {
            setSize(pixelWidth,pixelHeight);
      }
      public void paint(Graphics g) {
            if(trace == null)
                  return;
            Graphics2D g2 = (Graphics2D)g;
            GeneralPath gp;
            float userWidth = endx - beginx;
            float userHeight = endy - beginy;
            float fx = pixelWidth / (endx - beginx);
            float fy = pixelHeight / (endy - beginy);
            float ox = -fx * beginx;
            float oy = -fy * beginy;
            AffineTransform at = new AffineTransform(
                        fx,0f,
                        0f,fy,
                        ox,oy);
            g2.setTransform(at);
            for(int i=0; i<trace.getPointCount(); i++)
                  g2.fillOval((int)trace.x(i)-1,(int)trace.y(i)-1,2,2);
            g2.setColor(trace.getColor());
            g2.setStroke(trace.getBasicStroke());
            g2.drawLine(x1,y1,x2,y2);
      }
      public void setTrace(Trace trace) {
            this.trace = trace;
            float sx = 0f;
            float sy = 0f;
            float sxx = 0f;
            float sxy = 0f;
            int n = trace.getPointCount();
            float m;
            float b;
            for(int i=0; i<n; i++) {
                  float x = trace.x(i);
```

```
                    float y = trace.y(i);
                    sx += x;
                    sxx += x * x;
                    sy += y;
                    sxy += x * y;
                }
                m = (n * sxy) - (sy * sx);
                m /= (n * sxx) - (sx * sx);
                b = (sy * sxx) - (sx * sxy);
                b /= (n * sxx) - (sx * sx);

                x1 = (int)trace.x(0);
                y1 = (int)(m * x1 + b);
                x2 = (int)trace.x(n-1);
                y2 = (int)(m * x2 + b);
            }
        }
    }
```

The Commentary

LeastSquares.class reads a single trace into memory using the utility classes and performs the calculations using the equations described earlier. The result appears in Figure 10.5.

The method setTrace() in the inner class TracePanel performs the calculations. It uses the equations to derive the values of m and b, then uses

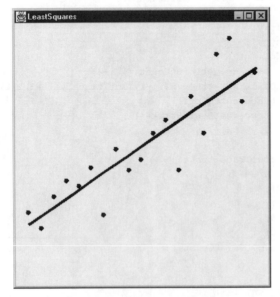

Figure 10.5 Least squares straight line representation of data.

those values to define the beginning and ending points of the line. With the values already calculated, all the paint() method needs to do is set the transform to fit the display window, draw the points (as small circles), and draw the line.

A Single Data Item

This class, the description of a data item, is used in the next two examples. Each data item has a magnitude and some descriptive attributes (color and name). This is used in the next two examples in much the same way Trace was used in the previous examples. It is used to load data in a form that can be displayed as a bar graph or a pie chart.

The Code

```java
import java.util.*;
import java.awt.*;
import java.awt.geom.*;
public class DataItems {
    Vector itemVector = new Vector();
    DataItems(String fileName) {
        Item item = null;
        Lex lex = new Lex(fileName);
        lex.gtkn();
        while(lex.getTokenType() != Lex.EOF) {
            if(lex.getToken().equals("item")) {
                if(item != null)
                    itemVector.addElement(item);
                if(lex.gtkn() != Lex.STRING)
                    lex.expected("quoted string");
                item = new Item(lex.getToken());
                lex.gtkn();
            } else if(lex.getToken().equals("color")) {
                lex.gtkn();
                int red = lex.getInteger();
                lex.gtkn();
                int green = lex.getInteger();
                lex.gtkn();
                int blue = lex.getInteger();
                lex.gtkn();
                if(item != null)
                    item.setColor(new Color(red,green,blue));
            } else if(lex.getToken().equals("number")) {
                lex.gtkn();
                float number = lex.getFloat();
                lex.gtkn();
```

```java
                            if(item != null)
                                item.setNumber(number);
                        } else {
                            lex.expected("a keyword");
                        }
                    }
                    if(item != null)
                        itemVector.addElement(item);
            }
            public int itemCount() {
                return(itemVector.size());
            }
            public String getName(int index) {
                if(index < itemVector.size())
                    return(((Item)itemVector.elementAt(index)).getName());
                return("Unnamed");
            }
            public float getNumber(int index) {
                if(index < itemVector.size())
                    return(((Item)itemVector.elementAt(index)).getNumber());
                return(0f);
            }
            public Color getColor(int index) {
                if(index < itemVector.size())
                    return(((Item)itemVector.elementAt(index)).getColor());
                return(Color.black);
            }
        class Item {
            String name;
            Color color = Color.black;
            float number = 0f;
            Item(String name) {
                this.name = name;
            }
            public void setColor(Color color) {
                this.color = color;
            }
            public void setNumber(float number) {
                this.number = number;
            }
            public Color getColor() {
                return(color);
            }
            public String getName() {
                return(name);
            }
            public float getNumber() {
                return(number);
            }
        }
    }
}
```

The Commentary

The DataItems class loads a collection of items into memory and makes their various parts accessible. It reads a data file that has this format:

```
item "First item"
number 943
color 255 0 0

item "Second item"
number 303
color 0 255 0

item "Third item"
number 82
color 0 0 255
```

This example is used in the following bar graph example. It contains three data items, each with a name, numeric value, and color defined for it. Each data item is loaded as a separate Item object, and they are all kept in a Vector. There are special get methods that can be used to retrieve the values.

Bar Graph

This example, and the next one, are different from the previous examples. This one represents a collection of values in such a way that their magnitudes can be compared quickly by noting the height of the bars for each one.

The Code

```
import java.io.*;
import java.awt.*;
import java.awt.geom.*;
import java.awt.event.*;
import java.util.*;
class BarGraph extends Frame {
    public static void main(String arg[]) {
        new BarGraph();
    }
    BarGraph() {
        super("BarGraph");
        addWindowListener(new WindowAdapter() {
            public void windowClosing(WindowEvent e)
```

```
                        { System.exit(0); } } );
            BarPanel bp = new BarPanel(new DataItems("items.data"));
            add(bp);
            pack();
            show();
        }
    class BarPanel extends Canvas {
        float pixelWidth = 400;
        float pixelHeight = 400;
        DataItems di;
        float in;
        float scaleFactor;
        BarPanel(DataItems dataItems) {
            setSize((int)pixelWidth,(int)pixelHeight);
            di = dataItems;
            float inCount = (4 * di.itemCount()) + 2;
            in = pixelWidth / inCount;
            float maxPixelHeight = pixelHeight - (3 * in);
            float maxWorldHeight = 0f;
            for(int i=0; i<di.itemCount(); i++) {
                if(di.getNumber(i) > maxWorldHeight)
                    maxWorldHeight = di.getNumber(i);
            }
            scaleFactor = maxPixelHeight / maxWorldHeight;
        }
        public void paint(Graphics g) {
            Graphics2D g2 = (Graphics2D)g;
            g2.drawLine(0,(int)pixelHeight,
                        (int)(3*in),(int)(pixelHeight - (3*in)));
            g2.drawLine((int)(3*in),(int)(pixelHeight - (3*in)),
                        (int)(3*in),0);
            g2.drawLine((int)(3*in),(int)(pixelHeight - (3*in)),
                        (int)(pixelWidth),(int)(pixelHeight - (3*in)));
            float xLeft = 2 * in;
            float yBottom = pixelHeight - in;
            for(int i=0; i<di.itemCount(); i++, xLeft += 4*in) {
                float height = di.getNumber(i) * scaleFactor;
                float yTop = yBottom - height;
                GeneralPath gp = new GeneralPath();
                gp.moveTo(xLeft,yTop);
                gp.lineTo(xLeft+(1.1f*in),yTop-in);
                gp.lineTo(xLeft+(3*in),yTop-in);
                gp.lineTo(xLeft+(3*in),yBottom-in);
                gp.lineTo(xLeft+(2*in),yBottom);
                gp.lineTo(xLeft+(2*in),yTop);
                gp.closePath();
                g2.setColor(di.getColor(i).darker());
                g2.fill(gp);
                g2.setColor(di.getColor(i));

    g2.fillRect((int)xLeft,(int)yTop,(int)(2*in),(int)height);
```

```
                        }
                    }
                }
            }
```

The Commentary

This program reads the data from the file "items.data" and displays it as the bar graph shown in Figure 10.6.

The inner class BarPanel is a Canvas object that loads the data from the file and does all the sizing and calculations necessary to position the bars on the display.

There are two variables calculated internally that are used to scale and place all the data. The variable in is determined from the width of the window and the number of bars to be displayed. The in value is used internally as the unit size from which everything else is built. For instance, the leftmost bar is two units from the left of the window, each bar is two units wide, and the bottom of the bar is one unit from the bottom of the window. The shadow to the top and right of each bar is one unit wide and there is one unit between the right side of the shadow of one bar to the left side of the next bar.

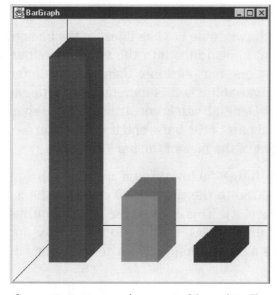

Figure 10.6   Bar graph generated from data file.

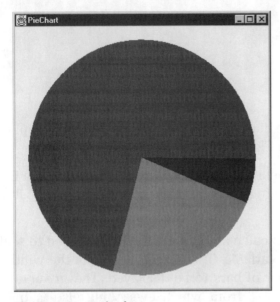

Figure 10.7   A pie chart.

The other variable is the scaleFactor. This value is multiplied by all the incoming data to scale the height of each bar. It is determined by setting the largest actual value two units from the top of the window and one unit from the bottom of the window. The rest of the bars are scaled accordingly.

The paint() method first draws some boxlike lines for the background to put a sort of dimensional appearance into the whole window. It then goes into a loop, drawing one bar per loop. Using the scale factor, the height is calculated. The variable xLeft is incremented with each iteration to position the bar. A GeneralPath is constructed in the shape of the shadow—the dimensional part of the bar—and it is drawn in a color one shade darker than the that of the face of the bar.

You may notice a little fudge factor thrown in. The top left of the shadow of the box is shifted to the right by 10 percent (the x value is multiplied by 1.1 to move it). This is because, if the outline of the shadow is made with parallel lines, the box looks clunky and out of shape. This fudging adds a bit of perspective without doing all the perspective drawing math.

A Pie Chart

A pie chart is really another form of a bar graph. It visually depicts the percentage of the whole consumed by any one item, as shown in Figure 10.7.

The Code

```
import java.io.*;
import java.awt.*;
import java.awt.geom.*;
import java.awt.event.*;
import java.util.*;
class PieChart extends Frame {
    public static void main(String arg[]) {
        new PieChart();
    }
    PieChart() {
        super("PieChart");
        addWindowListener(new WindowAdapter() {
            public void windowClosing(WindowEvent e)
                { System.exit(0); } } );
        PiePanel pp = new PiePanel(new DataItems("items.data"));
        add(pp);
        pack();
        show();
    }
class PiePanel extends Canvas {
    float pixelWidth = 400f;
    float pixelHeight = 400f;
    float margin = 20f;
    float pieHeight = pixelHeight - (2 * margin);
    float pieWidth = pixelWidth - (2 * margin);
    DataItems di;
    float totalNumber = 0f;
    PiePanel(DataItems dataItems) {
        setSize((int)pixelWidth,(int)pixelHeight);
        di = dataItems;
        for(int i=0; i<di.itemCount(); i++)
            totalNumber += di.getNumber(i);
    }
    public void paint(Graphics g) {
        Graphics2D g2 = (Graphics2D)g;
        float startAngle = 0f;
        float arcAngle;
        for(int i=0; i<di.itemCount(); i++) {
            arcAngle = 360f * (di.getNumber(i) / totalNumber);
            g2.setColor(di.getColor(i));
            if(i == 0) {
```

```
                           g2.fillArc((int)margin,(int)margin,
                                      (int)pieWidth,(int)pieHeight,
                                      (int)startAngle - 5,(int)arcAngle + 5);
                    } else {
                        g2.fillArc((int)margin,(int)margin,
                                   (int)pieWidth,(int)pieHeight,
                                   (int)startAngle,(int)arcAngle);
                    }
                    startAngle += arcAngle;
                }
            }
        }
    }
```

The Commentary

This example depicts the same set of data that was depicted in the bar graph of the previous example. Each slice of the pie begins at the start-Angle and continues for arcAngle degrees. The arcAngle is calculated as being a certain percentage of a full circle, 360 degrees.

There is a little fudging done to make sure the pie fills completely. Notice that the first slice of the pie starts five degrees before it is actually supposed to. This is to fill in a possible gap that could be left between the first slice of the pie and the last one. The gap could occur because of a cumulative rounding error as the circle is walked, and the fact that the drawing is done to the pixels "down and to the right" of the location instead of directly to an addressed pixel.

CHAPTER 11

Exploring Bitmapped Images

J ava has some innate capabilities to handle bitmapped images in the form of GIF and JPEG files. Further, it can be made to work with other bitmapped file formats (TIFF files, for example). Libraries are beginning to emerge to handle such formats. One company in Ottawa claims to have a CGM file-reader that reads and renders images only 10 percent slower than comparable C++ code on a Windows machine. Considering that this is software in development and that Java itself is undergoing performance improvements all the time, it's clear that rumors of the Java platform's lack of speed, at least in graphics, have been vastly exaggerated.

This chapter explores the mechanics of raster graphics in Java, generally, and particularly under Java2D.

Loading and Displaying an Image

This is a simple application that loads an image file from disk and displays it. The name of the image file can be specified on the command line, or it will default to earth.jpeg.

The Code

```java
import java.awt.*;
import java.awt.event.*;
public class DisplayImage extends Frame {
    public static void main(String[] arg) {
        if(arg.length == 0)
            new DisplayImage("earth.jpeg");
        else
            new DisplayImage(arg[0]);
    }
    public DisplayImage(String imageFileName) {
        super(imageFileName);
        Image image;
        addWindowListener(new WindowAdapter() {
            public void windowClosing(WindowEvent e)
                { System.exit(0); } } );
        image = Toolkit.getDefaultToolkit().getImage(imageFileName);
        MediaTracker mt = new MediaTracker(this);
        mt.addImage(image,1);
        try {
            mt.waitForAll();
        } catch(Exception e) {
            System.err.println(e);
            System.exit(1);
        }
        add(new DisplayImagePanel(image));
        pack();
        show();
    }
class DisplayImagePanel extends Canvas {
    Image image;
    DisplayImagePanel(Image image) {
        this.image = image;
        setSize(image.getWidth(this),image.getHeight(this));
    }
    public void paint(Graphics g) {
        g.drawImage(image,0,0,this);
    }
}
}
```

The Commentary

This is a small program, but a lot is going on here. The constructor of DisplayImage is supplied with the name of the file containing the image. The file extension for JPEG files can be either .jpg or .jpeg. Java also recognizes GIF files with the files extension .gif. There is the static method Toolkit.getDefaultToolkit() that returns a Toolkit object, and the image object is created with a call to the getImage() method of the default Toolkit.

The getImage() method creates an Image object, but the image itself is not loaded into RAM. It starts loading in another thread so the method can return immediately to the call and the program can continue with other activities while the image is loading. This can be handy if your program needs to load several images or if you have several different initializations to perform. Because of this asynchronous loading, however, it is necessary to make sure an image loaded before you try to use it. (Actually, you can start to use it right away; only part of the image will be displayed unless it has all been loaded. This may not be what you want.)

To make sure the image is fully loaded before the program starts working with it, a MediaTracker object is created to monitor the progress of the load. Once a MediaTracker has been created, it can be used to monitor the status of any number of images. To cause it to monitor the status of an Image object, it needs to be added to the list of those known to the MediaTracker. The method addImage() is used to add an Image to the list, and to assign an ID number. This number is not unique. Any number of Image objects can have the same ID number allowing the program to monitor the progress of groups of items as well as individuals. In this example, there is only one Image to be monitored, and the call to waitForAll() causes the program to pause until the Image is fully loaded and ready for display. There could, of course, be some sort of file error while it is loading, thus it is necessary to put the wait call inside a try/catch block.

The DisplayImagePanel class sizes itself to enclose the image exactly by calling setSize() with the dimensions of the image. The paint method simply draws the image at the upper-left hand corner of the window, thus filling it exactly. The result of the default display is shown in Figure 11.1.

Scaling an Image with Replication

The simplest way to scale an image is simply to replicate or delete pixels. That's what the ReplicateScaleFilter does in this example.

Figure 11.1   Home, in .GIF format.

The Code

```
import java.awt.*;
import java.awt.image.*;
import java.awt.event.*;
public class ReplicateUpDown extends Frame {
    public static void main(String[] arg) {
        if(arg.length == 0)
            new ReplicateUpDown("earthlet.jpeg");
        else
            new ReplicateUpDown(arg[0]);
    }
    public ReplicateUpDown(String imageFileName) {
        super(imageFileName);
        Image image;
        addWindowListener(new WindowAdapter() {
            public void windowClosing(WindowEvent e)
                { System.exit(0); } } );
        image = Toolkit.getDefaultToolkit().getImage(imageFileName);
        MediaTracker mt = new MediaTracker(this);
        mt.addImage(image,1);
        try {
```

```
                    mt.waitForAll();
            } catch(Exception e) {
                System.err.println(e);
                System.exit(1);
            }
            add(new ReplicatePanel(image));
            pack();
            show();
        }
    class ReplicatePanel extends Canvas {
        int h;
        int w;
        Image image;
        Image wider;
        Image taller;
        Image bigger;
        ReplicatePanel(Image image) {
            this.image = image;
            h = image.getHeight(this);
            w = image.getWidth(this);
            wider = getScaledImage(3*w,h);
            taller = getScaledImage(w,3*h);
            bigger = getScaledImage(3*w,3*h);
            setSize(4*w,4*h);
        }
        private Image getScaledImage(int width,int height) {
            ImageProducer ip = image.getSource();
            ReplicateScaleFilter rsf = new
    ReplicateScaleFilter(width,height);
            ImageProducer fis = new FilteredImageSource(ip,rsf);
            return(getToolkit().createImage(fis));
        }
        public void paint(Graphics g) {
            g.drawImage(image,0,0,this);
            g.drawImage(wider,w,0,this);
            g.drawImage(taller,0,h,this);
            g.drawImage(bigger,w,h,this);
        }
    }
}
```

The Commentary

The simplest form of scaling the size of an image is simply to duplicate or eliminate rows and columns of pixels. This example uses the ReplicateScaleFilter to double the size of an image along the x-axis, then along the y-axis, and then along both axes. As you can see from the results in Figure 11.2, this results in the "jaggies" so often associated with simple computer graphics.

The Image object is created from a disk file in the same way it was done in the previous example. The constructor of ReplicatePanel makes three copies, in different sizes, of the Image passed to it. The copies each have one or two dimensions multiplied by three.

The method getScaledImage() does the actual job of creating new images. An ImageProducer object is acquired from the original Image object. An ImageProducer will allow the program to read the same input image information as that used to create the original Image. A ReplicateScaleFilter is constructed that will automatically size any image to a specific width and height. These two, the ImageProducer and the ReplicateScaleFilter, are combined into a FilteredImageSource object that, in effect, becomes a new ImageProducer. This new ImageProducer is then passed to the createImage() method of the Toolkit and a new Image object is produced.

The getScaledImage() method is called three times—once for each newly scaled image. The images are all displayed as shown in Figure 11.2, with the original image in the upper left. The scaling is quick and accurate, but you can see that not only does it leave some jagged edges, it also generates that "blocky" appearance in the middle of the image.

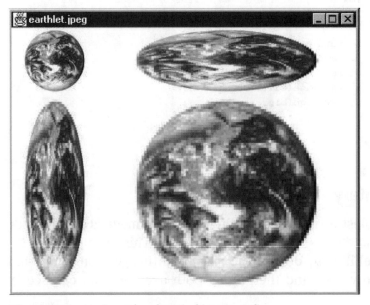

Figure 11.2 Horizontal and vertical image scaling.

Scaling an Image with Area Averaging

There are better ways to scale an image than in the previous example, and there are easier ways to do it. This example achieves the same result as the previous example, but does so directly from the Image object without having to deal with the details of creating a special filter to do the job.

The Code

```
import java.awt.*;
import java.awt.image.*;
import java.awt.event.*;
public class ImageScale extends Frame {
    public static void main(String[] arg) {
        if(arg.length == 0)
            new ImageScale("earthlet.jpeg");
        else
            new ImageScale(arg[0]);
    }
    public ImageScale(String imageFileName) {
        super(imageFileName);
        Image image;
        addWindowListener(new WindowAdapter() {
            public void windowClosing(WindowEvent e)
                { System.exit(0); } } );
        image = Toolkit.getDefaultToolkit().getImage(imageFileName);
        MediaTracker mt = new MediaTracker(this);
        mt.addImage(image,1);
        try {
            mt.waitForAll();
        } catch(Exception e) {
            System.err.println(e);
            System.exit(1);
        }
        add(new ScalePanel(image));
        pack();
        show();
    }
class ScalePanel extends Canvas {
    int h;
    int w;
    Image image;
    Image wider;
    Image taller;
    Image bigger;
```

```
        ScalePanel(Image image) {
            this.image = image;
            h = image.getHeight(this);
            w = image.getWidth(this);
            wider = image.getScaledInstance(3*w,h,Image.SCALE_REPLICATE);
            taller = image.getScaledInstance(w,3*h,Image.SCALE_REPLICATE);
            bigger = image.getScaledInstance(3*w,3*h,Image.SCALE_REPLICATE);
            setSize(4*w,4*h);
        }
        public void paint(Graphics g) {
            g.drawImage(image,0,0,this);
            g.drawImage(wider,w,0,this);
            g.drawImage(taller,0,h,this);
            g.drawImage(bigger,w,h,this);
        }
    }
}
```

The Commentary

The only difference between this example and the previous one is the process followed to create a scaled image. The method getScaledInstance() of the original Image object is called to create all of the three scaled images. Three arguments are passed to it. The first two are the width and height, in pixels, of the new image. The third one is a hint about what method should be used for scaling. The argument is called a hint because it can be ignored—there may be some reason why the requested method cannot be used.

There are constants defined in the Image class for all of the valid hint values. You can be sure that the one shown in the example, SCALE_REPLICATION, will be okay because it is such a simple algorithm that it is always available. If you ask for an algorithm that does not exist, the default (usually replication) will be used. The others, which may or may not be available, are as follows:

SCALE_AREA_AVERAGING. This will produce a scaled image that is more correct-looking than simple replication. When it has to insert new pixels, it creates the value of the new pixel from the average of the ones around it. This eliminates the look of the image being composed of little squares.

SCALE_DEFAULT. Choosing this as the hint will cause the default algorithm to be used, whatever that may be for this particular platform.

SCALE_FAST. This hint is a request to use whatever algorithm will work the fastest.

SCALE_REPLICATE. This is the replication method described in the previous example.

SCALE_SMOOTH. This method will, in many cases, generate a smoother-appearing image than the other methods.

Pixel by Pixel

If you want to work on graphics one pixel at time, you will need to do it inside an ImageFilter. You create an image of the correct size and pass it through your filter for processing. In this example, the image is created by being loaded from a disk file.

The Code

```java
import java.awt.*;
import java.awt.image.*;
import java.awt.event.*;
public class RecolorFilter extends Frame {
    public static void main(String[] arg) {
        if(arg.length == 0)
            new RecolorFilter("earthlet.jpeg");
        else
            new RecolorFilter(arg[0]);
    }
    public RecolorFilter(String imageFileName) {
        super(imageFileName);
        Image image;
        addWindowListener(new WindowAdapter() {
            public void windowClosing(WindowEvent e)
                { System.exit(0); } } );
        image = Toolkit.getDefaultToolkit().getImage(imageFileName);
        MediaTracker mt = new MediaTracker(this);
        mt.addImage(image,1);
        try {
            mt.waitForAll();
        } catch(Exception e) {
            System.err.println(e);
            System.exit(1);
        }
        add(new RecolorPanel(image));
        pack();
```

```
                    show();
            }
    class RecolorPanel extends Canvas {
        Image image;
        Image recolorImage;
        RecolorPanel(Image image) {
            this.image = image;
            ImageProducer ip = image.getSource();
            RecolorImageFilter rif = new RecolorImageFilter();
            FilteredImageSource fis = new FilteredImageSource(ip,rif);
            recolorImage = getToolkit().createImage(fis);
            setSize(image.getWidth(this),2*image.getHeight(this));
        }
        public void paint(Graphics g) {
            g.drawImage(image,0,0,this);
            g.drawImage(recolorImage,0,image.getHeight(this),this);
        }
    }
    }
    class RecolorImageFilter extends ImageFilter {
        public void setHints(int hint) {
            hint |= ImageConsumer.TOPDOWNLEFTRIGHT;
            super.setHints(hint);
        }
        public void setPixels(int x,int y,int width,int height,
                ColorModel model,byte pixels[],
                int offset,int scansize) {
            int[] co = null;
            byte[] pnew = new byte[width * height];
            for(int px=0; px<width; px++) {
                for(int py=0; py<height; py++) {
                    int index = px + (py*scansize) + offset;
                    co = model.getComponents(pixels[index],co,0);
                    co[0] /=  2; // Red
                    co[1] /=  2; // Green
                    co[2] /=  2; // Blue
                    pnew[index] = (byte)model.getDataElement(co,0);
                }
            }
            super.setPixels(x,y,width,height,model,pnew,offset,scansize);
        }
        public void setPixels(int x,int y,int width,int height,
                ColorModel model,int pixels[],
                int offset,int scansize) {
            int[] co = null;
            int[] pnew = new int[width * height];
            for(int px=0; px<width; px++) {
                for(int py=0; py<height; py++) {
                    int index = px + (py*scansize) + offset;
                    co = model.getComponents(pixels[index],co,0);
                    co[0] /=  2; // Red
                    co[1] /=  2; // Green
```

```
            co[2] /=  2; // Blue
            pnew[index] = (int)model.getDataElement(co,0);
        }
    }
    super.setPixels(x,y,width,height,model,pnew,offset,scansize);
    }
  }
  }
```

The Commentary

An image is loaded from disk into memory and passed through a filter that reduces the intensity of all its colors by half. Both the original and the filtered image are displayed.

The work of displaying the two images is done in RecolorPanel. Its constructor is supplied with an Image. The getSource() method of the Image is called so the program can access the ImageProducer. A new Image source, the FilteredImageSource object, is created by passing the original image source through the RecolorImageFilter. Finally, a new image, recolorImage, is constructed using the output of the FilteredImage-Source. The size of the window is set so it will hold both images, and the paint() method displays them both—the original on top and the filtered image on bottom as shown in Figure 11.3.

The pixel work is done in RecolorImageFilter. The setHints() method is overloaded to make certain that the image is passed to the filter in top-down left-right manner. If this is not set, it is possible that the image will come in some other form—even in separate pieces—and that may not be suitable for all filters. In this case it doesn't matter because we are simply transforming each pixel in place, but if the filter is designed to move

Figure 11.3   Halving the values of red, green, and blue.

pixels from one place to another in the image, it will be important that the entire image be present, and in the correct order.

There are two methods named setPixels(). These two methods do the actual work. They are identical in every way, except that one deals with 8-bit pixels and the other with 32-bit pixels. The super class, ImageFilter, has these two methods and simply passes data straight through it. In this example, a call is made to the getComponents() method of the color model to return the color components (red, green, and blue) in an array. Each of these individual components is divided in half, and a call is made to setComponents() to put the array of colors back into pixel format. It is necessary to unpack and repack the pixels this way because of portability—the exact internal format of a pixel will vary from one place to another, and using the components array this way allows the code to work no matter what the actual pixel format looks like. Finally, a call is made to super.setPixels() to pass the newly processed data on to the super class.

This design has some advantages. You can see that it is possible to scale an image by creating an array of the new size and passing the new height and width data to the super class. In fact, the input data can be completely ignored and an entirely new image created. Also, because of the way the data arrives and departs, it is possible to connect any number of these filters together. It is even possible to change the ColorModel by creating a new model and packing the pixels in a different way for output. Also, you can see where it would be a simple matter to extend the RecolorImageFilter class to add more processing, or, back in Recolor-Panel, it is possible to use the RecolorImageFilter as an image source and pass the result through another filter.

If you are new to this method of working with pixels, it will take a bit of getting used to, but it is very flexible. Version 1.1 of the API did not have all the methods available to do all the work necessary, but version 1.2 has added the key elements, and image filtering can be done quite easily.

Convolving

Images can be enhanced to bring out more details by using convolution. Each pixel is modified according to the values of the pixels around it. Each pixel has eight immediate neighbors and all of these can be involved in the calculations. Which pixels are involved, and how they are involved, is controlled by a matrix. The matrix itself is defined as a Kernel object.

The Code

```
import java.awt.*;
import java.awt.event.*;
import java.awt.image.*;
public class ConvolveImage extends Frame
        implements ActionListener {
    ConvolveImageCanvas cic;
    public static void main(String[] arg) {
        if(arg.length == 0)
            new ConvolveImage("trmm.jpeg");
        else
            new ConvolveImage(arg[0]);
    }
    public ConvolveImage(String imageFileName) {
        super(imageFileName);
        Image image;
        addWindowListener(new WindowAdapter() {
            public void windowClosing(WindowEvent e)
                { System.exit(0); } } );
        image = Toolkit.getDefaultToolkit().getImage(imageFileName);
        MediaTracker mt = new MediaTracker(this);
        mt.addImage(image,1);
        try {
            mt.waitForAll();
        } catch(Exception e) {
            System.err.println(e);
            System.exit(1);
        }
        cic = new ConvolveImageCanvas(image);
        setLayout(new BorderLayout());
        add("North",cic);
        add("South",makeButtonPanel());
        pack();
        show();
    }
    private Panel makeButtonPanel() {
        Panel panel = new Panel();
        Button button;
        button = new Button("Normal");
        button.addActionListener(this);
        panel.add(button);
        button = new Button("Soft");
        button.addActionListener(this);
        panel.add(button);
        button = new Button("Dark");
        button.addActionListener(this);
        panel.add(button);
        button = new Button("Light");
        button.addActionListener(this);
```

```java
        panel.add(button);
        button = new Button("Sharp");
        button.addActionListener(this);
        panel.add(button);
        button = new Button("Contrast");
        button.addActionListener(this);
        panel.add(button);
        return(panel);
    }
    public void actionPerformed(ActionEvent event) {
        if(event.getActionCommand().equals("Normal"))
            cic.setNormal();
        else if(event.getActionCommand().equals("Soft"))
            cic.setSoft();
        else if(event.getActionCommand().equals("Dark"))
            cic.setDark();
        else if(event.getActionCommand().equals("Light"))
            cic.setLight();
        else if(event.getActionCommand().equals("Sharp"))
            cic.setSharp();
        else if(event.getActionCommand().equals("Contrast"))
            cic.setContrast();
    }
class ConvolveImageCanvas extends Canvas {
    float[] IDENTITY = {0f,0f,0f,0f,1f,0f,0f,0f,0f};
    float[] SOFTEN = {0.1f,0.1f,0.1f,0.1f,0.2f,0.1f,0.1f,0.1f,0.1f};
    float[] DARKEN = {0f,0f,0f,0f,0.5f,0f,0f,0f,0f};
    float[] LIGHTEN = {0f,0f,0f,0f,1.5f,0f,0f,0f,0f};
    float[] SHARPEN = {0f,-0.5f,0f,-0.5f,3f,-0.5f,0f,-0.5f,0f};
    float[] CONTRAST = {-1f,-1f,-1f,-1f,9f,-1f,-1f,-1f,-1f};
    BufferedImage normal;
    BufferedImage current;
    ConvolveImageCanvas(Image image) {
        int w = image.getWidth(this);
        int h = image.getHeight(this);
        normal = new BufferedImage(w,h,BufferedImage.TYPE_INT_RGB);
        current = normal;
        Graphics2D g2 = normal.createGraphics();
        g2.drawImage(image,0,0,this);
        setSize(w,h);
    }
    public void paint(Graphics g) {
        g.drawImage(current,0,0,this);
    }
    public void setNormal() {
        Kernel kernel = new Kernel(3,3,IDENTITY);
        ConvolveOp co = new ConvolveOp(kernel);
        current = co.filter(normal,null);
        repaint();
    }
    public void setSoft() {
```

```
            Kernel kernel = new Kernel(3,3,SOFTEN);
            ConvolveOp co = new ConvolveOp(kernel);
            current = co.filter(normal,null);
            repaint();
        }
        public void setDark() {
            Kernel kernel = new Kernel(3,3,DARKEN);
            ConvolveOp co = new ConvolveOp(kernel);
            current = co.filter(normal,null);
            repaint();
        }
        public void setLight() {
            Kernel kernel = new Kernel(3,3,LIGHTEN);
            ConvolveOp co = new ConvolveOp(kernel);
            current = co.filter(normal,null);
            repaint();
        }
        public void setSharp() {
            Kernel kernel = new Kernel(3,3,SHARPEN);
            ConvolveOp co = new ConvolveOp(kernel);
            current = co.filter(normal,null);
            repaint();
        }
        public void setContrast() {
            Kernel kernel = new Kernel(3,3,CONTRAST);
            ConvolveOp co = new ConvolveOp(kernel);
            current = co.filter(normal,null);
            repaint();
        }
    }
}
```

The Commentary

A convolution is performed by placing the image to be performed in a BufferedImage object and calling the filter() method of ConvolveOp. A ConvolveOp object is created by being given a specific Kernel. The Kernel holds the matrix that, in effect, is the rule to be followed during convolution. The example program shows how to create and apply convoluting matrices.

This example loads an image and creates a Frame displaying an image at the top and a row of buttons at the bottom. The button labeled Normal shows the image without any convolution. The buttons labeled Soft, Dark, Light, Sharp, and Contrast each show the image after being convoluted with one of the Kernels.

The ConvolveOp class needs a BufferedImage to work with, so the constructor of the example creates one, called normal, and draws the image-loaded form disk onto it. This BufferedImage is set as the current one so the paint method will draw it on the display.

Whenever a button is pressed, a new BufferedImage is created using the ConvolveOp with one of the Kernels. The ConvolveOp filters the image from the normal BufferedImage to the current BufferedImage performing the convolution.

The image transformation that takes place is determined by the values in the matrix. The positions in the matrix correspond to the pixels in the image—in the 3-by-3 matrices used here, there is a center pixel and its eight surrounding pixels. Each pixel of an image is internally represented by a number—which encodes the color and intensity—and the values in the matrix are each multiplied by its corresponding pixel value, and then all the results are added together to form the resulting pixel. For example, this is the identity matrix:

$$\text{IDENTITY} \quad \begin{bmatrix} 0 & 0 & 0 \\ 0 & 1 & 0 \\ 0 & 0 & 0 \end{bmatrix}$$

In the identity matrix, the multipliers of all the neighboring pixels are set to zero, so they will play no part in the result. The center multiplier is set to one so there will be no change in the value of the center pixel. The result is that all the zero pixel values are added to the center pixel, generating a pixel value that is unchanged from the original, which results in the image being unmodified as shown in Figure 11.4.

Figure 11.4 The identity matrix does not alter the image.

Here is a matrix that softens an image by using almost the same value for all the pixels—each new pixel becomes an average of all the pixels around it:

SOFTEN
$$\begin{bmatrix} 0.1 & 0.1 & 0.1 \\ 0.1 & 0.2 & 0.1 \\ 0.1 & 0.1 & 0.1 \end{bmatrix} \begin{bmatrix} 0.1 & 0.1 & 0.1 \\ 0.1 & 0.2 & 0.1 \\ 0.1 & 0.1 & 0.1 \end{bmatrix} \begin{bmatrix} -1 & -1 & -1 \\ -1 & 9 & -1 \\ -1 & -1 & -1 \end{bmatrix}$$

The SOFTEN matrix has values that sum to one, so the intensity of the result will remain the same, but the sharp edges are gone. The new pixel becomes an average of all the pixels covered by the matrix. The softened image is shown in Figure 11.5.

A figure is darkened by having the sum of the matrix values result in less than one. This matrix discards all the surrounding pixels and reduces the intensity of the center pixel by half.

DARKEN
$$\begin{bmatrix} 0 & 0 & 0 \\ 0 & 0.5 & 0 \\ 0 & 0 & 0 \end{bmatrix}$$

The result of darkening an image is shown in Figure 11.6. Because the darkening is linear, some data could be lost. The size of the black area in the image is increased as pixel value approaches zero.

Just as a number less than 1.0 will darken an image, a number greater than 1.0 will lighten it. The image resulting from using the LIGHTEN matrix is shown in Figure 11.7. The only pixel involved in the result is the one in the center, and it is increased in intensity by 50 percent.

Figure 11.5   An image is softened by an even spreading of pixel values.

Figure 11.6 Reducing pixel intensity darkens a picture.

$$\text{LIGHTEN} \quad \begin{bmatrix} 0 & 0 & 0 \\ 0 & 1.5 & 0 \\ 0 & 0 & 0 \end{bmatrix}$$

The sharpening matrix ignores the pixels at the four corners, and subtracts half the value of the four at the sides and bottom.

$$\text{SHARPEN} \quad \begin{bmatrix} 0 & 0.5 & 0 \\ -0.5 & 3 & -0.5 \\ 0 & -0.5 & 0 \end{bmatrix} \begin{bmatrix} 0 & -1 & 0 \\ -1 & 5 & -1 \\ 0 & -1 & 0 \end{bmatrix}$$

Figure 11.7 Increasing pixel intensity lightens a picture.

The subtraction of the four outer pixels leaves the intensity at –2, so it necessary to multiply the center pixel by three to bring the summing total back to 1. This sharpening enhances the image, shown in Figure 11.8, brings out the lines in the swirling clouds below and emphasizes surface detail on the body of the satellite. Notice that different kinds of surfaces respond differently to the matrix. If you have some special image to be enhanced, you will have to experiment to find a matrix that does what you want to get done.

To increase the contrast of an image, emphasize the pixel in the middle while subtracting those surrounding it. In this matrix, the eight surrounding pixels are subtracted and the center pixel is added back in nine times—this leaves the overall intensity the same while emphasizing the difference between neighboring pixels.

$$\text{CONTRAST} \begin{bmatrix} -1 & -1 & -1 \\ -1 & 9 & -1 \\ -1 & -1 & -1 \end{bmatrix}$$

The CONTRAST matrix is a sort of emphasized version of the SHARPEN matrix. It uses all eight of the surrounding pixels for subtraction, and then multiplies the central pixel by 9. This produces a very high contrast image. Shown in Figure 11.9, the shape and texture of the body of the satellite is obscured, but the overall direction and shape of the swirls of the clouds in the storm below are immediately apparent.

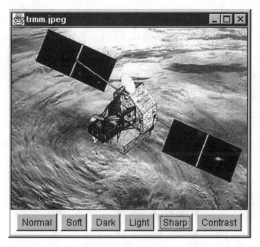

Figure 11.8 An image can be sharpened to bring out details.

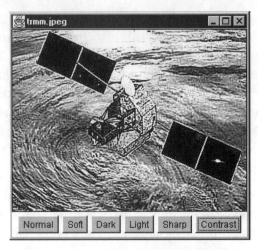

Figure 11.9　A highly contrasted image.

Image Transformation

The AffineTransform operations discussed earlier in Chapters 3 and 5 can also be applied to graphics. The same basic operations are available: rotation, shearing, and scaling. This example uses an AffineTransform to size and reshape a graphic.

The new pixels are derived from the old by using a nearest-neighbor, bilinear, or bicubic algorithm. There are a number of other settings used to control the actions of generating pixels—but they only exist in the form of hints. If the combination of settings you supply to the transform are valid, the transform will use them—otherwise, the transformation will ignore the hint and do something else instead. The result is that you can make a request, but you don't know whether or not it is being honored.

The passing of hints instead of supplying definite settings is a portability issue. Not all computer graphic systems have the same capabilities. Your program could be executed on a system that, say, does not have the ability to do antialiasing, and on another that does. If you specify the antialiasing hint, then the program will work on the system that has it and will cause no problem for the one that doesn't.

This example code is a little longer than it absolutely needs to be to demonstrate the fundamentals, but the addition of a dialog window turns it into a utility. You can specify the graphic file on the command line (or let it default to banana.jpeg). The utility makes it easy to set the options and quickly compare the different hint combinations, and to compare the effect of the three different pixel algorithms.

The Code

```
import java.awt.*;
import java.awt.event.*;
import java.awt.image.*;
import java.awt.geom.*;
public class TransformImage extends Frame
        implements ActionListener {
    TransformImageCanvas tic;
    TransformImageDialog tid;
    public static void main(String[] arg) {
        if(arg.length == 0)
            new TransformImage("banana.jpeg");
        else
            new TransformImage(arg[0]);
    }
    public TransformImage(String imageFileName) {
        super(imageFileName);
        addWindowListener(new WindowAdapter() {
            public void windowClosing(WindowEvent e)
                { System.exit(0); } } );
        tic = createCanvas(imageFileName);
        setLayout(new BorderLayout());
        add("North",tic);
        add("South",makeButtonPanel());
        pack();
        show();
        tid = new TransformImageDialog(tic);
    }
    private TransformImageCanvas createCanvas(String imageFileName) {
        Image image;
        image = Toolkit.getDefaultToolkit().getImage(imageFileName);
        MediaTracker mt = new MediaTracker(this);
        mt.addImage(image,1);
        try {
            mt.waitForAll();
        } catch(Exception e) {
            System.err.println(e);
            System.exit(1);
        }
        return(new TransformImageCanvas(image));
    }
```

```java
        private Panel makeButtonPanel() {
            Panel panel = new Panel();
            Button button;
            button = new Button("Identity");
            button.addActionListener(this);
            panel.add(button);
            button = new Button("Rotate");
            button.addActionListener(this);
            panel.add(button);
            button = new Button("Shear");
            button.addActionListener(this);
            panel.add(button);
            button = new Button("Scale Down");
            button.addActionListener(this);
            panel.add(button);
            button = new Button("Scale Up");
            button.addActionListener(this);
            panel.add(button);
            return(panel);
        }
        public void actionPerformed(ActionEvent event) {
            if(event.getActionCommand().equals("Identity"))
                tic.setIdentity();
            else if(event.getActionCommand().equals("Rotate"))
                tic.setRotate();
            else if(event.getActionCommand().equals("Shear"))
                tic.setShear();
            else if(event.getActionCommand().equals("Scale Down"))
                tic.setScaleDown();
            else if(event.getActionCommand().equals("Scale Up"))
                tic.setScaleUp();
        }
    }

import java.awt.*;
import java.awt.event.*;
import java.awt.image.*;
import java.awt.geom.*;
class TransformImageCanvas extends Canvas {
    private boolean needBuild = true;
    private BufferedImage normal;
    private BufferedImage current;
    private AffineTransform at;
    private RenderingHints hints;
    private int w;
    private int h;
    TransformImageCanvas(Image image) {
        w = image.getWidth(this);
        h = image.getHeight(this);
        at = new AffineTransform();
        normal = new BufferedImage(w,h,BufferedImage.TYPE_INT_RGB);
        current = normal;
```

```
            Graphics2D g2 = normal.createGraphics();
            g2.drawImage(image,0,0,this);
            setSize(w,h);
    }
    public void paint(Graphics g) {
        if(needBuild) {
            AffineTransformOp op = new AffineTransformOp(at,hints);
            current = op.filter(normal,null);
            needBuild = false;
        }
        g.drawImage(current,0,0,this);
    }
    public void setIdentity() {
        at = new AffineTransform();
        needBuild = true;
        repaint();
    }
    public void setRotate() {
        at.setToTranslation(w/2,h/2);
        at.rotate(Math.PI/4);
        at.translate(-w/2,-h/2);
        needBuild = true;
        repaint();
    }
    public void setShear() {
        at.setToTranslation(w/2,h/2);
        at.shear(0.7,0.7);
        at.translate(-w/2,-h/2);
        needBuild = true;
        repaint();
    }
    public void setScaleDown() {
        at.setToTranslation(0.3 * w/2,0.3 * h/2);
        at.scale(0.3,0.3);
        at.translate(-w/2,-h/2);
        needBuild = true;
        repaint();
    }
    public void setScaleUp() {
        at.setToTranslation(w/2,h/2);
        at.scale(1.5,1.5);
        at.translate(-w/2,-h/2);
        needBuild = true;
        repaint();
    }
    public void setHints(RenderingHints hints) {
        this.hints = hints;
        needBuild = true;
        repaint();
    }
}
```

```java
import java.awt.*;
import java.awt.event.*;
public class TransformImageDialog extends Frame
            implements ActionListener {
    static Object[][] option = {
        { RenderingHints.KEY_INTERPOLATION,
          RenderingHints.VALUE_INTERPOLATION_NEAREST_NEIGHBOR,
          "Interpolation is Nearest Neighbor" },
        { RenderingHints.KEY_INTERPOLATION,
          RenderingHints.VALUE_INTERPOLATION_BILINEAR,
          "Interpolation is Bilinear" },
        { RenderingHints.KEY_INTERPOLATION,
          RenderingHints.VALUE_INTERPOLATION_BICUBIC,
          "Interpolation is Bicubic" },
        { RenderingHints.KEY_ALPHA_INTERPOLATION,
          RenderingHints.VALUE_ALPHA_INTERPOLATION_DEFAULT,
          "Alpha Interpolation by Default" },
        { RenderingHints.KEY_ALPHA_INTERPOLATION,
          RenderingHints.VALUE_ALPHA_INTERPOLATION_QUALITY,
          "Alpha Interpolation for Quality" },
        { RenderingHints.KEY_ALPHA_INTERPOLATION,
          RenderingHints.VALUE_ALPHA_INTERPOLATION_SPEED,
          "Alpha Interpolation for Speed" },
        { RenderingHints.KEY_ANTIALIASING,
          RenderingHints.VALUE_ANTIALIAS_DEFAULT,
          "Antialiasing Default" },
        { RenderingHints.KEY_ANTIALIASING,
          RenderingHints.VALUE_ANTIALIAS_OFF,
          "Antialiasing Off" },
        { RenderingHints.KEY_ANTIALIASING,
          RenderingHints.VALUE_ANTIALIAS_ON,
          "Antialiasing On" },
        { RenderingHints.KEY_COLOR_RENDERING,
          RenderingHints.VALUE_COLOR_RENDER_DEFAULT,
          "Color Rendering Default" },
        { RenderingHints.KEY_COLOR_RENDERING,
          RenderingHints.VALUE_COLOR_RENDER_QUALITY,
          "Color Rendering for Quality" },
        { RenderingHints.KEY_COLOR_RENDERING,
          RenderingHints.VALUE_COLOR_RENDER_SPEED,
          "Color Rendering for Speed" },
        { RenderingHints.KEY_DITHERING,
          RenderingHints.VALUE_DITHER_DEFAULT,
          "Dithering Default" },
        { RenderingHints.KEY_DITHERING,
          RenderingHints.VALUE_DITHER_DISABLE,
          "Dithering Disabled" },
        { RenderingHints.KEY_DITHERING,
          RenderingHints.VALUE_DITHER_ENABLE,
          "Dithering Enabled" },
        { RenderingHints.KEY_FRACTIONALMETRICS,
          RenderingHints.VALUE_FRACTIONALMETRICS_DEFAULT,
```

```
          "Fractional Metrics Default" },
      { RenderingHints.KEY_FRACTIONALMETRICS,
        RenderingHints.VALUE_FRACTIONALMETRICS_OFF,
        "Fractional Metrics Off" },
      { RenderingHints.KEY_FRACTIONALMETRICS,
        RenderingHints.VALUE_FRACTIONALMETRICS_ON,
        "Fractional Metrics On" },
      { RenderingHints.KEY_RENDERING,
        RenderingHints.VALUE_RENDER_DEFAULT,
        "Render by Default" },
      { RenderingHints.KEY_RENDERING,
        RenderingHints.VALUE_RENDER_SPEED,
        "Render for Speed" },
      { RenderingHints.KEY_RENDERING,
        RenderingHints.VALUE_RENDER_QUALITY,
        "Render for Quality" },
    };
    private Checkbox[] box = new Checkbox[option.length];
    private TransformImageCanvas tic;

    TransformImageDialog(TransformImageCanvas tic) {
        super("Hints");
        setBackground(Color.lightGray);
        this.tic = tic;
        Button button;
        setLayout(new GridLayout(option.length+2,2));
        makeCheckboxes();
        button = new Button("Apply");
        button.addActionListener(this);
        add(button);
        button = new Button("Quit");
        button.addActionListener(this);
        add(button);
        pack();
        setVisible(true);
    }
    private void makeCheckboxes()

    CheckboxGroup group = null;
        boolean defaultSetting;
        Color color = Color.black;
        for(int i=0; i<option.length; i++) {
            if((group == null) || (option[i][0] != option[i-1][0])) {
                if(color == Color.black)
                    color = Color.blue;
                else
                    color = Color.black;
                defaultSetting = true;
                group = new CheckboxGroup();
            } else {
                defaultSetting = false;
            }
            box[i] = new Checkbox((String)option[i][2],defaultSetting);
```

```
                    box[i].setCheckboxGroup(group);
                    box[i].setForeground(color);
                    add(box[i]);
                    if(defaultSetting)
                        group.setSelectedCheckbox(box[i]);
                }
            }
            public void actionPerformed(ActionEvent event) {
                if(event.getActionCommand().equals("Quit")) {
                    setVisible(false);
                    System.exit(0);
                }
                if(event.getActionCommand().equals("Apply")) {
                    RenderingHints hints = null;
                    for(int i=0; i<option.length; i++) {
                        if(box[i].getState()) {
                            if(hints == null) {
                                hints = new RenderingHints(
                                    (RenderingHints.Key)option[i][0],
                                    option[i][1]);
                            } else {
                                hints.put(
                                    (RenderingHints.Key)option[i][0],
                                    option[i][1]);
                            }
                        }
                    }
                    tic.setHints(hints);
                }
            }
        }
    }
```

The Commentary

There are three classes here. The class TransformImageDialog allows the user to set the hints and interpolation algorithm. The class TransformImageCanvas converts the image to its new form and displays it in a Canvas window. The class TransformImage is the mainline of the program—it displays the TransformImageCanvas and the buttons along the bottom.

The TransformImage class loads an image in the same way as the previous examples did. The image is displayed in one of five different ways—it is displayed in its normal unmodified form, rotated by 45 degrees, sheared (squished) by 70 percent along both the x and y axes, scaled to 30 percent of its original size, and scaled to 130 percent of its original size.

The TransformImage constructor creates the main window to hold a TransformImageCanvas and the five buttons along the bottom. Each of the buttons is set to make a call to the TransformImageCanvas object to change the current algorithm setting. The Identity button uses an identity transform—that is, it doesn't resize or reshape the image in any way—but, like the other transforms, it will use the rendering hints shown in the TransformImageDialog window. The appearance of the window with everything set to their default values is shown in Figure 11.10.

The TransformImageCanvas class is an extension of the Canvas class—a Component that consists of a drawable rectangle. Its constructor receives the image to be displayed and saves it as a BufferedImage. This BufferedImage is used as the source for all transformations. There is a flag, named needBuild, to signify that a new transform and/or a new collection of hints has been supplied. If a new setting has been defined, the paint() method uses the current AffineTransform and RenderingHints to create a new current Image object before displaying it.

The TransformImageCanvas class has some methods that are called from the other classes to adjust the settings. The methods setIdentity(), setRotate(), setShear(), setScaleUp() and setScaleDown() correspond to the buttons on bottom of the window, and each one defines a new AffineTransform to be used on the image. The method setHints() is called from the TransformImageDialog to provide a new collection of hints. In each of these methods, the needBuild flag is set to indicate a change in the settings,

Figure 11.10 An image displayed using the default settings.

and the repaint() method is called to schedule a call to paint(). The paint() method will reconstruct the image as necessary.

The TransformImageDialog's constructor requires the TransformImage-Canvas object that it is to control. It creates a checkbox for each possible option—in each case, there are three settings for each option, but they are not entirely unique. As you can see in Figure 11.11 there are the three settings for interpolation (with nearest-neighbor being the default), and all the others have two settings and a default. For example, you can request that dithering be enabled or disabled, or you can allow dithering to default which will be on for some platforms and off for others.

The TransformDialog contains a table holding all the possible hints. Well, almost all. There are some that have to do with rendering text that are not included. Each table member has three entries: the key for the option, the value setting for the option, and the label for the Checkbox. The table is used to create the Checkboxes. Because the options come in groups—three settings for each key value—the makeCheckboxes() method changes the color of each group to make them easier to see on the display. Nothing happens as the selections are made, but, when the Apply button is clicked, all the settings are used to create a new Render-ingHints object which is passed on to the TransformImageCanvas causing a new image to be created and displayed.

Figure 11.11 Checkboxes for optional settings.

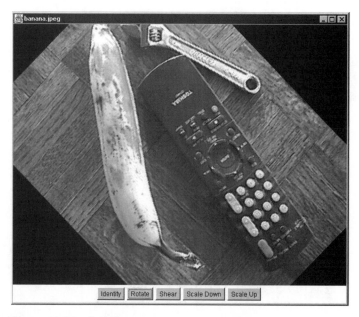

Figure 11.12   Rotation.

The results of setting the options may vary from one system to another. Figures 11.12 through 11.15 show our results on a Win32 system for rotation, shearing, shrinking, and enlarging by using the default hints.

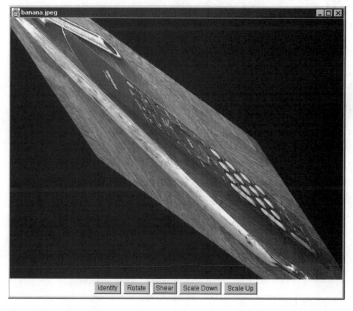

Figure 11.13   Shear.

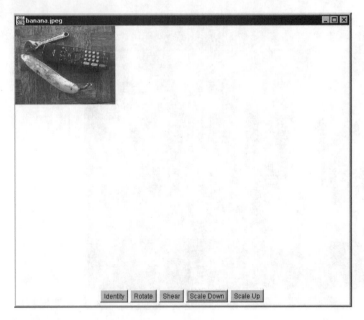

Figure 11.14 Scaling down.

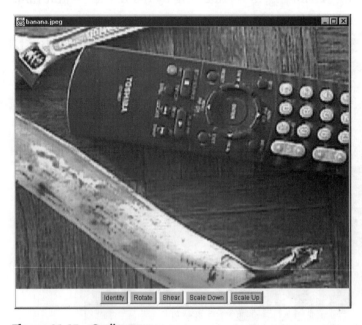

Figure 11.15 Scaling up.

Compositing

A composite image is one that is constructed from two or more images. This is done by superimposing one on top of the other.

Up to now, we have been dealing with opaque images. Along with the red, green, and blue components of a pixel, there is also an alpha component that determines the degree of transparency. An alpha value of 0 indicates total transparency (no color whatsoever), and a maximum value (a value of 255 is maximum for an 8-bit alpha field) is completely opaque.

When a BufferedImage is initially created, every pixel is transparent. As things are drawn on the image, they assume the alpha setting of the graphics being drawn—normally opaque.

This example shows how the alpha setting of a BufferedImage can be modified and then written on top of another image in such a way that the first image is partially transparent.

The Code

```java
import java.awt.*;
import java.awt.event.*;
import java.awt.image.*;
public class Compositing extends Frame
            implements ActionListener {
    private static String[] buttonLabel = {
        "100%","50%","Clear","DstIn","DstOut",
        "DstOver","Src","SrcIn","SrcOut","SrcOver"
    };
    private CompositingPanel cp;

    public static void main(String[] arg) {
        if(arg.length == 0)
            new Compositing("theseus.jpeg");
        else
            new Compositing(arg[0]);
    }
    public Compositing(String imageFileName) {
        super("Compositing");
        Image image;
        addWindowListener(new WindowAdapter() {
            public void windowClosing(WindowEvent e)
                { System.exit(0); } } );
        image = Toolkit.getDefaultToolkit().getImage(imageFileName);
```

```
        MediaTracker mt = new MediaTracker(this);
        mt.addImage(image,1);
        try {
            mt.waitForAll();
        } catch(Exception e) {
            System.err.println(e);
            System.exit(1);
        }
        cp = new CompositingPanel(image);
        Panel p = makeButtonPanel(cp);
        add("Center",cp);
        add("South",p);
        pack();
        show();
    }
    private Panel makeButtonPanel(CompositingPanel cp) {
        Button button;
        Panel p = new Panel();
        for(int i=0; i<buttonLabel.length; i++) {
            button = new Button(buttonLabel[i]);
            button.addActionListener(this);
            p.add(button);
        }
        return(p);
    }
    public void actionPerformed(ActionEvent e) {
        if(e.getActionCommand().equals("100%"))
            cp.setPercent(100);
        else if(e.getActionCommand().equals("50%"))
            cp.setPercent(50);
        else if(e.getActionCommand().equals("Clear"))
            cp.setComposite(AlphaComposite.Clear);
        else if(e.getActionCommand().equals("DstIn"))
            cp.setComposite(AlphaComposite.DstIn);
        else if(e.getActionCommand().equals("DstOut"))
            cp.setComposite(AlphaComposite.DstOut);
        else if(e.getActionCommand().equals("DstOver"))
            cp.setComposite(AlphaComposite.DstOver);
        else if(e.getActionCommand().equals("Src"))
            cp.setComposite(AlphaComposite.Src);
        else if(e.getActionCommand().equals("SrcIn"))
            cp.setComposite(AlphaComposite.SrcIn);
        else if(e.getActionCommand().equals("SrcOut"))
            cp.setComposite(AlphaComposite.SrcOut);
        else if(e.getActionCommand().equals("SrcOver"))
            cp.setComposite(AlphaComposite.SrcOver);
    }
class CompositingPanel extends Canvas {
    private BufferedImage background;
    private BufferedImage fore50;
    private BufferedImage fore100;
```

```java
    private Image image;
    private int w;
    private int h;
    private int percent = 100;
    private Composite composite = AlphaComposite.SrcOver;
    CompositingPanel(Image image) {
        Graphics g2;
        w = image.getWidth(this);
        h = image.getHeight(this);
        this.image = image;
        createBackground();
        createForeground();
        setSize(w,h);
    }
    private void createBackground() {
        background = new BufferedImage(w,h,BufferedImage.TYPE_INT_ARGB);
        Graphics2D g2 = background.createGraphics();
        g2.drawImage(image,0,0,this);
    }
    private void createForeground() {
        Graphics2D g2;
        Font font = new Font("TimesRoman",Font.BOLD,150);
        fore100 = new BufferedImage(w,h,BufferedImage.TYPE_INT_ARGB);
        g2 = fore100.createGraphics();
        g2.setFont(font);
        g2.drawString("FLY!",130,230);
        fore50 = new BufferedImage(w,h,BufferedImage.TYPE_INT_ARGB);
        g2 = fore50.createGraphics();
        g2.setFont(font);
        g2.drawString("FLY!",130,230);
        WritableRaster wr = fore50.getAlphaRaster();
        int[] array = null;
        for(int x=0; x<w; x++) {
            for(int y=0; y<h; y++) {
                array = wr.getPixel(x,y,array);
                array[0] /= 2;
                wr.setPixel(x,y,array);
            }
        }
    }
    public void paint(Graphics g) {
        Graphics2D g2 = (Graphics2D)g;
        g2.drawImage(background,0,0,this);
        g2.setComposite(composite);
        if(percent == 100)
            g2.drawImage(fore100,0,0,this);
        else
            g2.drawImage(fore50,0,0,this);
    }
    void setPercent(int setting) {
        percent = setting;
```

```
            repaint();
        }
        void setComposite(Composite setting) {
            composite = setting;
            repaint();
        }
    }
}
```

The Commentary

The Compositing constructor reads, from a file, the image to be used for the background. The display window will be sized to fit this image. The window is constructed with the CompositingPanel at the top and a row of buttons at the bottom. The first two buttons determine whether the overlaid figure will be opaque or 50 percent transparent.

The image is used by createBackground() to create a BufferedImage. Figure 11.16 shows the image being used as the background for the example code. The alpha settings for the background image are not modified. The image is assumed to be completely opaque but it doesn't really matter because it will be painted onto a blank BufferedImage, to be used as the picture that shows through the transparent part that will be painted later.

Note that the BufferedImages are created using TYPE_INT_ARGB instead of TYPE_INT_RGB. It is necessary to create a BufferedImage that has an alpha component with each pixel because it is this component that enables transparency. In fact, Compositing consists of adjusting the alpha component of the pixels to specify the degree to which the existing pixel will "show through" on the display.

Figure 11.16   The figure being used as a background.

Two other BufferedImages are created to hold the foreground graphics. One is at 100 percent (that is, fully opaque) and the other is at 50 percent (that is, one-half of the background pixel value will show through). The halftone BufferedImage is shown in Figure 11.17. This is achieved by simply creating BufferedImages the same size as the one being used for the background and then writing some text to it. After the text is written, the alpha settings for the text itself is opaque (255) and the alpha for the rest of the BufferedImage is completely transparent (0). The alpha settings were left this way for the 100 percent BufferedImage, and the result of using the SrcOver option is shown in Figure 11.18 (with with the letters completely obscuring the background, but the rest of the background being unaffected).

To add transparency to the figure, it is necessary to modify the alpha values of the BufferedImage. This is done in the loop in the method create-Foreground() after the 50 percent BufferedImage has been created and the text written to it. The method getAlphaRaster() returns a WritableRaster object that provides direct access to the alpha values of each individual pixel. For this example, we simply loop through all the pixels and divide the value in half giving the entire BufferedImage 50 percent transparency. The settings that are already zero—completely transparent—are not affected.

The WritableRaster object returns an array of values for each pixel. The reason this is an array is that this class can be used for direct access to the pixels, so more than one value can be returned for each pixel. In this example we retrieve a version of the WritableRaster object that contains only the alpha values, so it is array of size one.

Figure 11.17   The halftone BufferedImage.

Figure 11.18   Alpha at 100 percent using SrcOver.

There is one more thing to be done to achieve transparency. The rule must be set to determine how the transparent pixels are to be written over the top of the existing pixels. The rule itself, which can be quite complicated, is kept in a AlphaComposite object. The simplest way to achieve transparency is to use a predefined AlphaComposite object that implements the SrcOver rule. In the paint() method, the background is

Figure 11.19   Alpha at 50 percent using SrcOver.

Figure 11.20   Alpha at 100 percent using DstIn.

drawn, then the SrcOver rule is set in the Graphics2D object, and then the foreground is drawn. The results of doing this at 100 percent are shown in Figure 11.18 and the results of doing it at 50 percent are shown in Figure 11.19.

It is possible to select any of the rules from the AlphaComposite class by choosing the buttons at the bottom of the window. There are sixteen possible combinations, but some of them are less useful than others for this example—for mixing different kinds of images you may need to use different rules. The result can be modified, for example, by having both foreground and background defined with some sort of transparency. One interesting result is the 100 percent version using DstIn as shown in Figure 11.20.

Cross Fading with Transparency

This program demonstrates the pixel-by-pixel transparency control that a program has over an image. This program loads a pair of images and superimposes one over the other with a gradient fade from the center up to the top and down to the bottom.

The Code

```
import java.awt.*;
import java.awt.event.*;
import java.awt.image.*;
public class CrossFade extends Frame {
    public static void main(String[] arg) {
        new CrossFade();
    }
    public CrossFade() {
        super("CrossFade");
        Image edgeImage;
        Image centerImage;
        addWindowListener(new WindowAdapter() {
            public void windowClosing(WindowEvent e)
                { System.exit(0); } } );
        edgeImage = Toolkit.getDefaultToolkit().getImage("earth.jpeg");
        centerImage =
Toolkit.getDefaultToolkit().getImage("theseus2.jpeg");
        MediaTracker mt = new MediaTracker(this);
        mt.addImage(edgeImage,1);
        mt.addImage(centerImage,1);
        try {
            mt.waitForAll();
        } catch(Exception e) {
            System.err.println(e);
            System.exit(1);
        }
        add(new CrossFadePanel(edgeImage,centerImage));
        pack();
        show();
    }
}
class CrossFadePanel extends Canvas {
    BufferedImage edge;
    BufferedImage center;
    int w;
    int h;
    CrossFadePanel(Image edgeImage,Image centerImage) {
        Graphics g2;
        w =
Math.min(edgeImage.getWidth(this),centerImage.getWidth(this));
        h =
Math.min(edgeImage.getHeight(this),centerImage.getHeight(this));
        createEdge(edgeImage);
        createCenter(centerImage);
        setSize(w,h);
    }
    private void createEdge(Image image) {
        edge = new BufferedImage(w,h,BufferedImage.TYPE_INT_ARGB);
        Graphics2D g2 = edge.createGraphics();
        g2.drawImage(image,0,0,this);
```

```
        }
    private void createCenter(Image image) {
        center = new BufferedImage(w,h,BufferedImage.TYPE_INT_ARGB);
        Graphics2D g2 = center.createGraphics();
        g2.drawImage(image,0,0,this);
        WritableRaster wr = center.getAlphaRaster();
        double[] array = null;
        int h2 = h / 2;
        for(int y=0; y<h; y++) {
            double factor = Math.abs(y - h2);
            factor /= h2;
            for(int x=0; x<w; x++) {
                array = wr.getPixel(x,y,array);
                array[0] *= 1.0 - factor;
                wr.setPixel(x,y,array);
            }
        }
    }
    public void paint(Graphics g) {
        Graphics2D g2 = (Graphics2D)g;
        g2.drawImage(edge,0,0,this);
        g2.setComposite(AlphaComposite.SrcOver);
        g2.drawImage(center,0,0,this);
    }
}
}
```

The Commentary

The two images are loaded from disk and they are used to create a Cross-FadePanel object. The first image, named edge, is painted to cover the entire surface, and the second image is painted with gradient fill. The second image, named center, approaches complete transparency at the top and bottom, and is opaque in the center. This causes the background image, the one painted first, to be more visible at the top and bottom than in the center.

The method createEdge() creates a BufferedImage containing the image that is to be written second. Once the BufferedImage has been initialized with the image from the file, the alpha values of its pixels are adjusted. The nested loop with x and y for variables adjusts the alpha values according to the vertical position, the y value, of the pixel itself. To do this the getPixel() method that retrieves the values as doubles is used—the values still range from 0 to 255 in this color model, but the arithmetic is simpler if it is done with real numbers. A factor ranging from 0.0 to 1.0

Figure 11.21 Varying transparency from top to bottom.

is calculated—its value depends on the distance of the pixel from h2, which is the center of the image.

Multiplying an alpha value by 0.0 makes it transparent, and multiplying it by 1.0 leaves it opaque. This way, the gradient of transparency is made to vary smoothly from the center out to the top and bottom. The resulting image is shown in Figure 11.21.

CHAPTER 12

Understanding the Mouse

E ach time the mouse is moved or a mouse button is pressed, a mouse event is sent to the program. If your program has been written to process these events, you can, at all times, determine the position of the mouse and which buttons are currently being pressed. This chapter contains example programs demonstrating how to read information from the mouse.

Reading Mouse Events

This program reads events from the mouse and displays the current mouse position and status. If you need to know the position of the mouse only when it is clicked, implementing the MouseListener interface is probably the simplest way to do it. This program displays a window by extending the Canvas class and reports positions inside it where the mouse buttons are pressed and released. It also tracks when the mouse enters or exits the window.

The Code

```java
import java.awt.*;
import java.awt.event.*;
public class FollowMouse extends Frame {
    public static void main(String[] arg) {
        new FollowMouse();
    }
    FollowMouse() {
        super("FollowMouse");
        addWindowListener(new WindowAdapter() {
            public void windowClosing(WindowEvent e)
                { System.exit(0); } } );
        FollowMousePanel mp = new FollowMousePanel();
        add(mp);
        pack();
        show();
    }
}
class FollowMousePanel extends Canvas
            implements MouseListener {
    String enterExit = "";
    String click = "";
    String press = "";
    String release = "";
    FollowMousePanel() {
        addMouseListener(this);
        setSize(400,150);
    }
    public void paint(Graphics g) {
        g.drawString(enterExit,20,30);
        g.drawString(click,20,50);
        g.drawString(press,20,70);
        g.drawString(release,20,90);
    }
    public void mouseEntered(MouseEvent event) {
        enterExit = "Mouse Entered (" + event.getX() +
                "," + event.getY() + ")";
        repaint();
    }
    public void mouseExited(MouseEvent event) {
        enterExit = "Mouse Exited (" + event.getX() +
                "," + event.getY() + ")";
        repaint();
    }
    public void mouseClicked(MouseEvent event) {
        click = "Mouse Clicked (" + event.getX() +
                "," + event.getY() + ")";
        repaint();
    }
    public void mousePressed(MouseEvent event) {
```

```
            press = "Mouse Pressed (" + event.getX() +
                    "," + event.getY() + ")";
            repaint();
        }
        public void mouseReleased(MouseEvent event) {
            release = "Mouse Released (" + event.getX() +
                    "," + event.getY() + ")";
            repaint();
        }
    }
    }
```

The Commentary

The class FollowMousePanel extends a Canvas for drawing and implements the MouseListener interface for tracking mouse activities. The constructor of FollowMousePanel adds itself to the list of classes to be notified whenever a mouse event occurs. This notification comes in the form of calls to mouseEntered(), mouseExited(), mouseClicked(), mousePressed() or mouseReleased().

Whenever the mouse enters a visible region of the window, the method mouseEntered() is called, and whenever the mouse leaves the window, the method mouseExited() is called. The window does not need to have the current focus for this to happen—the window can be partially obscured by another window and the point of entry and exit will still be noted.

Every time a mouse button is pressed, the mousePressed() method is called. Every time a mouse button is released, the mouseReleased() method is called. Every time a mouse button is pressed and released without having its position changed while the button is held down, the mouseClicked() method is called. Figure 12.1 shows FollowMouse.class in action.

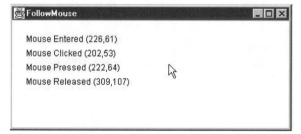

Figure 12.1   Detecting mouse positions.

Mouse Motion

It is possible to follow every movement of the mouse. This example is quite similar to the previous one where we tracked mouse buttons, except this example tracks every movement of the mouse and ignores the buttons.

The Code

```java
import java.awt.*;
import java.awt.event.*;
public class FollowMouseMotion extends Frame {
    public static void main(String[] arg) {
        new FollowMouseMotion();
    }
    FollowMouseMotion() {
        super("FollowMouseMotion");
        addWindowListener(new WindowAdapter() {
            public void windowClosing(WindowEvent e)
                { System.exit(0); } } );
        FollowMousePanel mp = new FollowMousePanel();
        add(mp);
        pack();
        show();
    }
class FollowMousePanel extends Canvas
            implements MouseMotionListener {
    String description = "";
    FollowMousePanel() {
        addMouseMotionListener(this);
        setSize(400,400);
    }
    public void paint(Graphics g) {
        g.drawString(description,20,30);
    }
    public void mouseMoved(MouseEvent event) {
        description = "Moved (" + event.getX() +
                "," + event.getY() + ")";
        repaint();
    }
    public void mouseDragged(MouseEvent event) {
        description = "Dragged (" + event.getX() +
                "," + event.getY() + ")";
        repaint();
    }
}
}
}
```

Figure 12.2   Following the mouse.

Figure 12.3   Following the mouse with a button held down.

The Commentary

This example is similar to the previous one except that this one implements the MouseMotionListener instead of the MouseListener interface. Two methods can be implemented to satisfy this interface. The method mouseMoved() is called each time the mouse moves to a different position without any of the buttons being pressed. The method mouseDragged() is called when the mouse is moved while any of the buttons are being held down.

Tracking the motion of the mouse requires monitoring a large number of events, and most applications don't need to know exactly where the pointer is at all times. The MouseMotionListener interface is separate from the MouseListener interface for the sake of efficiency. Figure 12.2 shows the mouse movement and Figure 12.3 shows mouse dragging movement.

Dissecting Mouse Events

The requirements of almost all applications will be satisfied by implementing one of the two interfaces just described. There can be circumstances where more detailed control is needed, however. This information can be found inside the MouseEvent. This example receives all mouse events in one method and displays all the information it receives.

The Code

```java
import java.awt.*;
import java.awt.event.*;
public class AllMouseEvents extends Frame {
    public static void main(String[] arg) {
        new AllMouseEvents();
    }
    AllMouseEvents() {
        super("AllMouseEvents");
        addWindowListener(new WindowAdapter() {
            public void windowClosing(WindowEvent e)
                { System.exit(0); } } );
        AllMousePanel ap = new AllMousePanel();
        add(ap);
        pack();
        show();
    }
}
class AllMousePanel extends Canvas
        implements MouseListener, MouseMotionListener {
    String when = "";
    String modifier = "";
    String eventID = "";
    String location = "";
    String clickCount = "";
    AllMousePanel() {
        addMouseListener(this);
        addMouseMotionListener(this);
        setSize(400,150);
    }
    public void paint(Graphics g) {
        g.drawString(modifier,20,30);
        g.drawString(eventID,20,50);
        g.drawString(location,20,70);
        g.drawString(clickCount,20,90);
        g.drawString(when,20,110);
    }
    public void mouseMoved(MouseEvent event) {
        showEvent(event);
    }
    public void mouseDragged(MouseEvent event) {
        showEvent(event);
    }
    public void mouseEntered(MouseEvent event) {
        showEvent(event);
    }
    public void mouseExited(MouseEvent event) {
        showEvent(event);
    }
    public void mouseClicked(MouseEvent event) {
```

```
        showEvent(event);
    }
    public void mousePressed(MouseEvent event) {
        showEvent(event);
    }
    public void mouseReleased(MouseEvent event) {
        showEvent(event);
    }
    private void showEvent(MouseEvent event) {
        modifier = "";
        if(event.isAltDown())
            modifier += "ALT ";
        if(event.isControlDown())
            modifier += "CTRL ";
        if(event.isMetaDown())
            modifier += "META ";
        if(event.isShiftDown())
            modifier += "SHIFT ";
        if((event.getModifiers() & InputEvent.BUTTON1_MASK) != 0)
            modifier += "BUTTON1 ";
        if((event.getModifiers() & InputEvent.BUTTON2_MASK) != 0)
            modifier += "BUTTON2 ";
        if((event.getModifiers() & InputEvent.BUTTON3_MASK) != 0)
            modifier += "BUTTON3 ";
        switch(event.getID()) {
        case MouseEvent.MOUSE_CLICKED:
            eventID = "Mouse clicked";
            break;
        case MouseEvent.MOUSE_DRAGGED:
            eventID = "Mouse dragged";
            break;
        case MouseEvent.MOUSE_ENTERED:
            eventID = "Mouse entered";
            break;
        case MouseEvent.MOUSE_EXITED:
            eventID = "Mouse exited";
            break;
        case MouseEvent.MOUSE_MOVED:
            eventID = "Mouse moved";
            break;
        case MouseEvent.MOUSE_PRESSED:
            eventID = "Mouse pressed";
            break;
        case MouseEvent.MOUSE_RELEASED:
            eventID = "Mouse released";
            break;
        default:
            eventID = "";
            break;
        }
        clickCount = "Click count: " + event.getClickCount();
```

```
            location = "(" + event.getX() + "," + event.getY() + ")";
            when = "When: " + event.getWhen();
            repaint();
        }
    }
}
```

The Commentary

AllMouseEvents.class receives all possible mouse events by implementing both the MouseListener and MouseMotionListener interfaces. The events arrive, according to type, in their separate methods and are immediately passed to the showEvent() method. The showEvent() method sets the values of several strings to descriptive contents of the event and calls repaint() to have the strings displayed.

The first few method calls (isAltDown(), isControlDown(), and so on) determine which keys were involved. The event not only reports which, if any, mouse button has been pressed, it also reports whether certain other keys were pressed at the moment of the event. The ALT key is a special key peculiar to PCs and the META key is peculiar to Sun and some other UNIX systems. There are systems with both keys. The ID of the event itself specifies whether it is click, release, drag or whatever.

There is a counter for the number of clicks. A bit of experimentation with the counter will show you how it works. For the counter to be greater than one, a mouse button must be pressed more than once without the mouse position having been moved, and it must have been pressed within a short period of time. There is no limit to the count of the number of clicks as long as they all continue to come at the same position and before the timer expires.

Each event carries a time stamp that was inserted into it to indicate the time that the event occurred. This can become important if your program is receiving events from more than one device (such as a mouse and a keyboard) and, through delays in transmission, they could arrive out of order.

This program displays as descriptive string for every combination of buttons. Figure 12.4 shows the results of a double click while the control key is being held down.

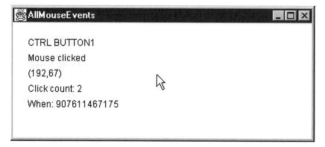

Figure 12.4 Double-click with the Ctrl key held down.

Changing Mouse Cursors

One of the basic requirements of a GUI interface is feedback to the user. One of the main ways of doing this is by changing the appearance of the mouse. It can be used to indicate that some activity is underway, or that the mouse pointer is over some special portion of the interface. This example shows how the mouse cursor's appearance can be modified.

The Code

```java
import java.awt.*;
import java.awt.event.*;
public class ShowCursor extends Frame {
    public static void main(String[] arg) {
        new ShowCursor();
    }
    ShowCursor() {
        super("ShowCursor");
        addWindowListener(new WindowAdapter() {
            public void windowClosing(WindowEvent e)
                { System.exit(0); } } );
        ShowCursorPanel mp = new ShowCursorPanel();
        add(mp);
        pack();
        show();
    }
class ShowCursorPanel extends Canvas
        implements MouseMotionListener {
    private Cursor cursor;
    private int cursorType = -1;
```

```java
        private int[] cursorTypeArray = {
            Cursor.CROSSHAIR_CURSOR,
            Cursor.DEFAULT_CURSOR,
            Cursor.HAND_CURSOR,
            Cursor.MOVE_CURSOR,
            Cursor.TEXT_CURSOR,
            Cursor.WAIT_CURSOR,
            Cursor.W_RESIZE_CURSOR,
            Cursor.NW_RESIZE_CURSOR,
            Cursor.N_RESIZE_CURSOR,
            Cursor.NE_RESIZE_CURSOR,
            Cursor.E_RESIZE_CURSOR,
            Cursor.SE_RESIZE_CURSOR,
            Cursor.S_RESIZE_CURSOR,
            Cursor.SW_RESIZE_CURSOR,
        };
        int x;
        ShowCursorPanel() {
            addMouseMotionListener(this);
            setSize(600,100);
        }
        public void paint(Graphics g) {
            Dimension dim = getSize();
            float delta = (float)dim.width / (float)cursorTypeArray.length;
            int index = (int)(x / delta);
            if(index < cursorTypeArray.length) {
                int newCursorType = cursorTypeArray[index];
                if(newCursorType != cursorType) {
                    cursorType = newCursorType;
                    cursor = Cursor.getPredefinedCursor(cursorType);
                    setCursor(cursor);
                }
            }
            g.setColor(Color.lightGray);
            for(float xPos=delta; xPos<dim.width; xPos += delta) {
                g.drawLine((int)xPos,0,(int)xPos,dim.height);
            }
            g.setColor(Color.black);
            g.drawString(cursor.toString(),20,30);
        }
        public void mouseMoved(MouseEvent event) {
            x = event.getX();
            repaint();
        }
        public void mouseDragged(MouseEvent event) {
            x = event.getX();
            repaint();
        }
    }
}
```

Figure 12.5 The standard hand cursor.

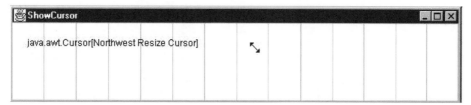

Figure 12.6 The standard northwest resizing cursor.

The Commentary

There are several cursors predefined as Cursor objects. It is possible to define your own cursor, but the ones already built in to Java are standard and are designed to be used on different platforms.

This example contains an array of the cursor type indicators as the cursorTypeArray. The window is divided into the same number of sections as there are cursors on the array. Each time the mouse pointer is discovered in a region associated with a different cursor, a new Cursor object (the one that matches the new position) is acquired with a call to getPredefinedCursor() and the method setCursor() is called to change the appearance of the active cursor.

Whenever you change the appearance of the cursor in a window, the change is only in effect while the mouse pointer is over that window. Figure 12.5 shows the hand cursor and Figure 12.6 the northwest resize cursor.

Locating and Dragging

This example shows how to move graphic objects from one location to another on the display. Four objects are drawn on the display. Any one of these can be selected with the mouse and dragged (by holding down the first mouse button) to a new location.

The Code

```java
import java.awt.*;
import java.awt.event.*;
import java.awt.geom.*;
public class Mover extends Frame {
    public static void main(String[] arg) {
        new Mover();
    }
    Mover() {
        super("Mover");
        addWindowListener(new WindowAdapter() {
            public void windowClosing(WindowEvent e)
                { System.exit(0); } } );
        MoverPanel mp = new MoverPanel();
        add(mp);
        pack();
        show();
    }
}
class MoverPanel extends Canvas
        implements MouseListener, MouseMotionListener {
    boolean moving = false;
    int moveIndex;
    int startx;
    int starty;
    int endx;
    int endy;
    Area[] area;
    AffineTransform at;
    BasicStroke dashes;
    MoverPanel() {
        addMouseListener(this);
        addMouseMotionListener(this);
        area = new Area[4];
        area[0] = new Area(new Ellipse2D.Float(10,10,40,40));
        area[1] = new Area(new Ellipse2D.Float(80,80,20,50));
        area[2] = new Area(new Ellipse2D.Float(130,130,60,60));
        area[3] = new Area(new Ellipse2D.Float(200,200,50,20));
        setSize(300,250);
        at = new AffineTransform();
        float[] pattern = { 5f,5f };
        dashes = new BasicStroke(1f,BasicStroke.CAP_BUTT,
                BasicStroke.JOIN_BEVEL,1f,pattern,0f);
    }
```

```
        public void paint(Graphics g) {
            Graphics2D g2 = (Graphics2D)g;
            for(int i=0; i<area.length; i++)
                g2.draw(area[i]);
            if(moving) {
                g2.setTransform(at);
                g2.setStroke(dashes);
                g2.draw(area[moveIndex]);
            }
        }
        public void mouseMoved(MouseEvent event) {
            moving = false;
        }
        public void mouseDragged(MouseEvent event) {
            if(!moving)
                return;
            endx = event.getX();
            endy = event.getY();
            at.setToTranslation(endx - startx,endy - starty);
            repaint();
        }
        public void mousePressed(MouseEvent event) {
            moving = false;
            startx = event.getX();
            starty = event.getY();
            for(int i=0; i<area.length; i++) {
                if(area[i].contains(startx,starty)) {
                    moving = true;
                    moveIndex = i;
                    at.setToTranslation(0,0);
                    break;
                }
            }
        }
        public void mouseReleased(MouseEvent event) {
            if(moving) {
                area[moveIndex].transform(at);
                moving = false;
                repaint();
            }
        }
        public void mouseEntered(MouseEvent event) { }
        public void mouseExited(MouseEvent event) { }
        public void mouseClicked(MouseEvent event) { }
    }
}
```

The Commentary

The MoverPanel class displays a window with four shapes on it. Each of these can be moved from one place to another with the mouse. Different-size ellipses were chosen to keep the example simple, but the actual shapes could be any Area object you care to define.

Both MouseListener and MouseMotionListener interfaces are implemented because we need to keep track of the mouse positions as well as the states of the buttons as they change.

The sequence of moving an object from one place to another is like this: A mouse button is pressed (this example doesn't care which button is used) while the mouse pointer is inside the Area object to be moved. This causes the method mousePressed() to be called. The method mouse-Pressed() has the job of determining which, if any, of the objects is to be moved, and the exact starting location of the mouse. The moving flag is set to true, signifying that one of the objects is being moved by the mouse. The AffineTransform is reset to a zero translation to prevent some value left over from the previous move from causing erroneous results.

As long the mouse is moved with a button held down, the method mouseMoved() will be called with an update of the mouse position. Each time this method is called, the AffineTransform is updated to translate the object to its new location.

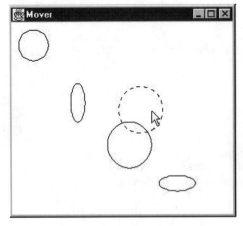

Figure 12.7 Mover lets you drag shapes around.

During the move, the paint() method uses the AffineTransform's translation position to draw a second image of the object. This second image is the one that follows the mouse. To make it distinct from the stationary version of the object, it is drawn with a dashed line. Figure 12.7 shows a circle being repositioned.

The final step in the move is when the mouse button is released. At this point, the method mouseReleased() is called. The AffineTransform object that has been used to follow the mouse is now used to modify the position of the area by calling its transform() method. The moving flag is turned off because the move has been completed.

CHAPTER 13

A Set of Basic Tools for Three-Dimensional Operations

There are ways to draw three-dimensional objects using the Java2D package. The fact is that a three-dimensional display is really the projection—sort of like the shadow—of a three-dimensional object onto a two-dimensional surface.

All the arithmetic for diagramming and positioning the object is done in three dimensions. As a final step, the coordinates are projected onto a flat plane for drawing. This is really simpler than it sounds. If the third dimension, z-axis, is considered to be perpendicular to the screen, the projection of the points automatically occurs by simply ignoring the z-axis values and drawing the x- and y-axis values.

The trick is finding out where the points x and y are when they are projected to the screen, and determining which ones should be joined by lines.

This chapter introduces some building-block classes that will be used in the following chapters to implement the hidden line suppression, perspective, and rotation.

A Point in Space

Each point in space requires three points, and the Vertex class is designed to hold a set of the three points.

The Code

```
import java.awt.geom.*
public class Vertex extends Point2D.Double {
    protected int ID;
    public double z;
    Vertex(int ID,double x,double y,double z) {
        super(x,y)
        this.z = z;
        this.ID = ID;
    }
    Vertex(double x,double y,double z) {
        this(0,x,y,z);
    }
    public final int getID() {
        return(ID);
    }
}
```

The Commentary

Vertex is a simple enough class. It just acts as a holder for the three coordinates of a point. This is done by simply adding the third dimension, z, to the normal two dimensions of x and y. There are times when we will be wanting to tag a Vertex with an ID number so we can have some way of referring to it. It is also possible to create a Vertex without an ID number—just let it default to zero.

The space being referred to here is the one in a Java window. The origin is in the upper-left-hand corner with x increasing to the right, y increasing downward, and z, the third dimension, increasing as it moves outward from the screen toward the viewer. This is shown in Figure 13.1.

The Edge of a Shape

In the two-dimensional world, a shape can be drawn by drawing a line from one point to the next, and to the next and then back to the beginning until the entire shape is outlined. The connection between two points is

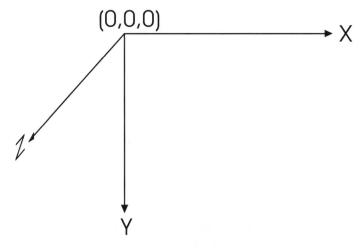

Figure 13.1   The three dimensions of our graphic system.

called an *edge*. In three dimensions, the same point can have several lines drawn from it to other points—that is, one point can be a vertex of several edges. For example, imagine the outline of a facet on a diamond. Also, the peak of a four-sided pyramid is the vertex of four edges that extend from its peak to the base—one for each corner of the base—and each corner of the base is the vertex of three edges.

The software we are going to be developing keeps three-dimensional object as a list of edges. To draw the object, just draw the edges.

The Code

```
public class Edge {
    public int vertexID1;
    public int vertexID2;
    Edge(int ID1,int ID2) {
        vertexID1 = Math.min(ID1,ID2);
        vertexID2 = Math.max(ID1,ID2);
    }
    public int compareTo(Edge that) {
        if(vertexID1 < that.vertexID1)
            return(-1);
        if(vertexID1 > that.vertexID1)
            return(1);
        if(vertexID2 < that.vertexID2)
            return(-1);
        if(vertexID2 > that.vertexID2)
            return(1);
        return(0);
    }
}
```

The Commentary

An edge is defined by two Vertex ID numbers. The constructor puts the two ID values in order simply so the Edge objects can easily be sorted and duplicates can easily be detected. The compareTo() method can be used to compare two Edge objects for equality and to determine a sorting order.

A Plane in Space

In three-dimensional space, it is possible to define a surface by three vertices. A single vertex is a point in space, two vertices define a line, and three define a surface. Since the three points also define a triangle, any object drawn in space has its surface defined as a collection of triangles.

Curved surfaces can be drawn this way. It's just that the triangles get pretty small. But that is not a real problem with computer graphics because we can make the curves smooth by making the vertices as close together as the pixels.

The Code

```
public class Triangle {
    protected Vertex[] v = new Vertex[3];
    Triangle(Vertex v0,Vertex v1,Vertex v2) {
        v[0] = v0;
        v[1] = v1;
        v[2] = v2;
    }
    public final Vertex getVertex(int vertexNumber) {
        return(v[vertexNumber]);
    }
    public final int getVertexID(int vertexNumber) {
        return(v[vertexNumber].getID());
    }
    public final double minimumX() {
        return(Math.min(v[0].x,Math.min(v[1].x,v[2].x)));
    }
    public final double minimumY() {
        return(Math.min(v[0].y,Math.min(v[1].y,v[2].y)));
    }
    public final double maximumX() {
        return(Math.max(v[0].x,Math.max(v[1].x,v[2].x)));
    }
    public final double maximumY() {
```

```
                    return(Math.max(v[0].y,Math.max(v[1].y,v[2].y)));
            }
    }
```

The Commentary

Three Vertex objects are used to describe a triangle. The constructor requires three Vertex references that are to be stored locally in the Triangle.

It is unnecessary for a Vertex to be duplicated because first, the same Vertex can be used to define the end points of any number of triangles and edges, and second, the code that performs operations (such as rotation) needs to adjust a Vertex only once and have it apply to all the objects that are defined by using it.

There is a set of minimum and maximum methods that can be used to quickly determine whether a point could not possibly be inside the triangle. If a point falls inside these minimums and maximums, further testing is required to determine its position.

A Face of an Object in Space

The internal representation of a three-dimensional object is a collection of flat surfaces. Any individual surface can be a triangle, square, rectangle, or some multisided polygon constructed from any number of line edges. It can even have holes in it. A face (or facet) is always a flat surface. It can be tilted at any angle in any direction, but the points defining its perimeter must define a level surface.

The Code

```
import java.util.*;
import java.io.*;
public class Face {
    private Vertex[] vertex = null;
    public void addVertex(Vertex v) {
        if(vertex == null) {
            vertex = new Vertex[1];
        } else {
            Vertex[] vNew = new Vertex[vertex.length+1];
            for(int i=0; i<vertex.length; i++)
                vNew[i] = vertex[i];
```

```
                    vertex = vNew;
                }
                vertex[vertex.length-1] = v;
        }
        public final Vertex getVertex(int index) {
            while(index >= vertex.length)
                index -= vertex.length;
            return(vertex[index]);
        }
        public final int getVertexCount() {
            return(vertex.length);
        }
        public Vector appendEdgeVector(Vector vec) {
            for(int i=0; i<vertex.length; i++) {
                if(i == vertex.length-1)
                    vec.add(new Edge(vertex[0].getID(),vertex[i].getID()));
                else
                    vec.add(new
    Edge(vertex[i].getID(),vertex[i+1].getID()));
            }
            return(vec);
        }
    }
```

The Commentary

A completely empty Face object can be created, but it really has no valid use until it contains at least three Vertex ID numbers to define a face of some shape. The Vertex ID numbers are added by the method addVertexID(), and they must be added in the correct order to circumscribe the outline of the face. There is no direction—the Vertex ID numbers can be added clockwise or counterclockwise. The edges of the face are defined as a line drawn from the first Vertex to the second one, then from the second to the third, and so on until the last one is reached. The first Vertex should not be added at the end—a final edge is assumed joining the last Vertex back to the first one to complete the figure.

The access method getVertexCount() returns the number of Vertex ID numbers that make up the face, and the method getVertexID() returns the ID number of the specified Vertex, or point, on the face.

A face can have one or more holes in it. A hole is defined as another Face—that is, a Face object is created that defines the exact outline of the hole and is then added to the Face with a call to addHole(). A call to the method getHole() returns the complete list of holes in this Face.

The write() method formats the ID numbers into an ASCII string and outputs them.

Describing a Shape in a File

A three-dimensional object is defined as a group of faces. Some of these faces have vertices in common. The contents of a file defining a three-dimensional object—like the one shown in Figure 13.2—look like this:

```
vertex 1 50.0 150.0 150.0
vertex 2 150.0 150.0 150.0
vertex 3 150.0 150.0 50.0
vertex 4 50.0 150.0 50.0
vertex 5 100.0 50.0 100.0
face   1 2 3 4
face   1 2 5
face   2 3 5
face   3 4 5
face   1 4 5
```

There is a total of five vertices that make up the pyramid. Each vertex is defined by the "vertex" keyword, followed by an ID number and the (x,y,z) values of its spatial coordinates. The rest of the file is defined in terms of the vertices; only the "vertex" lines contain spatial coordinates. As you can see, this pyramid begins 50 pixels from the origin and is 100 pixels wide, 100 deep, and 100 high. The ID numbers in the file match those shown in Figure 13.2.

You can also include edge definitions in the file to specify which portions are to be drawn. For example, say you appended this to the end of the pyramid file:

```
edge 1 2
edge 2 5
edge 5 1
```

This would cause the edges of that one face, and only that one face, to be drawn. If you do not supply any edge entries, every edge on every face is taken to be a displayable edge. That is, the array of Edge objects is automatically generated; it is done by the makeEdgeArray() method described in the next section.

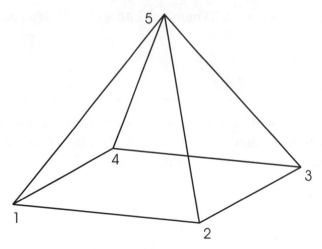

Figure 13.2 The wire frame pyramid.

The pyramid has five faces. The base is defined with its four corners 1, 2, 3, and 4. The four other faces, the sides of the pyramid, are each defined with the three vertices at their corners.

Each vertex is assigned an ID number and a value for x, y, and z. The faces are defined in terms of the vertex ID numbers. For a pyramid with a square base, there is a total of five faces. Being triangles, four of the faces have three vertices and the other one, being a square, has four.

Notice that the last two faces in the list share the Edge defined by vertex 4 and vertex 5. This is okay (quite normal, actually) because the drawing software will remove duplicate Edges and draw them only once. There are no triangles and no edges defined in the file. These will be generated internally as needed.

Loading a Three-Dimensional Shape

A computer graphic three-dimensional shape is composed of a collection of flat surfaces flying around the display in tight formation. This class uses the classes previously defined in this chapter and organizes them for display.

The class does two things. First, it holds the definition of a three-dimensional shape in RAM and makes its various parts available to the program that is to display it. Second, it has the ability to read and write the descriptions of the shape to and from the disk file. This second capability is important because a three-dimensional object is made up of lots of parts.

The Code

```java
import java.util.*;
import java.awt.*;
import java.io.*;
public class LoadableWireFrame {
    protected int largestVertexID = 0;
    protected Edge[] edgeArray = null;
    protected int nextEdge = 0;
    protected Face[] faceArray = null;
    protected int nextFace = 0;
    protected Vertex defaultVertex = new Vertex(0,0.0,0.0,0.0);
    protected Vertex[] vertex;
    {
        vertex = new Vertex[30];
        for(int i=0; i<30; i++)
            vertex[i] = defaultVertex;
    }
    LoadableWireFrame(String fileName) {
        Lex lex = new Lex(fileName);
        while(lex.getTokenType() != Lex.EOF) {
            if(lex.getToken().equals("vertex")) {
                lex.gtkn();
                int vertexID = lex.getInteger();
                lex.gtkn();
                double xVertex = lex.getDouble();
                lex.gtkn();
                double yVertex = lex.getDouble();
                lex.gtkn();
                double zVertex = lex.getDouble();
                addVertex(vertexID,xVertex,yVertex,zVertex);
                lex.gtkn();
            } else if(lex.getToken().equals("edge")) {
                lex.gtkn();
                int vertexID1 = lex.getInteger();
                lex.gtkn();
                int vertexID2 = lex.getInteger();
                addEdge(new Edge(vertexID1,vertexID2));
                lex.gtkn();
            } else if(lex.getToken().equals("face")) {
                Face face = new Face();
                while(lex.gtkn() == Lex.NUMBER)
                    face.addVertex(vertex[lex.getInteger()]);
                addFace(face);
            } else {
                lex.expected("a keyword");
            }
        }
        if((edgeArray == null) && (faceArray != null))
            makeEdgeArray();
    }
```

```java
public void addVertex(int ID,double x,double y,double z) {
    if(ID >= vertex.length) {
        int newSize = ID + 10;
        Vertex newVertex[] = new Vertex[newSize];
        for(int i=0; i<vertex.length; i++)
            newVertex[i] = vertex[i];
        for(int i=vertex.length; i<newSize; i++)
            newVertex[i] = defaultVertex;
        vertex = newVertex;
    }
    vertex[ID] = new Vertex(ID,x,y,z);
    if(ID > largestVertexID)
        largestVertexID = ID;
}
public void addEdge(Edge edge) {
    if(edgeArray == null) {
        edgeArray = new Edge[10];
        nextEdge = 0;
    } else if(nextEdge >= edgeArray.length) {
        Edge[] newEdge = new Edge[nextEdge + 10];
        for(int i=0; i<nextEdge; i++)
            newEdge[i] = edgeArray[i];
        edgeArray = newEdge;
    }
    for(int i=0; i<nextEdge; i++) {
        int cond;
        if((cond = edge.compareTo(edgeArray[i])) == 0)
            return; // Duplicate
        if(cond < 0) {
            Edge hold = edgeArray[i];
            edgeArray[i] = edge;
            edge = hold;
        }
    }
    edgeArray[nextEdge++] = edge;
}
public void addFace(Face face) {
    if(faceArray == null) {
        faceArray = new Face[10];
        nextFace = 0;
    } else if(nextFace >= faceArray.length) {
        Face[] newFace = new Face[nextFace + 10];
        for(int i=0; i<nextFace; i++)
            newFace[i] = faceArray[i];
        faceArray = newFace;
    }
    faceArray[nextFace++] = face;
}
public Vertex getVertexByID(int ID) {
    if(ID > largestVertexID)
        return(defaultVertex);
```

```
            return(vertex[ID]);
    }
    public Edge getEdge(int number) {
        if(number >= nextEdge)
            return(null);
        return(edgeArray[number]);
    }
    public int getEdgeCount() {
        return(nextEdge);
    }
    public Face getFace(int number) {
        if(number >= nextFace)
            return(null);
        return(faceArray[number]);
    }
    public int getFaceCount() {
        return(nextFace);
    }
    public double maxDimension() {
        double dim = vertex[0].x;
        for(int i=0; i<vertex.length; i++) {
            Vertex v = vertex[i];
            dim = Math.max(dim,Math.max(v.x,Math.max(v.y,v.z)));
        }
        return(dim);
    }
    public double minDimension() {
        double dim = vertex[0].x;
        for(int i=0; i<vertex.length; i++) {
            Vertex v = vertex[i];
            dim = Math.min(dim,Math.min(v.x,Math.min(v.y,v.z)));
        }
        return(dim);
    }
    private void makeEdgeArray() {
        int i;
        Vector vec = new Vector();
        for(i=0; i<nextFace; i++)
            vec = faceArray[i].appendEdgeVector(vec);
        i = 1;
        while(i < vec.size()) {
            Edge edge1 = (Edge)vec.elementAt(i-1);
            Edge edge2 = (Edge)vec.elementAt(i);
            int comparison = edge1.compareTo(edge2);
            if(comparison < 0) {
                vec.setElementAt(edge2,i-1);
                vec.setElementAt(edge1,i);
                if(i > 1)
                    i--;
            } else if(comparison == 0) {
                vec.removeElementAt(i);
```

```
              } else {
                  i++;
              }
          }
          for(i=0; i < vec.size(); i++)
              addEdge((Edge)vec.elementAt(i));
      }
  }
```

The Commentary

The LoadableWireFrame class is defined using the Vertex, Edge, Face, and Triangle classes, described earlier in this chapter, and the Lex class from Chapter 10. It has no default constructor—it can only be constructed from a file that contains a shape description.

The constructor creates a Lex object based on the file that contains the shape description. The file format (described in detail later) contains keywords defining all the parts of the shape and where each part is located. The constructor reads from the file and determines, by keyword, which of the shape descriptions are being loaded, and adds an object of that type to the object arrays defined in the class.

The add methods addVertex(), addEdge(), addTriangle(), and addFace() are used to add the objects to the arrays. Note that these are public methods, which makes them accessible externally; this way, a program can add as many of these objects as it wishes to the defined shape. As we shall see later, this capability comes in very handy for automatically generating some shape metrics.

There is one thing to note about the vertex array. The Vertex objects are stored in the array at the index point of their ID numbers—that is, a vertex with an ID number of 4 will be stored at vertex[4]. This is a simple matter of efficiency to prevent the necessity of requiring the extra step of a lookup table to find a Vertex by its ID number. This has the consequence that the ID numbers need to be selected so they are small to keep the size of the array down. The array can have holes in it—the missing members of the array refer to a dummy Vertex called defaultVertex.

There are some get methods that can be used to access the internal shape definition, and extract some information about it. There are methods that can be used to find the total number of Vertex, Edge, Triangle, and Face objects, as well as retrieve any one of them by its index number. The methods maxDimension() and minDimension() can be used to determine the extent of the object—a sort of crude way of determining where an object is in 3D space, and calculating its center.

The write() method writes the contents of the LoadableWireFrame to a file in the form that is readable. That is, another LoadableWireFrame object can be created from the contents of the file.

An Oblique Cubelike Thing

This is a very simple program that loads a simple shape and displays it. The shape is an oblique view of a cube—that is, the vertices of the cube have been skewed in the file (meaning that it isn't really a cube) because the program just loads and displays what is there and, with it skewed this way, you will be able to see all the edges and vertices.

By the way, we are using the oblique cube because it is more demonstrative of the 3D appearance of things. The pyramid described in the previous section simply shows up as a triangle unless it can be rotated. The ability to perform three-dimensional rotation is in the next chapter.

The file doesn't contain any face or triangle information, just a bunch of edges. The file, oblique.data, looks like this:

```
vertex 0 100 50 50
vertex 1 200 50 50
vertex 2 50 100 100
vertex 3 150 100 100
vertex 4 100 150 50
vertex 5 200 150 50
vertex 6 50 200 100
vertex 7 150 200 100
edge 0 1
edge 0 2
edge 1 3
edge 2 3
edge 0 4
edge 1 5
edge 2 6
edge 3 7
edge 6 7
edge 4 6
edge 4 5
edge 5 7
```

A cube has 6 faces, 8 vertices, and 12 edges. The eight vertices of the cube are assigned the ID numbers 0 through 7. The twelve vertices are defined in terms of the vertices (each vertex occurs three times because there are three edges arriving at each vertex).

The Code

```
import java.awt.*;
import java.awt.event.*;
class ObliqueCube extends Frame {
    public static void main(String arg[]) {
        new ObliqueCube();
    }
    ObliqueCube() {
        super("ObliqueCube");
        addWindowListener(new WindowAdapter() {
            public void windowClosing(WindowEvent e)
                { System.exit(0); } } );
        add(new CubeCanvas());
        pack();
        show();
    }
class CubeCanvas extends Canvas {
    LoadableWireFrame frame;
    CubeCanvas() {
        setSize(250,250);
        frame = new LoadableWireFrame("oblique.data");
    }
    public void paint(Graphics g) {
        for(int i=0; i<frame.getEdgeCount(); i++) {
            Edge e = frame.getEdge(i);
            Vertex v1 = frame.getVertexByID(e.vertexID1);
            Vertex v2 = frame.getVertexByID(e.vertexID2);
            g.drawLine((int)v1.getX(),(int)v1.getY(),
                    (int)v2.getX(),(int)v2.getY());
        }
    }
}
}
```

The Commentary

As you can see, it doesn't take much code to display the object. The LoadableWireFrame object is constructed from the file oblique.data. The paint() method loops through the list of edges and extracts the beginning and ending vertex from each one. The actual line is drawn between the two (x,y) endpoints of the line—the z-axis is ignored. The z-axis is never actually drawn, but it is used in calculations to determine hidden lines, create perspective, and perform rotations, as you will see in the upcoming chapters.

The resulting window is shown in Figure 13.3. This example is simply to demonstrate the mechanism used to load and draw a three-dimensional object.

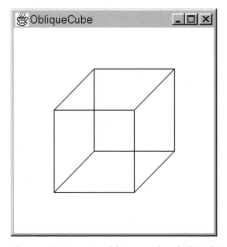

Figure 13.3   An oblique cube defined in a file.

CHAPTER 14

Rotating Wire Frame Shapes in Three Dimensions

T he WireFrame class in the previous chapter has some extensions and modifications made in this chapter to enable shapes to be rotated in three-dimensional space.

An Adjustable Wire Frame

This class extends the LoadableWireFrame class in the previous chapter and adds some methods that can be used to change the position and size of the object to be displayed.

The Code

```
class AdjustableWireFrame extends LoadableWireFrame {
    private double centerX;
    private double angleX;
    private double sineX;
    private double cosineX;
    private double centerY;
    private double angleY;
    private double sineY;
    private double cosineY;
    private double centerZ;
    private double angleZ;
```

```java
    private double sineZ;
    private double cosineZ;
    private int edgeIndex;
    AdjustableWireFrame(String fileName) {
        super(fileName);
        setAngleX(0.0);
        setAngleY(0.0);
        setAngleZ(0.0);
        setRotationCenter(0.0,0.0,0.0);
    }
    public void setRotationCenter(double x,double y,double z) {
        centerX = x;
        centerY = y;
        centerZ = z;
    }
    public void scale(double scaleFactor) {
        double pct = 1.0 - scaleFactor;
        for(int i=0; i<vertex.length; i++) {
            Vertex v = vertex[i];
            v.x = v.x - pct * (v.x - centerX);
            v.y = v.y - pct * (v.y - centerX);
            v.z = v.z - pct * (v.z - centerX);
        }
    }
    public void setAngleX(double angle) {
        angleX = angle;
        cosineX = Math.cos(angle);
        sineX = Math.sin(angle);
    }
    public void setAngleY(double angle) {
        angleY = angle;
        cosineY = Math.cos(angle);
        sineY = Math.sin(angle);
    }
    public void setAngleZ(double angle) {
        angleZ = angle;
        cosineZ = Math.cos(angle);
        sineZ = Math.sin(angle);
    }
    public void rotate() {
        rotateAroundX();
        rotateAroundY();
        rotateAroundZ();
    }
    public void rotateAroundX(double angle) {
        setAngleX(angle);
        rotateAroundX();
    }
    public void rotateAroundY(double angle) {
        setAngleY(angle);
        rotateAroundY();
```

```
    }
    public void rotateAroundZ(double angle) {
        setAngleZ(angle);
        rotateAroundZ();
    }
    private void rotateAroundX() {
        for(int i=0; i<vertex.length; i++) {
            Vertex v = vertex[i];
            double dz = v.z - centerZ;
            double dy = v.y - centerY;
            v.y = centerY + dz*sineX + dy*cosineX;
            v.z = centerZ + dz*cosineX - dy*sineX;
        }
    }
    private void rotateAroundY() {
        for(int i=0; i<vertex.length; i++) {
            Vertex v = vertex[i];
            double dz = v.z - centerZ;
            double dx = v.x - centerX;
            v.x = centerX + dz*sineY + dx*cosineY;
            v.z = centerZ + dz*cosineY - dx*sineY;
        }
    }
    private void rotateAroundZ() {
        for(int i=0; i<vertex.length; i++) {
            Vertex v = vertex[i];
            double dx = v.x - centerX;
            double dy = v.y - centerY;
            v.x = centerX + dx*cosineZ - dy*sineZ;
            v.y = centerY + dx*sineZ + dy*cosineZ;
        }
    }
}
```

The Commentary

There are two possible location adjustments—one is rotation and the other is size scaling. In both cases, these adjustments occur in relation to a center of rotation. This center—a point in three-dimensional space—can be set and reset any number of times by making calls to setRotationCenter(). The default center is the origin.

The scale() method will adjust the position of every point either closer to or farther from the center of rotation. The argument, the scale factor, is the size multiplier. For example, a scale factor of 0.5 will reduce the shape to half its size. A factor of 0.333 will reduce it to one-third of its original size. A factor of 2 will double it, and a factor of 4 will multiply the size by four. A factor of 1 will not change the current size.

The rotate() method will rotate the points of the shape around each of the three axes in space. The angles of rotation are previously set with calls to setAngleX(), setAngleY(), and setAngleZ(). All angle values are in radians. Both the sine and cosine values of the angles are stored so they won't need to be recalculated for each rotation. Each time the rotate() method is called, a rotation is performed around each of the three axes independently by a call to each of the methods rotateAroundX(), rotateAroundY() and rotateAroundZ().

Chapter 3 discusses the equations required for rotating points on a two-dimensional coordinate system which is, in effect, rotating around the z-axis. The equations look like this:

$$x' = x\cos\phi - y\sin\phi$$
$$y' = x\sin\phi + y\cos\phi$$

These equations are the ones implemented in the method rotateAroundZ(). Similar equations are used for rotating around the x-axis:

$$z' = z\cos\alpha - y\sin\alpha$$
$$y' = z\sin\alpha + y\cos\alpha$$

and around the x-axis:

$$z' = z\cos\beta - y\sin\beta$$
$$y' = z\sin\beta + y\cos\beta$$

These last four equations are implemented in rotateAroundY() and rotateAroundX(). In these methods, the values of x, y, and z are offset by the desired center of rotation so the rotation is not around the actual axis; instead it is around the defined center point.

An Automatic Rotater

This class opens a window, loads a three-dimensional shape from a data file, and then rotates the shape around the three axes. At the same time, it continuously scales the size of the object up and down.

The Code

```
import java.awt.*;
import java.awt.event.*;
```

```
class AutoRotate extends Frame {
    public static void main(String arg[]) {
        if(arg.length != 1) {
            System.out.println("Usage: AutoRotate <filename>");
            System.exit(1);
        }
        new AutoRotate(arg[0]);
    }
    AutoRotate(String fileName) {
        super("AutoRotate");
        addWindowListener(new WindowAdapter() {
            public void windowClosing(WindowEvent e)
                { System.exit(0); } } );
        AdjustableWireFrame awf = new AdjustableWireFrame(fileName);
        AutoRotatePanel arPanel = new AutoRotatePanel(awf);
        add(arPanel);
        pack();
        show();
    }
}
class AutoRotatePanel extends Canvas implements Runnable {
    private AdjustableWireFrame awf;
    private int pause = 30;
    private Rectangle rectangle;
    private Thread looper;
    private Image image;

    private final int REANGLE = 30;
    private final int RESCALE = 21;
    private int reangleCount = REANGLE;
    private int rescaleCount = RESCALE;
    private double scaleFactor = 0.93;

    AutoRotatePanel(AdjustableWireFrame awf) {
        this.awf = awf;
        setSize((int)awf.maxDimension()+50,
            (int)awf.maxDimension()+50);
        rectangle = new Rectangle();
        looper = new Thread(this);
        looper.start();
    }
    public void run() {
        try {
            while(true) {
                repaint();
                Thread.sleep(pause);
            }
        } finally {
            return;
        }
    }
}
```

```java
        public void update(Graphics g) {
            if(looper.isAlive()) {
                if(!rectangle.equals(getBounds()) || (image == null)) {
                    rectangle = getBounds();
                    image = createImage(rectangle.width,rectangle.height);
                    firstFrame();
                }
                if(nextFrame()) {
                    paint(image.getGraphics());
                    g.drawImage(image,0,0,null);
                }
            }
        }

        public void paint(Graphics g) {
            g.setColor(Color.white);
            g.fillRect(0,0,getSize().width,getSize().height);
            g.setColor(Color.black);
            for(int i=0; i<awf.getEdgeCount(); i++) {
                Edge e = awf.getEdge(i);
                Vertex v1 = awf.getVertexByID(e.vertexID1);
                Vertex v2 = awf.getVertexByID(e.vertexID2);
                g.drawLine((int)v1.getX(),(int)v1.getY(),
                        (int)v2.getX(),(int)v2.getY());
            }
        }
        private void firstFrame() {
            awf.setRotationCenter(rectangle.width / 2,
                    rectangle.height / 2,
                    rectangle.width / 2);
            awf.setAngleX(0.02);
            awf.setAngleY(0.03);
            awf.setAngleZ(0.05);
        }
        private boolean nextFrame() {
            if(reangleCount-- < 0) {
                awf.setAngleX(0.08 * Math.random());
                awf.setAngleY(0.08 * Math.random());
                awf.setAngleZ(0.08 * Math.random());
                reangleCount = REANGLE;
            }
            if(rescaleCount-- < 0) {
                scaleFactor = 1.0 / scaleFactor;
                rescaleCount = RESCALE;
            }
            awf.scale(scaleFactor);
            awf.rotate();
            return(true);
        }
    }
}
```

The Commentary

The AutoRotate class creates an AdjustableWireFrame object from a file and then uses it to create an AutoRotatePanel object and displays it in a window. The name of the file containing the vertex and edge definitions is supplied on the command line. For example, to display the edges defined in the file named pyramid.data, enter:

```
java AutoRotate pyramid.data
```

Figure 14.1 shows typical output from pyramid.data at three different points of revolution and scaling. AutoRotatePanel will rotate any shape that can be loaded from a file by an AdjustableWireFrame object.

The method firstFrame()sets up the center of rotation as being the center of the display window. It also sets up some initial rotation angles for each of the three axes.

The nextFrame() method is called once the shape is to be repainted. If the reangleCount has reached zero, a new random set of angles are passed to the AdjustableWireFrame. To be able to view a good mix of rotations it is necessary change these angles from time to time because if they are left constant the shape will continue to revolve, in all three planes, through the same repeated loops. The rescaleCount reaching zero will convert the scale factor from increasing to decreasing (or decreasing to increasing, depending) by simply taking the reciprocal of the scale factor value. Recall that numbers less than one will decrease the size, and numbers larger than one will increase the size. Finally, the nextFrame() method calls the scale() and rotate() methods of the AdjustableWireFrame to adjust the positions of the points.

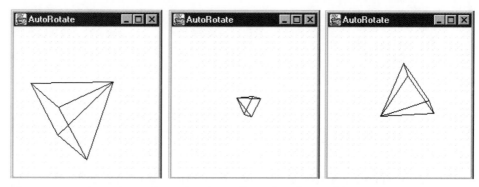

Figure 14.1 A moving and rotating three-dimensional pyramid.

The paint() method clears the window and performs a loop that draws all edges. The loop retrieves each edge object form the AdjustableWire-Frame and draws a line between its two vertices.

Figure 14.2 shows one of the positions from rotating the data shape defined in the file tbar.data. The contents of the file, defining the vertices and edges of the T-shaped object, look like this:

```
vertex 1 50 50 50
vertex 2 300 50 50
vertex 3 50 50 100
vertex 4 300 50 100
vertex 5 300 100 75
vertex 6 50 100 75
vertex 7 150 50 100
vertex 8 200 50 100
vertex 9 150 300 100
vertex 10 200 300 100
vertex 11 150 50 50
vertex 12 200 50 50
vertex 13 150 300 50
vertex 14 200 300 50
vertex 15 200 100 75
vertex 16 150 100 75
edge 1 2
edge 1 3
edge 1 6
edge 2 4
edge 2 5
edge 3 4
edge 3 6
edge 4 5
edge 5 6
edge 5 15
edge 7 9
edge 7 16
edge 8 10
edge 8 15
edge 9 10
edge 9 13
edge 10 14
edge 11 13
edge 11 16
edge 12 14
edge 12 15
edge 13 14
```

As you can see, this is simply a collection of points and edges. Figure 14.3 shows the dimensions of the bar and the ID number of each of the vertices.

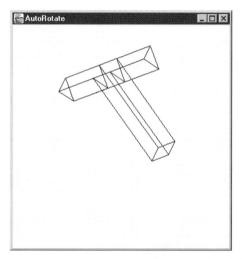

Figure 14.2   A moving and rotating three-dimensional shape.

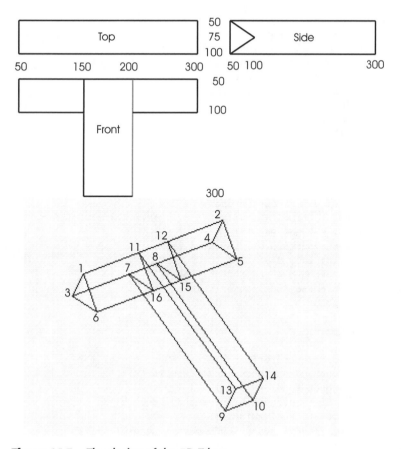

Figure 14.3   The design of the 3D T-bar.

Manual Rotater

This program is very similar to the previous one except the rotation is controlled manually instead of proceeding automatically.

The Code

```
import java.awt.*;
import java.awt.event.*;
class ManualRotate extends Frame
        implements ActionListener {
    RotatePanel rotatePanel;
    public static void main(String arg[]) {
        if(arg.length != 1) {
            System.out.println("Usage: ManualRotate <filename>");
            System.exit(1);
        }
        new ManualRotate(arg[0]);
    }
    ManualRotate(String fileName) {
        super("ManualRotate");
        addWindowListener(new WindowAdapter() {
            public void windowClosing(WindowEvent e)
                { System.exit(0); } } );
        setLayout(new BorderLayout());
        AdjustableWireFrame awf = new AdjustableWireFrame(fileName);
        rotatePanel = new RotatePanel(awf);
        add("Center",rotatePanel);
        add("East",makeButtonPanel());
        pack();
        show();
    }
    private Panel makeButtonPanel() {
        String[] label = {"X+","X-","Y+","Y-","Z+","Z-","S+","S-"};
        Panel p = new Panel();
        p.setLayout(new GridLayout(4,2));
        for(int i=0; i<8; i++) {
            Button b = new Button(label[i]);
            b.addActionListener(this);
            p.add(b);
        }
        return(p);
    }
    public void actionPerformed(ActionEvent event) {
        if(event.getActionCommand().equals("X+"))
            rotatePanel.xPlus();
        else if(event.getActionCommand().equals("X-"))
            rotatePanel.xMinus();
        else if(event.getActionCommand().equals("Y+"))
            rotatePanel.yPlus();
        else if(event.getActionCommand().equals("Y-"))
            rotatePanel.yMinus();
```

```
                else if(event.getActionCommand().equals("Z+"))
                    rotatePanel.zPlus();
                else if(event.getActionCommand().equals("Z-"))
                    rotatePanel.zMinus();
                else if(event.getActionCommand().equals("S+"))
                    rotatePanel.sPlus();
                else if(event.getActionCommand().equals("S-"))
                    rotatePanel.sMinus();
        }
    class RotatePanel extends Canvas {
        private AdjustableWireFrame awf;
        private Rectangle rectangle;
        private Image image;

        private double scaleFactor = 0.93;
        private double rotationAngle = 0.02;

        RotatePanel(AdjustableWireFrame awf) {
            this.awf = awf;
            int dim = (int)awf.maxDimension()+50;
            setSize(dim,dim);
            awf.setRotationCenter(dim/2,dim/2,dim/2);
            awf.setAngleX(0.02);
            awf.setAngleY(0.02);
            awf.setAngleZ(0.02);
        }
        public void paint(Graphics g) {
            g.setColor(Color.white);
            g.fillRect(0,0,getSize().width,getSize().height);
            g.setColor(Color.black);
            for(int i=0; i<awf.getEdgeCount(); i++) {
                Edge e = awf.getEdge(i);
                Vertex v1 = awf.getVertexByID(e.vertexID1);
                Vertex v2 = awf.getVertexByID(e.vertexID2);
                g.drawLine((int)v1.getX(),(int)v1.getY(),
                        (int)v2.getX(),(int)v2.getY());
            }
        }
        public void xPlus() {
            awf.rotateAroundX(rotationAngle);
            repaint();
        }
        public void xMinus() {
            awf.rotateAroundX(-rotationAngle);
            repaint();
        }
        public void yPlus() {
            awf.rotateAroundY(rotationAngle);
            repaint();
        }
        public void yMinus() {
            awf.rotateAroundY(-rotationAngle);
            repaint();
        }
```

```
public void zPlus() {
    awf.rotateAroundZ(rotationAngle);
    repaint();
}
public void zMinus() {
    awf.rotateAroundZ(-rotationAngle);
    repaint();
}
public void sPlus() {
    awf.scale(1.0 / scaleFactor);
    repaint();
}
public void sMinus() {
    awf.scale(scaleFactor);
    repaint();
}
}
```

The Commentary

The program takes the name of a data file on the command line and displays its edges in the window. The window has eight buttons to its right as shown in Figure 14.4.

When the figure is first displayed, it is unrotated and shows up as a flat outline. Selecting the button labeled X+ will rotate the figure by 0.02 radians around the x-axis. Selecting X– will do the same thing, but in the opposite direction. This way, the buttons can be pressed moving the figure back and forth until the desired position is achieved. The same is true for rotation around the y-axis with Y+ and Y–, and around the z-axis with Z+ and Z–.

The figure can be sized, both larger and smaller, by selecting the S+ and S– buttons.

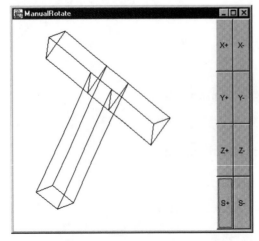

Figure 14.4 A manually rotated figure.

CHAPTER 15

Hidden Line Suppression

In the previous chapters we rendered figures in wire frames. Things looked as if they were composed of some sort of clear material like glass or plastic. In this chapter the lines drawing the back part of the figures will be invisible—that is, you will not be able to see through the object.

Imagine, if you will, all the surfaces of a three-dimensional object being divided into triangles—nothing but triangles. Then, we devise some ways of determining the positions of some points in relation to a triangle so we can find out whether or not a point is hidden by the triangle. Knowing where a point is can be very handy, but it is not quite enough. We are trying to find hidden line segments, and a line segment is made up of an infinite number of points—including the two important ones at each end of the segment.

There are a lot of ways that a triangle can hide (or not hide) a line. The three-dimensional vertexes of the triangle and of the line segment are projected onto the screen, the third dimension—the z-axis—can be used to determine whether the line or the triangle is in front. It gets a little complicated because the two can interact in several ways. A line segment can be completely hidden, partially hidden, or completely visible. If a segment is partially visible, the segment is split into two and the whole process is applied to both parts. Here is a list of the cases the software will need to consider for a segment:

- If both z-axis values of the endpoints of the segment are greater than the z-axis values of all three triangle points, the segment is completely visible.

- If the two endpoints of a line segment are both hidden by the triangle, the entire segment is hidden by the triangle.

- If the piercing point (the point at which the line segment intersects the plane of the triangle) is inside the triangle, the segment can be divided into two segments—one that is on front of the triangle and one that is completely or partially obscured behind it.

- If one endpoint is hidden by the triangle and the other is not, the segment can be divided into two segments. The division will come at the point where the line segment intersects an edge of the triangle.

- If both endpoints are visible, but the segment intersects an edge of the triangle, and, at the crossing point the segment is behind the triangle, the segment is broken into two at that point.

If this seems a bit complicated, that's because it is. There are two cases where a single line segment can be split into as many as three parts. This can happen when both endpoints are visible but the segment passes behind the triangle, and it can also happen when both endpoints are visible and the segment pierces the triangle. When we start splitting up the line segments we can wind up with points in five positions:

- Outside the triangle
- Inside the triangle and behind it
- Inside the triangle and in front of it
- Inside the triangle and on its surface
- On an edge of the triangle

Once segments have been split into their components, the visibility of a segment can be determined by checking the position of its two endpoints. It comes down to this: If either endpoint is visible, the entire segment is visible. Points on the surface or on an edge are neither visible nor hidden and are not considered—the visibility is determined by the other point.

However, even with all this, it is much simpler with triangles than with polygons having more than three sides, so that is why we break the surface into a collection of triangles to determine what is hidden. The algorithm is simple: Start off assuming that a segment is visible and go from one triangle to the next snipping off the invisible portions until all that is left is the visible portion, or the segment is gone completely (meaning it is totally obscured).

That's what this chapter is all about. The process is complicated enough so that there are just about as many ways to do it as there are graphics packages. This chapter shows one way of doing it, but there are others.

XYZPoint

This class is the container of a point in three-dimensional space. Two of these can be used to define a line segment, and three can be used to define a triangle.

The Code

```
public class XYZPoint extends Vertex {
    private boolean back;
    private boolean front;
    private boolean surface;
    private boolean inside;
    private boolean outside;
    private boolean edge;
    private boolean endpoint;

    XYZPoint(double x,double y,double z) {
        super(x,y,z);
    }
    XYZPoint(Vertex v) {
        super(v.x,v.y,v.z);
    }
    XYZPoint(double x,double y) {
        this(x,y,0.0);
    }
    public int compareTo(XYZPoint that) {
        if(this.x < that.x)
            return(-1);
        if(this.x > that.x)
            return(1);
        if(this.y < that.y)
            return(-1);
```

```java
        if(this.y > that.y)
            return(1);
        if(this.z < that.z)
            return(-1);
        if(this.z > that.z)
            return(1);
        return(0);
    }
    public boolean near(XYZPoint that) {
        if(Math.abs(this.x - that.x) < 1.0) {
            if(Math.abs(this.y - that.y) < 1.0) {
                if(Math.abs(this.z - that.z) < 1.0) {
                    return(true);
                }
            }
        }
        return(false);
    }
    public XYZPoint combine(XYZPoint that) {
        XYZPoint p = new XYZPoint(
                (this.x + that.x) / 2,
                (this.y + that.y) / 2,
                (this.z + that.z) / 2);
        if(this.back && that.back)
            p.back = true;
        else if(this.front && that.front)
            p.front = true;
        else
            p.surface = true;
        if(this.inside && that.inside)
            p.inside = true;
        else if(this.outside && that.outside)
            p.outside = true;
        else
            p.edge = true;
        p.endpoint = this.endpoint || that.endpoint;
        return(p);
    }
    public final boolean isBack() {
        return(back);
    }
    public final boolean isFront() {
        return(front);
    }
    public final boolean isSurface() {
        return(surface);
    }
    public final boolean isInside() {
        return(inside);
    }
    public final boolean isOutside() {
```

```
        return(outside);
    }
    public final boolean isEdge() {
        return(edge);
    }
    public final boolean isEndpoint() {
        return(endpoint);
    }
    public final void setBack(boolean setting) {
        back = setting;
    }
    public final void setFront(boolean setting) {
        front = setting;
    }
    public final void setSurface(boolean setting) {
        surface = setting;
    }
    public final void setInside(boolean setting) {
        inside = setting;
    }
    public final void setOutside(boolean setting) {
        outside = setting;
    }
    public final void setEdge(boolean setting) {
        edge = setting;
    }
    public final void setEndpoint(boolean setting) {
        endpoint = setting;
    }
}
```

The Commentary

This class contains the location of a point in three-dimensional space. It contains the *x-y-z* coordinates. A pair of these points can be used to describe a line segment in space.

This class can optionally contain information as to the visibility of the point in relationship to a triangle. It does this in two ways. The variable XYPosition specifies whether the point is inside, outside, or on one of the edges of the triangle. The variable Zposition specifies whether the point is in front of the triangle, behind it, or on its surface.

There is also a compareTo() method that can be used to place the points in order. This ordering is somewhat arbitrary but it comes in handy to have things in order when determining the relative positions of line segments and triangles in space.

A Line Segment

This class is a container for a line segment. A line segment is defined by two points in three-dimensional space. It has three constructors allowing it to be instantiated from a pair of XYZPoint objects, a pair of Vertex objects, or a set of six raw coordinate values.

The line segment is stored as six points in (x1,y1,z1) and (x2,y2,z2). There are four other values calculated during construction. The values for u, v, and w are a set of constants that are used with the parametric form of the equation of the line, and m is the slope of the line projected against the two-dimensional (x,y) plane.

The parametric form of the equation of a line in space has an advantage over other forms: there are far fewer calculations required to derive locate points on the line. In the following, (x0, y0, z0) is any point on the line and the three values u, v, and w are a set of constant values calculated for this particular line. The parametric equation of a line in space is this:

$$x = x_0 + u$$
$$y = y_0 + v$$
$$z = z_0 + w$$

which can be also be written in this form:

$$u = x - x_0$$
$$v = v - y_0$$
$$w = z - z_0$$

There is a simple relationship among all three equations allowing for them to be written this way:

$$\frac{x - x_0}{u} = \frac{y - y_0}{v} = \frac{z - z_0}{w}$$

The constants determine the angle of the line in all three dimensions. There is more than one set of constants that will define the same line—the values relate to one another rather than to any specific position in space. Applying the parametric equation to any two points on a line, a set of constants can be derived.

The Code

```java
public class Segment {
    private XYZPoint p1;
    private XYZPoint p2;
    private double u;
    private double v;
    private double w;
    private double m;
    private double length;
    public Segment(double x1,double y1,double z1,
            double x2,double y2,double z2) {
        p1 = new XYZPoint(x1,y1,z1);
        p2 = new XYZPoint(x2,y2,z2);
        calculate();
    }
    public Segment(Vertex v1,Vertex v2) {
        p1 = new XYZPoint(v1);
        p2 = new XYZPoint(v2);
        calculate();
    }
    private void calculate() {
        u = p2.x - p1.x;
        v = p2.y - p1.y;
        w = p2.z - p1.z;
        length = Math.sqrt(u*u + v*v + w*w);
        if(u == 0.0)
            m = Double.MAX_VALUE;
        else
            m = v / u;
    }
    public Segment(XYZPoint p1,XYZPoint p2) {
        this(p1.x,p1.y,p1.z,p2.x,p2.y,p2.z);
    }
    public final double getSlope() {
        return(m);
    }
    public final double getZfromXY(double x,double y) {
        if(u != 0)
            return(((w * (x - p1.x)) / u) + p1.z);
        else if(v != 0)
            return(((w * (y - p1.y)) / v) + p1.z);
        return(0);
    }
    public final double getYfromX(double x) {
        if(u != 0)
            return(((v * (x - p1.x)) / u) + p1.y);
        return(0);
    }
    public final double getXfromY(double y) {
```

```
        if(v != 0)
            return(((u * (y - p1.y)) / v) + p1.x);
        return(0);
    }
    public final double getZfromX(double x) {
        if(u != 0)
            return(((w * (x - p1.x)) / u) + p1.z);
        return(0);
    }
    public final double getLength() {
        return(length);
    }
    public final double x1() {
        return(p1.x);
    }
    public final double y1() {
        return(p1.y);
    }
    public final double z1() {
        return(p1.z);
    }
    public final double x2() {
        return(p2.x);
    }
    public final double y2() {
        return(p2.y);
    }
    public final double z2() {
        return(p2.z);
    }
    public final double u() {
        return(u);
    }
    public final double v() {
        return(v);
    }
    public final double w() {
        return(w);
    }
    public XYZPoint makeXYZPoint(Segment that) {
        double x;
        double y;
        if(this.m == that.m)
            return(null);
        if(that.m == Double.MAX_VALUE) {
            x = that.p1.x;
            y = getYfromX(x);
        } else if(this.m == Double.MAX_VALUE) {
            x = p1.x;
            y = that.getYfromX(x);
        } else {
            x = this.m * this.p1.x - this.p1.y;
```

```
        x -= that.m * that.p1.x - that.p1.y;
        x /= this.m - that.m;
        y = getYfromX(x);
    }

    if(x + 0.1 < Math.min(this.p1.x,this.p2.x))
        return(null);
    if(x - 0.1 > Math.max(this.p1.x,this.p2.x))
        return(null);
    if(y + 0.1 < Math.min(this.p1.y,this.p2.y))
        return(null);
    if(y - 0.1 > Math.max(this.p1.y,this.p2.y))
        return(null);
    if(x + 0.1 < Math.min(that.p1.x,that.p2.x))
        return(null);
    if(x - 0.1 > Math.max(that.p1.x,that.p2.x))
        return(null);
    if(y + 0.1 < Math.min(that.p1.y,that.p2.y))
        return(null);
    if(y - 0.1 > Math.max(that.p1.y,that.p2.y))
        return(null);
    return(new XYZPoint(x,y));
  }
}
```

The Commentary

Our line segment is defined by its two endpoints, so the constructor can use (x1,y1,z1) and (x2,y2,z2) to precalculate the constant values and be ready with them when they are needed later. This way, the constants are only calculated once. The values u, v, and w are simply the differences between the coordinates of the two endpoints.

The length of the line segment uses a formula for the distance between two points in space, which is the three-dimensional form of the Pythagorean theorem:

$$d^2 = a^2 + b^2 + c^2$$

Another special value is the slope of the line that is projected on the two dimensional display. The slope is called m, and it is calculated by dividing u into v. There is one pesky problem with using the slope in calculations—the value of the slope is infinite for a vertical line. However, because we are dealing with the real world of rounding off the actual point at the end of line to the nearest pixel width, we can use a close approximation and achieve the same results. Vertical lines are awarded a slope value of Float.MAX_VALUE.

Even though we are in three dimensions, we are still dealing with a line, so knowing any one of the three coordinates of a point on the line is sufficient information to calculate the other two. There are size methods that take advantage of this characteristic—the ones with the names like getXfromY(), getXfromZ(), and so on.

Access to the individual coordinate points, as well as the other precalculated values, is required in the processing to come, so there is a method that returns each of these values. With efficiency in mind (because these methods are used a lot), the methods were all declared as final so the Java compiler could optimize the method calls into direct access reads.

The method makeXYZPoint() calculates the point of intersection of two line segments after they have been projected to the two-dimensional world of the display. The value returned from this method is an XYZPoint object, but the z component of the coordinate of the point is left to its default. If the segments—after being projected to the display—do not intersect, a null object is returned. The purpose of the repeated calls to isInOrder() is to determine whether the segments actually intersect.

Link

This class contains a pair of Vertex objects and defines some special operations on them. Using objects of this class, it is possible to determine how and where lines will cross or join at their ends.

The Code

```
import java.awt.geom.*;
public class Link {
    public Vertex v1;
    public Vertex v2;
    private Line2D line;
    Link(Vertex vertex1,Vertex vertex2) {
        v1 = vertex1;
        v2 = vertex2;
        line = new Line2D.Double(v1.x,v1.y,v2.x,v2.y);
    }
    public boolean intersects(Link that) {
        switch(getCommonVertexCount(that)) {
        case 1: // Cannot intersect--joined at one end
            return(false);
```

```
            case 2: // Same link
                return(true);
            default:
                return(line.intersectsLine(that.line));
        }
    }
    public boolean hasCommonVertex(Link that) {
        return(getCommonVertexCount(that) > 0);
    }
    private int getCommonVertexCount(Link that) {
        int count = 0;
        if((v1 == that.v1) || (v1 == that.v2))
            count++;
        if((v2 == that.v1) || (v2 == that.v2))
            count++;
        return(count);
    }
}
```

The Commentary

A Link object, constructed from two Vertex objects, is a utility object that is used later in this chapter in the process of breaking up a polygon into its triangular components. Although a Vertex is a point in three-dimensional space, a Link does its work in a two-dimensional space using the x and y components of the Vertex.

The intersects() method compares this Link to another one and returns true if the line segments defined by the two of them intersect one another. If the two links are joined at either end, they are not considered to be intersecting. A Link compared to itself will be considered to be intersecting.

The method getCommonVertexCount() compares this Link to another one and returns a count of the number of vertexes they have in common. If they are disjoint, the return is 0. If they are joined at one end, the return count is 1. If the two represent the same Link, the returned count is 2.

TriangleMetrics

In Chapter 13 we introduced a simple class named Triangle that was simply a container of three Vertex objects used to define a triangle. This class extends that one, adding some methods that can be used to perform calculations on the plane defined by the three points of the triangle.

The Code

```java
import java.util.*;
import java.awt.geom.*;
public class TriangleMetrics extends Triangle {
protected Segment[] segment = new Segment[3];
protected double a;
protected double b;
protected double c;
protected double d;
protected Area area;
TriangleMetrics(Vertex v0,Vertex v1,Vertex v2) {
super(v0,v1,v2);
calculate();
}
public Segment[] getSegments() {
return(segment);
}
protected void calculate() {
makeArea();
makePlaneEquation();
segment[0] = new Segment(v[0],v[1]);
segment[1] = new Segment(v[1],v[2]);
segment[2] = new Segment(v[2],v[0]);
}
private void makeArea() {
GeneralPath gp = new GeneralPath();
gp.moveTo((float)v[0].x,(float)v[0].y);
gp.lineTo((float)v[1].x,(float)v[1].y);
gp.lineTo((float)v[2].x,(float)v[2].y);
gp.closePath();
area = new Area(gp);
}
private void makePlaneEquation() {
double dx01 = v[0].x - v[1].x;
double dy01 = v[0].y - v[1].y;
double dz01 = v[0].z - v[1].z;
double dx02 = v[0].x - v[2].x;
double dy02 = v[0].y - v[2].y;
double dz02 = v[0].z - v[2].z;
a = dy01 * dz02 - dz01 * dy02;
b = dz01 * dx02 - dx01 * dz02;
c = dx01 * dy02 - dy01 * dx02;
d = -(a * v[0].x + b * v[0].y + c * v[0].z);
}
public static Triangle makeTriangle(Link link1,
Link link2,Link link3) {
Vertex v[] = new Vertex[3];
v[0] = link1.v1;
v[1] = link1.v2;
v[2] = null;
```

```
if(link2.v1 == v[0])
v[2] = link2.v2;
else if(link2.v2 == v[0])
v[2] = link2.v1;
else if(link2.v1 == v[1])
v[2] = link2.v2;
else if(link2.v2 == v[1])
v[2] = link2.v1;
else
return(null);
int matchCount = 0;
for(int i=0; i<3; i++) {
if(link2.v1 == v[i])
matchCount++;
if(link2.v2 == v[i])
matchCount++;
if(link3.v1 == v[i])
matchCount++;
if(link3.v2 == v[i])
matchCount++;
}
if(matchCount != 4)
return(null);
return(new Triangle(v[0],v[1],v[2]));
}
}
```

The Commentary

The constructor calls the super class constructor with the three Vertex objects to store the basic information defining the triangle. The calculate() method then sets the internal values that can be used in future calculations.

The makeArea() method creates a GeneralPath object, based on the two-dimensional components of x and y, that can be used by classes that extend this one to draw or fill the triangle. The makePlaneEquation() method calculates the coordinates for the equation of a plane in space. The coordinates a, b, c, and d are chosen so that, for any point (x,y,z) on the plane, this equation holds:

$$ax + by + cz + d = 0$$

This equation is not for the triangle. It is for the plane in which the triangle lies—the plane that extends to infinity in all directions. Finally, the constructor creates an array of three Segment objects—one for each side of the triangle that defines the plane.

The Line Splitter

This is a class that extends the TriangleMetrics class to add the ability of determining which portions of a line are hidden and which are visible. The class is instantiated, holding the information about a single triangle. The method getVisibleSegments() is called with a collection of Segment objects. Each Segment is broken up into zero, one, or three Segments according to its visibility.

The Code

```
import java.util.*;
import java.awt.geom.*;
public class Splitter extends TriangleMetrics {
    private XYZPoint center;
    private final static double EPSILON = 1.1;
    Segment[] workSeg = new Segment[2];
    public Splitter(Vertex v0,Vertex v1,Vertex v2) {
        super(v0,v1,v2);
        calculate();
    }
    public Splitter(Triangle t) {
        super(t.getVertex(0),t.getVertex(1),t.getVertex(2));
        calculate();
    }
    public void calculate() {
        super.calculate();
        double px = (v[0].x + v[1].x) / 2.0;
        double py = (v[0].y + v[1].y) / 2.0;
        double pz = (v[0].z + v[1].z) / 2.0;
        px = (px + v[2].x) / 2.0;
        py = (py + v[2].y) / 2.0;
        pz = (pz + v[2].z) / 2.0;
        center = new XYZPoint(px,py,pz);
    }
    public Vector getVisibleSegments(Vector vec) {
        calculate();
        Vector newVec = new Vector();
        for(int i=0; i<vec.size(); i++) {
            Segment s = (Segment)vec.elementAt(i);
            switch(fragment(s)) {
            case 0:
                break;
            case 1:
                newVec.addElement(workSeg[0]);
                break;
            case 2:
```

```
                newVec.addElement(workSeg[0]);
                newVec.addElement(workSeg[1]);
                break;
            }
        }
        return(newVec);
    }
    private int fragment(Segment s) {
        int count = 0;
        XYZPoint p;
        XYZPoint p1 = null;
        XYZPoint p2 = null;
        Vector pVec = makeXYZPoints(s);
        for(int index=0; index<pVec.size(); index++) {
            p = (XYZPoint)pVec.elementAt(index);
            if(p1 == null) {
                p1 = p;
            } else if(p2 == null) {
                if(ppVisibility(p1,p))
                    p2 = p;
                else
                    p1 = p;
            } else {
                if(ppVisibility(p2,p)) {
                    p2 = p;
                } else {
                    workSeg[count++] = new Segment(p1,p2);
                    p1 = p;
                    p2 = null;
                }
            }
        }
        if((p1 != null) && (p2 != null))
            workSeg[count++] = new Segment(p1,p2);
        return(count);
    }

    private boolean ppVisibility(XYZPoint p1,XYZPoint p2) {
        if(p1.isEdge() && p2.isEdge()) {
            if(p1.isBack() || p2.isBack())
                return(false);
        }
        if(p1.isOutside() || p2.isOutside())
            return(true);
        if(p1.isFront() || p2.isFront())
            return(true);
        if(p1.isSurface() && p2.isSurface())
            return(true);
        if(p1.isFront() && p2.isSurface())
            return(true);
        if(p1.isSurface() && p2.isFront())
```

```java
            return(true);
        return(false);
    }

    private Vector makeXYZPoints(Segment s) {
        Vector pVec = new Vector();
        XYZPoint p;
        XYZPoint pe1;
        XYZPoint pe2;

        // The two end points of the segment
        p = new XYZPoint(s.x1(),s.y1(),s.z1());
        p.setEndpoint(true);
        setInsideOutside(p);
        setFrontBack(p);
        pVec.addElement(p);
        p = new XYZPoint(s.x2(),s.y2(),s.z2());
        p.setEndpoint(true);
        setInsideOutside(p);
        setFrontBack(p);
        pVec.addElement(p);

        // The point where the segment pierces the plane.
        double t = -(a * s.x1() + b * s.y1() + c * s.z1() + d);
        t /= a * s.u() + b * s.v() + c * s.w();
        double px = s.x1() + t * s.u();
        double py = s.y1() + t * s.v();
        double pz = s.z1() + t * s.w();

        if(!Double.isNaN(px) && !Double.isNaN(py)) {
            p = new XYZPoint(px,py,pz);
            setInsideOutside(p);
            p.setSurface(true);
            pVec.addElement(p);
        }

        // Intersections with the segment and the edges of the triangle.
        for(int i=0; i<3; i++) {
            if((p = s.makeXYZPoint(segment[i])) != null) {
                p.z = s.getZfromXY(p.x,p.y);
                p.setEdge(true);
                setFrontBack(p);
                pVec.addElement(p);
            }
        }
        pVectorSort(pVec);
        pVectorTrim(pVec);
        return(pVec);
    }
    private void pVectorSort(Vector pVec) {
        int i=1;
```

```
            while(i < pVec.size()) {
                XYZPoint p1 = (XYZPoint)pVec.elementAt(i-1);
                XYZPoint p2 = (XYZPoint)pVec.elementAt(i);
                if(p1.compareTo(p2) > 0) {
                    pVec.setElementAt(p2,i-1);
                    pVec.setElementAt(p1,i);
                    if(i > 1)
                        i--;
                } else {
                    i++;
                }
            }
        }
        private void pVectorTrim(Vector pVec) {
            XYZPoint p;
            XYZPoint p1;
            XYZPoint p2;
            int index = 0;
            p = (XYZPoint)pVec.elementAt(index);
            while(!p.isEndpoint()) {
                pVec.removeElementAt(index);
                p = (XYZPoint)pVec.elementAt(index);
            }
            p = (XYZPoint)pVec.elementAt(++index);
            while(!p.isEndpoint()) {
                p = (XYZPoint)pVec.elementAt(++index);
            }
            index++;
            while(index < pVec.size()) {
                pVec.removeElementAt(index);
            }
            index = 1;
            while(index < pVec.size()) {
                p1 = (XYZPoint)pVec.elementAt(index-1);
                p2 = (XYZPoint)pVec.elementAt(index);
                if(p1.near(p2)) {
                    pVec.setElementAt(p1.combine(p2),index-1);
                    pVec.removeElementAt(index);
                } else {
                    index++;
                }
            }
        }
        boolean isInBack(double x,double y,double z) {
            return(z < -((a*x + b*y + d) / c) - EPSILON);
        }
        boolean isInFront(double x,double y,double z) {
            return(z > -((a*x + b*y + d) / c) + EPSILON);
        }
        private void setInsideOutside(XYZPoint p) {
            double pDelta;
```

```
double cDelta;
for(int i=0; i<3; i++) {
    Segment s = segment[i];
    // If it is close to an edge, we are done.
    if(Math.abs(p.x - s.getXfromY(p.y)) < 1.0) {
        if(Math.abs(p.y - s.getYfromX(p.x)) < 1.0) {
            p.setEdge(true);
            return;
        }
    }
    // If it is outside the rectangle, we are done.
    if(p.x < minimumX()) {
        p.setOutside(true);
        return;
    }
    if(p.x > maximumX()) {
        p.setOutside(true);
        return;
    }
    if(p.y < minimumY()) {
        p.setOutside(true);
        return;
    }
    if(p.y > maximumY()) {
        p.setOutside(true);
        return;
    }
    // The distance indicators
    if(Math.abs(s.getSlope()) > 1.0) {
        pDelta = p.y - s.getYfromX(p.x);
        cDelta = center.y - s.getYfromX(center.x);
    } else {
        pDelta = p.x - s.getXfromY(p.y);
        cDelta = center.x - s.getXfromY(center.y);
    }
    if((pDelta > -0.1) && (pDelta < 0.1)) {
        p.setEdge(true);
        return;
    }
    // If close to zero, call it zero
    if((cDelta > -0.1) && (cDelta < 0.1))
        cDelta = 0.0;
    // If opposite directions, it is outside
    if((pDelta) < 0.0) {
        if((cDelta) > 0.0) {
            p.setOutside(true);
            return;
        }
    }
    if((pDelta) > 0.0) {
```

```
                    if((cDelta) < 0.0) {
                        p.setOutside(true);
                        return;
                    }
                }
            }
        p.setInside(true);
        }
        private void setFrontBack(XYZPoint p) {
            if(isInFront(p.x,p.y,p.z))
                p.setFront(true);
            else if(isInBack(p.x,p.y,p.z))
                p.setBack(true);
            else
                p.setSurface(true);
        }
    }
```

The Commentary

The constructor stores the vertex values of the triangle and, with a call to calculate(), creates a point that is at the center of the triangle. The center is found by locating the midpoint of one side, and then locating the midpoint between it and the opposite vertex.

The method getVisibleSegments() breaks up segments into those that are visible. The method fragment() is called once for each segment. A call to the method fragment() may result in no segments, one segment, or two segments. If segments are returned by fragment(), they are added to new collection and, once all the segments have been processed, the new collection is returned to the caller.

The fragment() method calls the method makeXYZPoints() to create an array of points to be considered in the generation of a new segment. If two adjacent points are visible, then the portion of the segment between them is visible. If fragment() finds more than two adjacent points that are visible, it combines all of them into one visible segment. The resulting segments (there can never be more than two) are stored in the work-Seg array and the count is returned.

The ppVisibility() method determines—by examining the positions of the endpoints—whether or not a segment is visible. This method tests for the cases described at the beginning of this chapter, and then returns true if the segment is visible and false if not.

The makeXYZPoints() method compares the segment to the triangle to create an array of points at which the segment could possibly be broken. Included in the list are the two endpoints, the point at which the point pierces the plane of the triangle, and the points where the segment crosses an edge of the triangle. These points all have their flags set indicating their relative positions to the plane and the triangle. The points are sorted by pVectorSort() because they are not created in any particular order and are probably not in the order they appear along the segment. The method pVectorTrim() removes some unnecessary points.

The method pVectorSort() simply puts the points in order according to their position on the line. At the very most there can only be five points, so a simple swap sort is used.

The method pVectorTrim() removes unnecessary points. The points, front and back, that are outside of the endpoints can be removed since the segment doesn't extend that far. After that, any points that are at the same location—that is, their separation is less than one pixel—are combined. This can happen if, for example, a segment crosses the triangle at a vertex—this crossing could be reported for both of the adjacent sides. Also, because two adjacent triangles could be using the same vertex, the endpoint can match up with both a surface point and two crossing points. If two points are very close (determined by a call to near() of XYZPoint) the points are combined into one point (by calling combine() of XYZPoint).

The methods isInBack() and isInFront() return information about the position of a point. There is an EPSILON value included in the equation to leave a little area for the point being on the surface.

The method setInsideOutside() examines a point to determine whether it is inside the triangle, outside the triangle, or on the edge. If the point is less than a pixel away from a vertex of the triangle, it is considered to be on an edge. If either the x or the y value of the point is completely above, below, or on either side of the triangle, it is considered outside the triangle. The value of pDelta is calculated to be the directed distance from the point to the segment. The value of cDelta is calculated to be the directed distance from the center of the triangle to the edge. If the signs of these two values differ, the points are on opposite sides of the segment, and the point is outside.

The method setFrontBack() uses isInFront() and isInBack() to set the z-axis position to in back, in front, or on the surface.

Obscuring Lines behind a Triangle

This example program shows how line segments can be obscured by a triangle. In this program, there is a triangle waving back and forth like a flag in the center of the display. Moving around in the background is another triangle. It moves around and resizes itself in the x and y directions, but always stays behind the obscuring "flag" triangle (the z-axis value of the background triangle is constant). There is a line running from one side of the display to the other (its x-axis values are constant), but it moves about in the y and z axes and can be behind, in front, or piercing the triangle. There is a point that moves around in all three axes and has lines drawn from it to the three vertices of the triangle. As all these objects move around, the lines describing any of them may be obscured by the flag in the center.

To make the positions clearer, the objects are displayed in both a top view and a front view.

The Code

```
import java.util.*;
import java.awt.*;
import java.awt.geom.*;
import java.awt.event.*;
class Crossing extends Frame {
    public static void main(String arg[]) {
        new Crossing();
    }
    Crossing() {
        super("Crossing");
        addWindowListener(new WindowAdapter() {
            public void windowClosing(WindowEvent e)
                { System.exit(0); } } );
        CrossingPanel loPanel = new CrossingPanel();
        add(loPanel);
        pack();
        show();
    }
class CrossingPanel extends Canvas implements Runnable {
    private int pause = 120;
    private Rectangle rectangle;
    private Thread looper;
    private Image image;
    private boolean ready = false;
    private Splitter splitter;
    private Vector polyVector;
```

```java
    private Vector lineVector;
    private Vector focusVector;
    private AffineTransform trans1;
    private AffineTransform trans2;

    // Dimensions for the red (background) polygon
    MovingPoint poly1 = new MovingPoint(0,400,5,0,200,5,-5,-5,0);
    MovingPoint poly2 = new MovingPoint(0,400,4,0,200,4,-5,-5,0);
    MovingPoint poly3 = new MovingPoint(0,400,3,0,200,3,-5,-5,0);
    MovingPoint poly4 = new MovingPoint(0,400,2,0,200,2,-5,-5,0);

    // Positon of the dot
    MovingPoint dot = new MovingPoint(-30,430,2,25,125,1,10,100,1);

    // Dimensions for the black triangle (flag)
    MovingPoint flag1 = new MovingPoint(200,200,0,0,0,0,0,0,0);
    MovingPoint flag2 = new MovingPoint(200,200,0,150,150,0,0,0,0);
    MovingPoint flag3 = new MovingPoint(0,400,7,75,75,0,200,200,0);

    // Dimensions for the line
    MovingPoint line1 = new MovingPoint(0,0,0,0,200,4,-100,200,5);
    MovingPoint line2 = new MovingPoint(400,400,0,0,200,3,-100,200,4);

    CrossingPanel() {
        setSize(500,500);
        rectangle = new Rectangle();
        looper = new Thread(this);
        looper.start();
    }
    public void run() {
        try {
            while(true) {
                repaint();
                Thread.sleep(pause);
            }
        } finally {
            return;
        }
    }

    public void update(Graphics g) {
        if(looper.isAlive()) {
            if(!rectangle.equals(getBounds()) || (image == null)) {
                rectangle = getBounds();
                image = createImage(rectangle.width,rectangle.height);
                firstFrame();
            }
            if(nextFrame()) {
                paint(image.getGraphics());
                g.drawImage(image,0,0,null);
            }
```

```
        }
    }

    public void paint(Graphics g) {
        if(!ready)
            return;
        Graphics2D g2 = (Graphics2D)g;
        Segment[] ts = splitter.getSegments();
        Vector bVector = splitter.getVisibleSegments(polyVector);
        Vector lVector = splitter.getVisibleSegments(lineVector);
        Vector fVector = splitter.getVisibleSegments(focusVector);

        g2.setColor(Color.white);
        g2.fillRect(0,0,getSize().width,getSize().height);

        // Set location of top view
        g2.setTransform(trans1);

        // The top view of the flag
        g2.setColor(Color.black);
        g2.drawLine((int)ts[1].x1(),(int)ts[1].z1(),
                (int)ts[1].x2(),(int)ts[1].z2());

        // Top view of the red polygon
        g2.setColor(Color.red);
        g2.drawLine(poly1.x,poly1.z,poly2.x,poly2.z);
        g2.drawLine(poly2.x,poly2.z,poly3.x,poly3.z);
        g2.drawLine(poly3.x,poly3.z,poly4.x,poly4.z);

        // Top view of the dot
        g2.setColor(Color.black);
        g2.fillOval(dot.x-2,dot.z-2,4,4);

        // Top view of the line
        g2.setColor(Color.blue);
        g2.drawLine(line1.x,line1.z,line2.x,line2.z);

        // Switch to front view
        g2.setTransform(trans2);

        // The front view of the flag
        g2.setColor(Color.black);
        for(int i=0; i<3; i++)
            g2.drawLine((int)ts[i].x1(),(int)ts[i].y1(),
                    (int)ts[i].x2(),(int)ts[i].y2());

        // Front view of the red polygon
        g2.setColor(Color.red);
        for(int i=0; i<bVector.size(); i++) {
            Segment s = (Segment)bVector.elementAt(i);
```

```
g2.drawLine((int)s.x1(),(int)s.y1(),(int)s.x2(),(int)s.y2());
    }

        // Front view of the dot-to-flag lines
        g2.setColor(Color.green);
        for(int i=0; i<fVector.size(); i++) {
            Segment s = (Segment)fVector.elementAt(i);

g2.drawLine((int)s.x1(),(int)s.y1(),(int)s.x2(),(int)s.y2());
    }

        // Front view of the dot
        if(fVector.size() > 0) {
            g2.setColor(Color.black);
            g2.fillOval(dot.x-2,dot.y-2,4,4);
        }

        // Front view of the line
        g2.setColor(Color.blue);
        for(int i=0; i<lVector.size(); i++) {
            Segment s = (Segment)lVector.elementAt(i);

g2.drawLine((int)s.x1(),(int)s.y1(),(int)s.x2(),(int)s.y2());
    }

        // The annotation at the bottom
        String description = "The red polygon ";
        if(bVector.size() == 0)
            description += "completely obscured.";
        else
            description += "is drawn in " + bVector.size() + " seg-
ments.";
        g2.drawString(description,10,180);
        if(splitter.isInBack(dot.x,dot.y,dot.z))
            description = "The dot is in back of the plane.";
        else if(splitter.isInFront(dot.x,dot.y,dot.z))
            description = "The dot is in front of the plane.";
        else
            description = "The dot is on the surface of the plane.";
        g2.drawString(description,10,200);
        description = "The blue line ";
        if(lVector.size() == 0)
            description += "is completely visible";
        else if(lVector.size() == 1)
            description += "is in one segment.";
        else
            description += "is in " + lVector.size() + " segments.";
        g2.drawString(description,10,220);
    }
    private void firstFrame() {
        trans1 = new AffineTransform();
```

```
            trans1.setToTranslation(25,25);
            trans2 = new AffineTransform();
            trans2.setToTranslation(25,250);
            ready = true;
        }
        private boolean nextFrame() {
            // The triangle used for masking (flag)
            flag1.next();
            flag2.next();
            flag3.next();
            Vertex v0 = new Vertex(flag1.x,flag1.y,flag1.z);
            Vertex v1 = new Vertex(flag2.x,flag2.y,flag2.z);
            Vertex v2 = new Vertex(flag3.x,flag3.y,flag3.z);
            splitter = new Splitter(v0,v1,v2);

            // The backgrond polygon
            poly1.next();
            poly2.next();
            poly3.next();
            poly4.next();
            Vertex sv1 = new Vertex(poly1.x,poly1.y,poly1.z);
            Vertex sv2 = new Vertex(poly2.x,poly2.y,poly2.z);
            Vertex sv3 = new Vertex(poly3.x,poly3.y,poly3.z);
            Vertex sv4 = new Vertex(poly4.x,poly4.y,poly4.z);
            polyVector = new Vector();
            polyVector.addElement(new Segment(sv1,sv2));
            polyVector.addElement(new Segment(sv2,sv3));
            polyVector.addElement(new Segment(sv3,sv4));
            polyVector.addElement(new Segment(sv4,sv1));

            // The moving dot
            dot.next();

            // The lines that focus on the dot
            Vertex v = new Vertex(dot.x,dot.y,dot.z);
            focusVector = new Vector();
            focusVector.addElement(new Segment(v,v0));
            focusVector.addElement(new Segment(v,v1));
            focusVector.addElement(new Segment(v,v2));

            // The line that pierces the surface
            line1.next();
            line2.next();
            sv1 = new Vertex(line1.x,line1.y,line1.z);
            sv2 = new Vertex(line2.x,line2.y,line2.z);
            lineVector = new Vector();
            lineVector.addElement(new Segment(sv1,sv2));

            return(true);
        }
    }
```

```
class MovingPoint {
    private int xMax;
    private int yMax;
    private int zMax;
    private int xMin;
    private int yMin;
    private int zMin;
    private int xDelta;
    private int yDelta;
    private int zDelta;
    private boolean xDown;
    private boolean yDown;
    private boolean zDown;
    public int x;
    public int y;
    public int z;
    MovingPoint(
            int xMin,int xMax,int xDelta,
            int yMin,int yMax,int yDelta,
            int zMin,int zMax,int zDelta) {
        this.xMax = xMax;
        this.yMax = yMax;
        this.zMax = zMax;
        this.xMin = xMin;
        this.yMin = yMin;
        this.zMin = zMin;
        this.xDelta = xDelta;
        this.yDelta = yDelta;
        this.zDelta = zDelta;
        x = (xMax + xMin) / 2;
        y = (yMax + yMin) / 2;
        z = (zMax + zMin) / 2;
    }
    public void next() {
        if(xDown) {
            if((x -= xDelta) <= xMin)
                xDown = false;
        } else {
            if((x += xDelta) >= xMax)
                xDown = true;
        }
        if(yDown) {
            if((y -= yDelta) <= yMin)
                yDown = false;
        } else {
            if((y += yDelta) >= yMax)
                yDown = true;
        }
        if(zDown) {
            if((z -= zDelta) <= zMin)
                zDown = false;
```

```
        } else {
            if((z += zDelta) >= zMax)
                zDown = true;
        }
    }
}
}
```

The Commentary

Most of this program is involved with the animation details of calculating the next position of the various parts.

The class MovingPoint is used to define points in space that can be moved. A MovingPoint object has settings for its maximum and minimum bounds in all three dimensions, and how fast movement is to be along any axis. Each time a point reaches a bound, its direction is reversed. This causes points to bounce around in a three-dimensional space like the puck in the old Pong game—they bounce off the left, right, top, bottom, front, and back. All of these values are supplied on the constructor.

The Boolean values in MovingPoints determine which way each point is to be moved, and the delta values are either added to or subtracted from each point, according to the direction in which it is moving. Once a moving point reaches one of its extremes, the Boolean that controls it is toggled, causing it to start in the opposite direction on the next frame. See Figure 15.1.

The CrossingPanel class does all the work. It is a Canvas (so it can display) and implements Runnable (so it can have an animated thread). It defines a MovingPoint describing all the items to be displayed. The MovingPoints poly1 through poly4 define the background polygon; flag1 through flag2 define the blocking triangle, line1 and line2 define the horizontal moving line, and dot defines the apex of the three lines drawn from the triangle.

The firstFrame() method is called once to set up the initial values of the triangle and the line. A couple of AffineTransforms are created—one to position the top view and the other to position the front view.

The nextFrame() method is called repeatedly—once for each time the points are shifted to a new position. The next() method is called for all the moving points and, once the position values are adjusted, the new positions are stored to be available to the paint() method. Finally, a Splitter

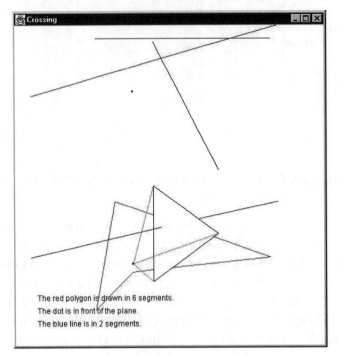

Figure 15.1 The Crossing window in action.

object is constructed based on three Vertex objects that define the triangle location.

The paint() method expects all the positional calculations to have been completed, and for a Splitter object to have been defined. To draw the top view, it is simply a matter of using an AffineTransform to position the drawing in the window, using the and transposing x and y values, and drawing a single line for the triangle and the polygon. The Splitter is then used to break up the Segments, leaving only the portions that are visible. The front view is drawn in a loop because all three sides of the triangle are to be drawn. If there is more than one segment to be drawn, that means that part of the line was obscured in some way, so the line is drawn in red.

TriangleFace

The class will break up a closed polygon into its component triangles. The polygon is planar (that is, it is completely flat) and can be of any degree of complexity, including holes, and can be at any angle floating in space. This class will create an array of Triangle objects that, when pieced together edge to edge, will exactly cover the polygon.

The Code

```java
import java.util.*;
import java.awt.geom.*;
public class TriangleFace {
    Face face;
    Area area;
    Vector triVector;
    Vector linkVector;
    TriangleFace(Face f) {
        face = f;
        if(face.getVertexCount() < 3)
            return;
        boolean success = makeTriangles();
        if(!success) {
            skewX();
            success = makeTriangles();
            skewX();
        }
        if(!success) {
            skewY();
            success = makeTriangles();
            skewY();
        }
    }
    private boolean makeTriangles() {
        makeArea();
        makeLinkList();
        makeNewLinks();
        makeTriVector();
        return(triVector.size() > 0);
    }
    public Triangle[] getTriangleArray() {
        Triangle[] tArray = new Triangle[triVector.size()];
        for(int i=0; i<triVector.size(); i++)
            tArray[i] = (Triangle)triVector.get(i);
        return(tArray);
    }
    private void skewX() {
        for(int i=1; i<face.getVertexCount(); i++) {
            Vertex v = face.getVertex(i);
            double hold = v.x;
            v.x = v.z;
            v.z = hold;
        }
    }
    private void skewY() {
```

```
            for(int i=1; i<face.getVertexCount(); i++) {
                Vertex v = face.getVertex(i);
                double hold = v.y;
                v.y = v.z;
                v.z = hold;
            }
        }
        private boolean isOutside(Vertex v1,Vertex v2) {
            double x = (v1.x + v2.x) / 2.0;
            double y = (v1.y + v2.y) / 2.0;
            return(!area.contains(x,y));
        }
        private void makeArea() {
            GeneralPath gp = new GeneralPath();
            Vertex vertex = face.getVertex(0);
            gp.moveTo((float)vertex.x,(float)vertex.y);
            for(int index=1; index<face.getVertexCount(); index++) {
                vertex = face.getVertex(index);
                gp.lineTo((float)vertex.x,(float)vertex.y);
            }
            gp.closePath();
            area = new Area(gp);
        }
        private void makeLinkList() {
            linkVector = new Vector();
            for(int i=0; i<face.getVertexCount(); i++) {
                Link link = new Link(face.getVertex(i),
                        face.getVertex(i+1));
                linkVector.addElement(link);
            }
        }
        private void makeNewLinks() {
            for(int i=0; i<face.getVertexCount(); i++) {
                jloop: for(int j=i+1; j<face.getVertexCount(); j++) {
                    if(isOutside(face.getVertex(i),face.getVertex(j)))
                        continue jloop;
                    Link newLink = new Link(face.getVertex(i),
                            face.getVertex(j));
                    for(int k=0; k<linkVector.size(); k++) {
                        Link link = (Link)linkVector.get(k);
                        if(link.intersects(newLink))
                            continue jloop;
                    }
                    linkVector.addElement(newLink);
                }
            }
        }
        private void makeTriVector() {
            triVector = new Vector();
            int size = linkVector.size();
            link1loop: for(int i1=0; i1<size; i1++) {
```

```
            Link link1 = (Link)linkVector.get(i1);
            for(int i2=i1+1; i2<size; i2++) {
                Link link2 = (Link)linkVector.get(i2);
                if(link1.hasCommonVertex(link2)) {
                    for(int i3=i2+1; i3<size; i3++) {
                        Triangle t;
                        Link link3 = (Link)linkVector.get(i3);
                        t = TriangleMetrics.makeTriangle(link1,
                                link2,link3);
                        if(t != null) {
                            triVector.addElement(t);
                            continue link1loop;
                        }
                    }
                }
            }
        }
    }
}
```

The Commentary

The constructor requires the polygon in the form of a Face object. To create the triangles, the calculations are done using only the x and y coordinates of each point. This means that if the polygon is on a plane that is horizontal to the z axis (that is, it is on edge from the direction of the viewer), it will be necessary to skew the points just a bit so their relationships can be discerned.

The constructor completes all calculations by calling a series of methods. A call is made to makeTriangles() and, if the call fails, the x-axis points are skewed and the call is made again—it that fails, the y-axis points are skewed and a final attempt is made. The method makeArea() creates a Java 2D Area object from the Face. The methods makeLinkList() and makeNewLinks() create an array of Link objects joining the points of the polygon. Finally, triVector() is called to create an array of Triangle objects that fill the polygon.

The makeArea() method creates a Java2D Area object for the polygon. The polygon may have holes in it, so it is necessary to create Area objects for them also. The purpose of the Area object is so we will be able to easily determine whether or not a point is inside or outside the polygon (being in a hole is considered being outside).

The makeGeneralPath() method is used by makeArea() to create the Area objects. It simply traces the polygon from one point to another inscribing its shape, and draws the shape into a GeneralPath object. This object, in turn, is used to create the Area objects in makeArea().

The methods skewX() and skewY() reposition the face in an attempt to open the shape so the points can be discerned on the x-y plane. If a plane is parallel to the z-axis, it will appear as a line and there is no way to find the triangles. A plane can be parallel to any two axes, but there is no way a plane can be parallel to all three, so swapping the Z values with either the X or Y values will expose the shape of the face to the algorithm. These skew methods are their own inverses—that is, call once and the values are reversed; call twice and the original action is undone

The makeLinkList() method simply makes an array of Link objects—one for each line segment along the edge of the face, and along the edge of any holes in the face. Because all of these are edges of the polygon, all of them will be one edge of a triangle.

The makeNewLinks() method takes the list created by makeLinkList() and adds new Link objects by connecting points along the polygon. To make all possible connections, it is simply a matter of connecting all points that can be connected without causing two Links to cross. Each Link is created by joining any two points that do not require the crossing of another Link. Once done, the polygon has been broken into its component triangles.

The method makeTriVector() scans through the Links that were created by the previous methods and creates all the triangles that can be made from them. This is done in three nested loops. The outer loop is executed once for every Link in the list. The next loop is executed once for every Link after the one specified by the outer loop, and the inner loop is executed once for each Link after the one of the middle loop. If, in the inner loop, the three are all connected end to end, they make a triangle. Because the outer loop goes through the Links only once, and the inner loops never visit a Link that has been visited by an outer loop, no triangles are duplicated.

HiddenLineWireFrame

This wire frame class extends the AdjustableWireFrame class, in the previous chapter, to render three-dimensional drawings with hidden line suppression. The actions of loading the diagram of the object, and of scaling and rotation, are inherited. This class adds methods to suppress hidden lines.

The Code

```java
import java.util.*;
class HiddenLineWireFrame extends AdjustableWireFrame {
    private Splitter[] splitterArray;
    private int nextSplitter = 0;
    private Vector segmentVector;
    private Triangle[] triangleArray = null;
    private int nextTriangle = 0;
    public HiddenLineWireFrame(String fileName) {
        super(fileName);
        triangulate();
    }
    private void triangulate() {
        triangleArray = null;
        for(int i=0; i<nextFace; i++) {
            Face face = faceArray[i];
            TriangleFace tf = new TriangleFace(face);
            addTriangle(tf.getTriangleArray());
        }
        nextSplitter = nextTriangle;
        splitterArray = new Splitter[nextSplitter];
        for(int i=0; i<nextSplitter; i++)
            splitterArray[i] = new Splitter(triangleArray[i]);
        segmentize();
    }
    public void segmentize() {
        segmentVector = new Vector();
        for(int i=0; i<nextEdge; i++) {
            Edge edge = edgeArray[i];
            Segment s = new Segment(vertex[edge.vertexID1],
                    vertex[edge.vertexID2]);
            segmentVector.addElement(s);
        }
        for(int i=0; i<nextSplitter; i++) {
            segmentVector =
                splitterArray[i].getVisibleSegments(segmentVector);
        }
    }
    public Segment getSegment(int number) {
        Segment s;
        try {
            s = (Segment)segmentVector.elementAt(number);
        } catch(ArrayIndexOutOfBoundsException e) {
            s = null;
        }
        return(s);
```

```
    }
    public int getSegmentCount() {
        return(segmentVector.size());
    }
    private void addTriangle(Triangle t) {
        if(triangleArray == null) {
            triangleArray = new Triangle[10];
            nextTriangle = 0;
        } else if(nextTriangle >= triangleArray.length) {
            Triangle[] newTriangle = new Triangle[nextTriangle + 10];
            for(int i=0; i<nextTriangle; i++)
                newTriangle[i] = triangleArray[i];
            triangleArray = newTriangle;
        }
        triangleArray[nextTriangle++] = t;
    }
    private void addTriangle(Triangle[] t) {
        for(int i=0; i<t.length; i++)
            addTriangle(t[i]);
    }
    public Triangle getTriangle(int number) {
        if(number >= nextTriangle)
            return(null);
        return(triangleArray[number]);
    }
    public int getTriangleCount() {
        return(nextTriangle);
    }
}
```

The Commentary

The method triangulate() creates a TriangleFace object for each face of the object to be drawn. Each of these triangles are used to create a Splitter object to be used to clip invisible lines.

The method segmentize() does the work of breaking up the segments into their visible portions and returning an array of them to the caller. To do this, Vector object is created as the Segment representation of all the Edges. This array of Segments is processed by every splitter—each one trimming of any parts segments that are obscured. This method can be called after the diagram has been rotated or scaled because all positions are based on the same array of Vertex objects—the one that defines the outline of the object being drawn.

The getSegmentCount() and getSegment() methods are used to access the drawable segments—the ones that are left over after the suppressed sections have been omitted.

Every face that should be opaque must be specified. That is, even though the edges of a face are defined fully by other faces , it is still necessary to specify the face if you wish it to be opaque. For example, the file box1.data contains this:

```
vertex 1 50 100 100
vertex 2 100 50 90
vertex 3 150 100 100
vertex 4 100 150 110
vertex 5 50 130 100
vertex 6 100 80 90
vertex 7 150 130 100
vertex 8 100 180 110
face 1 2 3 4
face 5 6 7 8
face 1 4 8 5
face 2 3 7 6
face 1 2 6 5
face 4 3 7 8
```

The box that will display from this file is shown in Figure 15.2. Any combination of the six faces of the box can be removed by having their face declaration removed. For example, removing the face defining the top (as in the file box2.data) the display looks like the one in Figure 15.3. If the top face is left in place and the two on the front are removed (as in the file box3.data), the display looks like Figure 15.4.

A Triangulation Demonstration

This demo application uses the TriangleFace capabilities inside the HiddenLineWireFrame class to demonstrate the results of breaking a face of a polygon into its component triangles.

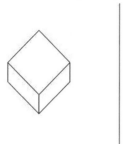

Figure 15.2 A box with all faces.

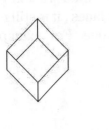

Figure 15.3 A box with all faces except the top.

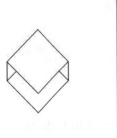

Figure 15.4 A box with all faces except the front two.

The Code

```
import java.io.*;
import java.awt.*;
import java.awt.event.*;
class Triangulation extends Frame
        implements ActionListener {
    private FrameTriangleCanvas fc;
    public static void main(String arg[]) {
        if(arg.length != 1) {
            System.out.println("Usage: Triangulation infile [ outfile ]");
            System.exit(1);
        }
        Triangulation tri = new Triangulation(arg[0]);
    }
    Triangulation(String fileName) {
        super("Triangulation");
        addWindowListener(new WindowAdapter() {
            public void windowClosing(WindowEvent e)
                { System.exit(0); } } );
        HiddenLineWireFrame hlwf = new HiddenLineWireFrame(fileName);
        fc = new FrameTriangleCanvas(hlwf);
        add(fc,BorderLayout.CENTER);
        Panel p = new Panel();
        Button button = new Button("None");
        button.addActionListener(this);
```

```
            p.add(button,BorderLayout.WEST);
            button = new Button("All");
            button.addActionListener(this);
            p.add(button,BorderLayout.CENTER);
            button = new Button("Next");
            button.addActionListener(this);
            p.add(button,BorderLayout.EAST);
            add(p,BorderLayout.SOUTH);
            pack();
            show();
    }
    public void actionPerformed(ActionEvent event) {
        if(event.getActionCommand().equals("All"))
            fc.showAllTriangles();
        else if(event.getActionCommand().equals("None"))
            fc.showNoTriangles();
        else if(event.getActionCommand().equals("Next"))
            fc.showNextTriangle();
    }
class FrameTriangleCanvas extends Canvas {
    private HiddenLineWireFrame hlwf;
    private final int SHOW_NONE = -1;
    private final int SHOW_ALL = -2;
    private int triangleToShow = SHOW_NONE;
    private int side;
    FrameTriangleCanvas(HiddenLineWireFrame hlwf) {
        this.hlwf = hlwf;
        side = (int)(hlwf.maxDimension() + 50);
        setSize(side,side);
    }
    public void showAllTriangles() {
        triangleToShow = SHOW_ALL;
        repaint();
    }
    public void showNoTriangles() {
        triangleToShow = SHOW_NONE;
        repaint();
    }
    public void showNextTriangle() {
        if(hlwf.getTriangleCount() == 0) {
            triangleToShow = SHOW_NONE;
        } else if(triangleToShow < 0) {
            triangleToShow = 0;
        } else if(++triangleToShow >= hlwf.getTriangleCount()) {
            triangleToShow = 0;
        }
        repaint();
    }
    public void paint(Graphics g) {
        Vertex v1;
        Vertex v2;
```

```
            String description;
            for(int i=0; i<hlwf.getFaceCount(); i++) {
                Face face = hlwf.getFace(i);
                outlineFace(g,face);
            }
            g.setColor(Color.red);
            switch(triangleToShow) {
            case SHOW_ALL:
                for(int i=0; i<hlwf.getTriangleCount(); i++)
                    outlineTriangle(g,hlwf.getTriangle(i));
            case SHOW_NONE:
                description = "There are " +
                        hlwf.getTriangleCount() + " triangles.";
                break;
            default:
                outlineTriangle(g,hlwf.getTriangle(triangleToShow));
                description = "Triangle " + (triangleToShow+1) +
                        " of " + hlwf.getTriangleCount();
                break;
            }
            g.setColor(Color.black);
            g.drawString(description,5,side-10);
        }
        private void outlineFace(Graphics g,Face face) {
            Vertex v1;
            Vertex v2;
            v1 = face.getVertex(0);
            for(int j=1; j<=face.getVertexCount(); j++) {
                v2 = face.getVertex(j);
                g.drawLine((int)v1.x,(int)v1.y,(int)v2.x,(int)v2.y);
                v1 = v2;
            }
        }
        private void outlineTriangle(Graphics g,Triangle t) {
            Vertex v1 = t.getVertex(0);
            Vertex v2 = t.getVertex(1);
            Vertex v3 = t.getVertex(2);
            g.drawLine((int)v1.x,(int)v1.y,(int)v2.x,(int)v2.y);
            g.drawLine((int)v1.x,(int)v1.y,(int)v3.x,(int)v3.y);
            g.drawLine((int)v2.x,(int)v2.y,(int)v3.x,(int)v3.y);
        }
    }
}
```

The Commentary

This application will load any object, create the triangles that make up
its faces, and allow the user to display the triangles all at once, or one at
a time. Entering the command line

```
java Triangulation jface.data
```

will load the face object (which is not a three-dimensional object; it is simply a face with a complex outline) and display it with its triangles showing. Figure 15.5 shows the figure with no triangle being displayed. Selecting the Next button will display the triangles one at a time. Figure 15.6 shows the window with a single triangle being displayed. Figure 15.7 shows all the triangles.

Most of the program is involved with displaying the object and its triangles. The triangulation works for faces that have their edges turned toward the viewer, but, without being rotated, they cannot be seen except as an edge.

The constructor requires an input file name to be fed to the HiddenLineWireFrame object. The HiddenLineWireFrame is not used for its ability to suppress hidden lines—it is used for its ability to load Vertexes and Faces, create triangles from each face, and to store the array of Triangles and return information about them. For example, the FrameTriangleCanvas sizes itself according to the size of the loaded wire frame.

The FrameTriangleCanvas has methods that are called according to the buttons selected on the display, and flags are set before the window is repainted. The paint() method first displays the entire frame and then, according to the selection, it may display no triangles, one triangle, or all

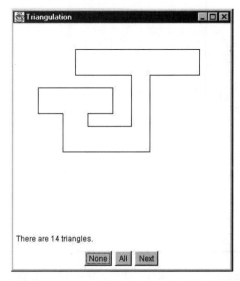

Figure 15.5 The jface displayed without triangles.

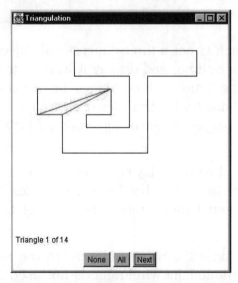

Figure 15.6   The jface object with one of its triangles.

triangles. The method outlineFace() is used to display the entire Face and the method outlineTriangle() is used to display one triangle.

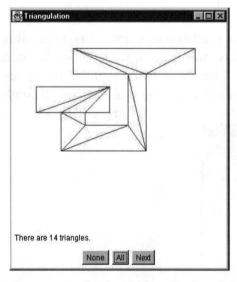

Figure 15.7   The jface object showing all the triangles.

ManualHide

ManualHide allows you to manipulate a three-dimensional shape, just as you did in the previous chapter. The difference here is that hidden lines are concealed. This program allows you to play with the shape to see exactly when and how lines are "turned off."

The syntax for running ManualHide is this:

```
java ManualHide tface.data
```

where `tface.data` is a data file that defines a three-dimensional shape.

The Code

```java
import java.awt.*;
import java.awt.event.*;
class ManualHide extends Frame
        implements ActionListener {
    ManualHidePanel manualHidePanel;
    public static void main(String arg[]) {
        if(arg.length != 1) {
            System.out.println("Usage: ManualHide <filename>");
            System.exit(1);
        }
        new ManualHide(arg[0]);
    }
    ManualHide(String fileName) {
        super("ManualHide");
        addWindowListener(new WindowAdapter() {
            public void windowClosing(WindowEvent e)
                { System.exit(0); } } );
        setLayout(new BorderLayout());
        HiddenLineWireFrame hlwf = new HiddenLineWireFrame(fileName);
        manualHidePanel = new ManualHidePanel(hlwf);
        add("Center",manualHidePanel);
        add("East",makeButtonPanel());
        pack();
        show();
    }
    private Panel makeButtonPanel() {
        String[] label = {"X+","X-","Y+","Y-","Z+","Z-","S+","S-"};
        Panel p = new Panel();
        p.setLayout(new GridLayout(4,2));
        for(int i=0; i<8; i++) {
            Button b = new Button(label[i]);
            b.addActionListener(this);
            p.add(b);
        }
        return(p);
    }
    public void actionPerformed(ActionEvent event) {
        if(event.getActionCommand().equals("X+"))
```

```
            manualHidePanel.xPlus();
        else if(event.getActionCommand().equals("X-"))
            manualHidePanel.xMinus();
        else if(event.getActionCommand().equals("Y+"))
            manualHidePanel.yPlus();
        else if(event.getActionCommand().equals("Y-"))
            manualHidePanel.yMinus();
        else if(event.getActionCommand().equals("Z+"))
            manualHidePanel.zPlus();
        else if(event.getActionCommand().equals("Z-"))
            manualHidePanel.zMinus();
        else if(event.getActionCommand().equals("S+"))
            manualHidePanel.sPlus();
        else if(event.getActionCommand().equals("S-"))
            manualHidePanel.sMinus();
    }
class ManualHidePanel extends Canvas {
    private HiddenLineWireFrame hlwf;
    private Rectangle rectangle;
    private Image image;

    private double scaleFactor = 0.93;
    private double rotationAngle = 0.02;

    ManualHidePanel(HiddenLineWireFrame hlwf) {
        this.hlwf = hlwf;
        int dim = (int)hlwf.maxDimension()+50;
        setSize(dim,dim);
        hlwf.setRotationCenter(dim/2,dim/2,dim/2);
        hlwf.setAngleX(0.02);
        hlwf.setAngleY(0.02);
        hlwf.setAngleZ(0.02);
    }
    public void paint(Graphics g) {
        g.setColor(Color.white);
        g.fillRect(0,0,getSize().width,getSize().height);
        g.setColor(Color.black);
        for(int i=0; i<hlwf.getSegmentCount(); i++) {
            Segment s = hlwf.getSegment(i);
            g.drawLine((int)s.x1(),(int)s.y1(),(int)s.x2(),(int)s.y2());
        }
    }
    public void xPlus() {
        hlwf.rotateAroundX(rotationAngle);
        hlwf.segmentize();
        repaint();
    }
    public void xMinus() {
        hlwf.rotateAroundX(-rotationAngle);
        hlwf.segmentize();
```

```
                    repaint();
            }
            public void yPlus() {
                hlwf.rotateAroundY(rotationAngle);
                hlwf.segmentize();
                repaint();
            }
            public void yMinus() {
                hlwf.rotateAroundY(-rotationAngle);
                hlwf.segmentize();
                repaint();
            }
            public void zPlus() {
                hlwf.rotateAroundZ(rotationAngle);
                hlwf.segmentize();
                repaint();
            }
            public void zMinus() {
                hlwf.rotateAroundZ(-rotationAngle);
                hlwf.segmentize();
                repaint();
            }
            public void sPlus() {
                hlwf.scale(1.0 / scaleFactor);
                hlwf.segmentize();
                repaint();
            }
            public void sMinus() {
                hlwf.scale(scaleFactor);
                hlwf.segmentize();
                repaint();
            }
        }
    }
```

The Commentary

Figures 15.8 and 15.9 show the file tface.data rotated into a couple of different positions. The program is really quite simple. Most of the code is for responding to the buttons to scale or rotate the drawing. Whenever a button is pressed, the HiddenLineWireFrame is passed the rotation angle (or scale factor) causing the adjustments to be made. A call is then made to segmentize() to cause the HiddenLineWireFrame to create a new array of visible segments. After segmentize() is called, there is a call to repaint() causing the paint() method to retrieve and draw each of the line segments.

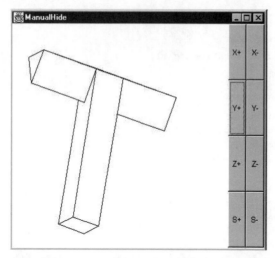

Figure 15.8   A rotation of the file tface.data.

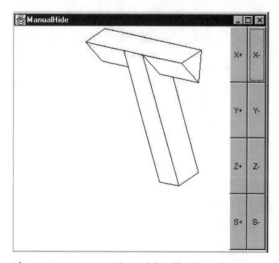

Figure 15.9   A rotation of the file tface.data.

AutoHide

This program continuously and randomly rotates and scales a wire frame object.

The syntax for running AutoHide is this:

```
java ManualHide tface.data
```

where `tface.data` is a data file that defines a three-dimensional shape.

The Code

```
import java.awt.*;
import java.awt.event.*;
class AutoHide extends Frame {
public static void main(String arg[]) {
if(arg.length != 1) {
System.out.println("Usage: AutoHide <filename>");
System.exit(1);
}
new AutoHide(arg[0]);
}
AutoHide(String fileName) {
super("AutoHide");
addWindowListener(new WindowAdapter() {
public void windowClosing(WindowEvent e)
{ System.exit(0); } } );
HiddenLineWireFrame hlwf = new HiddenLineWireFrame(fileName);
AutoHidePanel arPanel = new AutoHidePanel(hlwf);
add(arPanel);
pack();
show();
}
class AutoHidePanel extends Canvas implements Runnable {
private HiddenLineWireFrame hlwf;
private int pause = 30;
private Rectangle rectangle;
private Thread looper;
private Image image;

private final int REANGLE = 30;
private final int RESCALE = 21;
private int reangleCount = REANGLE;
private int rescaleCount = RESCALE;
private double scaleFactor = 0.93;

AutoHidePanel(HiddenLineWireFrame hlwf) {
this.hlwf = hlwf;
setSize((int)hlwf.maxDimension()+50,
(int)hlwf.maxDimension()+50);
rectangle = new Rectangle();
looper = new Thread(this);
looper.start();
}
public void run() {
try {
while(true) {
repaint();
Thread.sleep(pause);
}
```

```
    } finally {
    return;
    }
    }

    public void update(Graphics g) {
    if(looper.isAlive()) {
    if(!rectangle.equals(getBounds()) || (image == null)) {
    rectangle = getBounds();
    image = createImage(rectangle.width,rectangle.height);
    firstFrame();
    }
    if(nextFrame()) {
    paint(image.getGraphics());
    g.drawImage(image,0,0,null);
    }
    }
    }

    public void paint(Graphics g) {
    g.setColor(Color.white);
    g.fillRect(0,0,getSize().width,getSize().height);
    g.setColor(Color.black);
    for(int i=0; i<hlwf.getSegmentCount(); i++) {
    Segment s = hlwf.getSegment(i);
    g.drawLine((int)s.x1(),(int)s.y1(),(int)s.x2(),(int)s.y2());
    }
    }
    private void firstFrame() {
    hlwf.setRotationCenter(rectangle.width / 2,
    rectangle.height / 2,
    rectangle.width / 2);
    hlwf.setAngleX(0.02);
    hlwf.setAngleY(0.03);
    hlwf.setAngleZ(0.05);
    }
    private boolean nextFrame() {
    if(reangleCount-- < 0) {
    hlwf.setAngleX(0.08 * Math.random());
    hlwf.setAngleY(0.08 * Math.random());
    hlwf.setAngleZ(0.08 * Math.random());
    reangleCount = REANGLE;
    }
    if(rescaleCount-- < 0) {
    scaleFactor = 1.0 / scaleFactor;
    rescaleCount = RESCALE;
    }
    hlwf.scale(scaleFactor);
    hlwf.rotate();
```

```
hlwf.segmentize();
return(true);
}
}
}
```

The Commentary

This program is almost identical to AutoRotate. The only differences are that, instead of an AdjustableWireFrame, a HiddenLineWireFrame is used, and the drawing is done by segments instead of by edges. Figure 15.10 shows the file tface.data being rotated and scaled.

Figure 15.10 Continuous rotation and scaling with hidden lines.

CHAPTER 16

Perspective

W e look at things in the real world and, to an extent, determine how far away or close they are according to their size. A single object will have parts that are further away from us and thus appear smaller. Parallel lines will get closer and closer together as they get further away from us. This is called perspective.

Vanishing Points

Drawing in perspective can be achieved more than one way. The most common method used for drawing on a page is to establish one or more vanishing points, and use the points as guides to skew the drawn lines. An example of this is shown in Figure 16.1. As you can see, by having the lines converging on two points along the horizon, the eye is given the information it needs to place the cube in space.

Even though the procedure in Figure 16.1 is quite simple and intuitive, it turns out that it works better for pencil and paper than it does for computer graphics. To use the vanishing point method, it is necessary to establish a pair of points on the horizon and then, using triangulation, calculate the x and y coordinates of each point after they have been moved around to fit on the line coming from the pair of points.

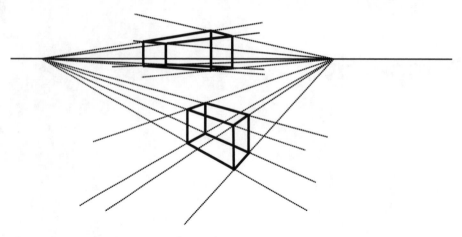

Figure 16.1 Boxes in space with vanishing points.

It turns out there is another method that makes the entire process very simple.

Screen Projection

Imagine that the object you want to draw is suspended in space inside your CRT, and you are looking at it through your screen, which is simply a glass window. If you draw a line in space from your eye to each point on the object being viewed, as shown in Figure 16.2, these lines will pass through the screen in such a way that they will be repositioned according to the depth perception of the eye. This screen image, or projection, shows us exactly where we want to paint the object. This is because a single point (your eye) is viewing multiple points (the object outline) and the lines all converge, from the object to your eye, in conical sort of arrangement.

Because we know the x and y coordinates of every point, and we can make up distances to the screen and the eye, it is very simple to calculate the x and y coordinates of each point on the projected image of the object. The calculations required are very simple.

In the coordinate system we are working with, the origin is in the far-back upper-left-hand corner of the virtual three-dimensional space inside the CRT. The values for x increase to the right, y increases going downward, and z increases as it comes out toward the screen and your eye. We know all the values describing the object—it is only necessary to get some values for location of the screen and your eye. These can be

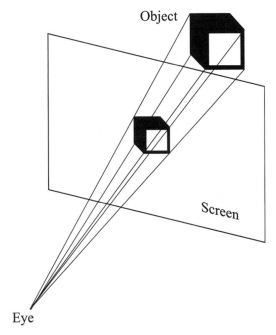

Object

Screen

Eye

Figure 16.2 Projecting a 3D object onto a 2D screen.

arbitrary, but modifying will modify the size and sharpness of the dimensional gradient. For example, if the eye is very close to the screen, the
object will become very small because the converging lines are very
close together when they pass through the screen. If the eye is very far
back, the object will appear closer to its full size, but there will be very
few dimensional effects because the distance from the front to the back
of the object is a very small percentage of the distance of the eye from
either the front or back of the object.

Once a z-axis value has been selected for the screen, and the three-
dimensional coordinates of the eye have been selected, it is just a matter
of plugging the values into a simple equation to calculate the location of
each point on the object. As we can see in the diagram in Figure 16.3,
which shows how to calculate the position of a single point, the information we need requires only the most fundamental relationships. The same
relationships can be used for both the x- and y-axis—one is vertical and
the other is horizontal. The value of a is the distance from the eye to the
point on the object. The value of b is the lateral distance (horizontal to calculate x and vertical to calculate y) from the point on the object to the eye.
On a similar triangle, the value e is the distance from the point to the
screen and f is the lateral distance to the screen position of the point.

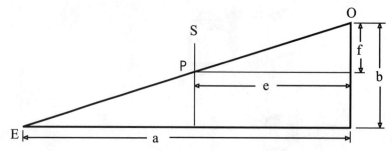

Figure 16.3 The relationship of the object point to the screen point.

The relationship of these values is simply this:

$$\frac{b}{a} = \frac{f}{e}$$

And, because simple subtraction will give us all the values except f, this is the form we need:

$$f = \frac{e\,b}{a}$$

We use this principle in deriving a new kind of wire frame class.

PerspectiveWireFrame

This class is an extension of the AdjustableWireFrame class to add perspective to the wire frame object being displayed.

The Code

```
public class PerspectiveWireFrame extends AdjustableWireFrame {
    private Vertex[] pVertex = null;
    private double eyeX;
    private double eyeY;
    private double eyeZ;
    private double screenZ;
    PerspectiveWireFrame(String fileName) {
        super(fileName);
        screenZ = maxDimension() + 50;
        eyeX = 0;
        eyeY = 0;
        eyeZ = 2*screenZ;
        pVertex = new Vertex[vertex.length];
        makePerspectiveVector();
    }
    public Vertex getVertexByID(int ID) {
```

```
            if(ID > largestVertexID)
                return(defaultVertex);
            return(pVertex[ID]);
        }
        public void setView(double eyeX,double eyeY,double eyeZ,double
    screenZ) {
            this.eyeX = eyeX;
            this.eyeY = eyeY;
            this.eyeZ = eyeZ;
            this.screenZ = screenZ;
        }
        public void scale(double scaleFactor) {
            super.scale(scaleFactor);
            makePerspectiveVector();
        }
        public void rotate() {
            super.rotate();
            makePerspectiveVector();
        }
        public void rotateAroundX(double angle) {
            super.rotateAroundX(angle);
            makePerspectiveVector();
        }
        public void rotateAroundY(double angle) {
            super.rotateAroundY(angle);
            makePerspectiveVector();
        }
        public void rotateAroundZ(double angle) {
            super.rotateAroundZ(angle);
            makePerspectiveVector();
        }
        private void makePerspectiveVector() {
            double delta;
            double dx;
            double dy;
            for(int i=0; i<vertex.length; i++) {
                delta = screenZ - vertex[i].z;
                delta /= eyeZ - vertex[i].z;
                dx = delta * (eyeX - vertex[i].x);
                dy = delta * (eyeY - vertex[i].y);
                pVertex[i] = new Vertex(vertex[i].ID,
                    vertex[i].x+dx,vertex[i].y+dy,screenZ);
            }
        }
    }
```

The Commentary

This class extends its parent class and adds only the perspective calculations. The parent class makes adjustments to the points (for rotation

and scaling) and keeps the adjusted points in an array of Vertex objects. Other classes access the Vertex values through the method getVertexByID(). To be able to extend the class to make some other adjustments, it is necessary to overload the key methods to perform the local actions. It will also be necessary to invoke the methods of the superclass so the normal adjustments will take place.

The constructor calls the constructor of the superclass so the data file is loaded. It then sets some default values for the location of the eye and the screen. The screen is placed 50 virtual pixels in front of the largest dimension defined for the object. This way, no matter what the rotation, the object should remain behind the screen. The eye is positioned directly in front of the origin at twice the distance the screen is from the origin. This should put everything in order and in some semblance of a reasonable relationship. There is the method setView() that can be used to set the locations for screen and eye.

By the way, if all or part of the object passes through the screen, everything still works okay, but if the eye gets inside the object, the points start flying all around and behind the viewer, and spend lots of time in areas where they can't actually be seen. Looking from inside an object that you can only see in one direction makes the shape really hard to discern.

The method makePerspectiveVector() creates a local array of Vertex objects from the one in the parent class. When this method is called, it is assumed that the parent has adjusted the Vertex points in the array and they are ready for display. It is this method that applies the projection equation that places the points into their projected location. There is a loop that maps each Vertex, one at a time. This is the equation developed earlier, and it is applied once in the x-axis direction and once in the y-axis direction. Some intermediate values (the ones in the variable named delta) are used for both instead of being calculated twice. Because the new Vertex objects are simply aliases of the ones in the other array, they are given the same ID numbers.

The method getVertexByID() simply overrides the same method in the parent class. This is the only method by which the Vertex array can be accessed, so replacing the returned Vertex with a local one is a simple matter.

The other methods are scale(), rotate(), rotateAroundX(), rotateAroundY(), and rotateAroundZ(). These all override methods of the parent class just so there will be a call made to makePerspectiveVector() every time the Vertex values are adjusted.

With these overloadings, this class can be used anywhere the AdjustableWireFrame class can be used and the only difference will be the perspective adjustment to the Vertex values.

AutoPerspective

This application loads data from a wire frame file and randomly rotates it around all three axes. The wire frame is drawn in perspective on the display.

The Code

```java
import java.awt.*;
import java.awt.event.*;
class AutoPerspective extends Frame
        implements ActionListener {
    private TextField eyeXText;
    private TextField eyeYText;
    private TextField eyeZText;
    private TextField screenZText;
    private PerspectivePanel pPanel;
    public static void main(String arg[]) {
        if(arg.length != 1) {
            System.out.println("Usage: AutoPerspective <filename>");
            System.exit(1);
        }
        new AutoPerspective(arg[0]);
    }
    AutoPerspective(String fileName) {
        super("AutoPerspective");
        addWindowListener(new WindowAdapter() {
            public void windowClosing(WindowEvent e)
                { System.exit(0); } } );
        setLayout(new BorderLayout());
        PerspectiveWireFrame pFrame = new PerspectiveWireFrame(fileName);
        pPanel = new PerspectivePanel(pFrame);
        add("Center",pPanel);
        add("South",makeAdjustmentPanel());
        pack();
        show();
    }
    private Panel makeAdjustmentPanel() {
        Button button;
        Panel p = new Panel();
```

```
            p.setLayout(new GridLayout(2,5));
            eyeXText = new TextField(pPanel.getEyeXString());
            p.add(eyeXText);
            eyeYText = new TextField(pPanel.getEyeYString());
            p.add(eyeYText);
            eyeZText = new TextField(pPanel.getEyeZString());
            p.add(eyeZText);
            screenZText = new TextField(pPanel.getScreenZString());
            p.add(screenZText);
            button = new Button("Set");
            button.addActionListener(this);
            p.add(button);
            p.add(new Label("eyeX",Label.CENTER));
            p.add(new Label("eyeY",Label.CENTER));
            p.add(new Label("eyeZ",Label.CENTER));
            p.add(new Label("screenZ",Label.CENTER));
            button = new Button("Defaults");
            button.addActionListener(this);
            p.add(button);
            return(p);
        }
        public void actionPerformed(ActionEvent event) {
            if(event.getActionCommand().equals("Set")) {
                pPanel.setView(
                    Integer.parseInt(eyeXText.getText()),
                    Integer.parseInt(eyeYText.getText()),
                    Integer.parseInt(eyeZText.getText()),
                    Integer.parseInt(screenZText.getText()));
                setTextFields();
            } else if(event.getActionCommand().equals("Defaults")) {
                pPanel.setDefaults();
                setTextFields();
            }
        }
        private void setTextFields() {
            eyeXText.setText(pPanel.getEyeXString());
            eyeYText.setText(pPanel.getEyeYString());
            eyeZText.setText(pPanel.getEyeZString());
            screenZText.setText(pPanel.getScreenZString());
        }
    class PerspectivePanel extends Canvas implements Runnable {
        private PerspectiveWireFrame frame;
        private int pause = 100;
        private Rectangle rectangle;
        private Thread looper;
        private Image image;

        private int side;
        private int eyeX;
        private int eyeY;
        private int eyeZ;
        private int screenZ;
```

```java
    private final int REANGLE = 30;
    private int reangleCount = REANGLE;

    PerspectivePanel(PerspectiveWireFrame frame) {
        this.frame = frame;
        side = (int)frame.maxDimension() + 50;
        setSize(side,side);
        setDefaults();
        rectangle = new Rectangle();
        looper = new Thread(this);
        looper.start();
    }
    public void setDefaults() {
        eyeX = side / 2;
        eyeY = side / 2;
        eyeZ = side + (side / 2);
        screenZ = side;
        frame.setView(eyeX,eyeY,eyeZ,screenZ);
    }
    public void setView(float eX,float eY,float eZ,float sZ) {
        eyeX = (int)eX;
        eyeY = (int)eY;
        eyeZ = Math.max((int)sZ,Math.max((int)eZ,side));
        screenZ = Math.max((int)sZ,side);
        frame.setView(eyeX,eyeY,eyeZ,screenZ);
    }
    public String getEyeXString() {
        return(Integer.toString(eyeX));
    }
    public String getEyeYString() {
        return(Integer.toString(eyeY));
    }
    public String getEyeZString() {
        return(Integer.toString(eyeZ));
    }
    public String getScreenZString() {
        return(Integer.toString(screenZ));
    }
    public void run() {
        try {
            while(true) {
                repaint();
                Thread.sleep(pause);
            }
        } finally {
            return;
        }
    }

    public void update(Graphics g) {
        if(looper.isAlive()) {
            if(!rectangle.equals(getBounds()) || (image == null)) {
```

```
                rectangle = getBounds();
                image = createImage(rectangle.width,rectangle.height);
                firstFrame();
            }
            if(nextFrame()) {
                paint(image.getGraphics());
                g.drawImage(image,0,0,null);
            }
        }
    }

    public void paint(Graphics g) {
        g.setColor(Color.white);
        g.fillRect(0,0,getSize().width,getSize().height);
        g.setColor(Color.black);
        for(int i=0; i<frame.getEdgeCount(); i++) {
            Edge e = frame.getEdge(i);
            Vertex v1 = frame.getVertexByID(e.vertexID1);
            Vertex v2 = frame.getVertexByID(e.vertexID2);
            g.drawLine((int)v1.x,(int)v1.y,(int)v2.x,(int)v2.y);
        }
    }
    private void firstFrame() {
        frame.setRotationCenter((float)(rectangle.width / 2),
                (float)(rectangle.height / 2),
                (float)(rectangle.width / 2));
        frame.setAngleX(0.02f);
        frame.setAngleY(0.03f);
        frame.setAngleZ(0.05f);
    }
    private boolean nextFrame() {
        if(reangleCount-- < 0) {
            frame.setAngleX((float)(0.08 * Math.random()));
            frame.setAngleY((float)(0.08 * Math.random()));
            frame.setAngleZ((float)(0.08 * Math.random()));
            reangleCount = REANGLE;
        }
        frame.rotate();
        return(true);
    }
    }
    }
```

The Commentary

This program is similar to AutoRotate, presented in Chapter 14. This program uses the same techniques for rotating a wire frame in three-dimensional space.

There are two parts to the display window—a Canvas is used to draw the object and a Panel is used to hold the collection of text fields and push buttons. There are four values that can be entered. There are the x, y, and z coordinates of the location of the eye and the z coordinate used to position the screen. There are some limitations placed on the positioning. The screen must be positioned at or beyond the end of the object, and the eye must be positioned at or beyond the screen. These limitations are imposed in the method setView(). There is another method, setDefaults(), that is used to set the positions.

Figures 16.4 and 16.5 show a couple of views of the rotating object defined in tbar.data. As it rotates, it appears to get larger and smaller, but there is no scaling being done on the drawing—the size results from the perspective of the object being closer or farther away. The default values seem to be the ones that are most intuitive to the eye. That is, with the settings shown in Figure 16.4 the object looks about right as it moves around the screen.

As the eye is moved farther away from the screen, as shown in Figure 16.6, the object flattens out and takes on less of a perspective appearance. This is true in the real world also—things seen from a great distance appear flat. You will notice that in Figure 16.6 the screen was left at its original position. This gives the object its size. Moving the screen back and forth has no effect on the degree of perspective appearance,

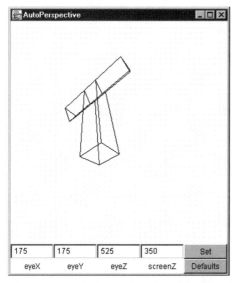

Figure 16.4 A view using the default settings.

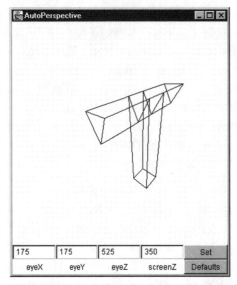

Figure 16.5 Another view using the default settings.

but it does change the size of the object being viewed—the farther away the screen moves, the smaller the object appears. So, to simulate the real world, it is necessary to move back and forth with the eye along the z-axis.

As the eye approaches the screen, the perspective appearance of the object becomes more enhanced. Figure 16.7 shows the eye moved closer to the screen, and the object appears greatly elongated as if it comes close to the viewer and extends much farther into the distance. You can

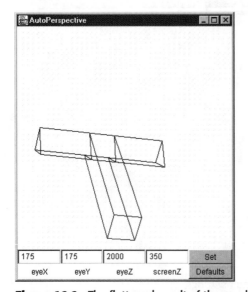

Figure 16.6 The flattened result of the eye being moved far away.

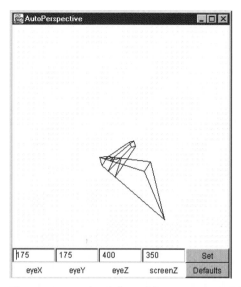

Figure 16.7 The enhanced perspective with the eye close to the screen.

experiment with the eye, moving it closer and closer to the screen, and you will see the object appear to dart rapidly toward and away from the screen as the distance along the z-axis is enhanced.

It is possible to move the eye to a location other than the window, but it can make the appearance of the perspective of the object confusing. Figure 16.8 shows the eye being moved to the upper-left-hand corner of the screen. The projection on the screen, then, is as if it were being viewed

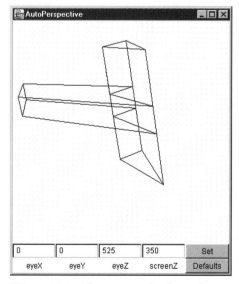

Figure 16.8 The perspective from the upper-left-hand corner.

from the corner instead of the direction you are in as a viewer. The perspective becomes a bit skewed—it still makes some sense, but the object appears misshapen.

CHAPTER 17

Exploring the Advanced Imaging API

The Advanced Imaging API is designed to provide a standard set of Java tools for creating, displaying, and manipulating the sorts of images required by medical technicians, scientists, professional photographers, and others whose imaging needs exceed the capabilities of core Java. Sun Microsystems developed the Advanced Imaging API in cooperation with several imaging-centric companies like Eastman Kodak and Siemens, and the result is that the resources it provides are not garden-variety GIF and JPEG display utilities.

The Advanced Imaging API enables you to implement such image-manipulation services as selecting an area of interest, manipulating the color distribution in an image (via histograms), managing time-sequential images, networking images, and generally adjusting the appearance of raster images through such operations as focusing and softening. Further, the Advanced Imaging API provides support for many more image formats than does standard Java. The Advanced Imaging API also supports images of infinitely large size, in theory.

Further, the Advanced Imaging API allows for deferred execution, giving software developers considerable flexibility in optimizing the performance of the programs they create. It also allows the developer to make decisions regarding memory use, performance, and hardware acceleration, making it possible to trade something in plentiful supply (like memory, perhaps) for something that's needed (like speedy performance).

Perhaps best of all, the Advanced Imaging API is designed to be eminently expandable and extensible. If a tool you need isn't present in the API, or if a data format you need to work with isn't supported, it's possible to define your own classes and expect them to be granted the same authority as those that are part of the standard Advanced Imaging API. If you plan to work with unusual or specialized imaging tools, you'll be happy to hear about this ease of extensibility. There's been considerable excitement on the Java imaging newsgroups and mailing lists regarding the use of this API in medical imaging applications.

For instance, Sun expects that the Advanced Imaging API will enable Java programmers someday to write software for a magnetic resonance imaging (MRI) machine. Such software might need to recognize and highlight key anatomical structures. Alternately, it could be used to write image-enhancement routines for surveillance cameras, or to create informative graphical representations of scientific data. Basically, if you're running up against a problem that involves pixels and you can't seem to solve it with the standard Java classes, you need to take a look at the Advanced Imaging API.

NOTE

The Advanced Imaging API isn't very far along the path to usefulness at this point—we based this chapter upon a preview release. That's why there's not as much illustrative code and informed commentary here as we would like. So it goes, here on the Planet of Shaky Preview Releases. Mainly, we've relied upon Sun's Advanced Imaging API White Paper and other advance documentation from Sun.

No doubt, like every piece of Java, the Advanced Imaging API will experience changes, both subtle and dramatic, as imaging experts scrutinize it and Sun makes alterations. When you read this, the Advanced Imaging API may be substantially different from what we've written about here. That's why you need to visit the JavaSoft site for the latest news and information. References to that site and other recommended resources appear at the end of this chapter.

How It Fits into Java

The Advanced Imaging API is a standard Java extension library, and is not part of any core Java distribution. Therefore, if you are going to write programs that take advantage of the Advanced Imaging API, you'll have to make sure it's installed on the user's computer. For this reason, the Advanced Imaging API probably won't find much use in applets and applications for public consumption. It will prove more useful in custom vertical applications that will run repeatedly on particular workstations.

Essentially, the Advanced Imaging API is designed to be extended—more on that later. You'd be hard-pressed to write a Java version of Adobe Photoshop without writing a lot of extensions and modifications to the Advanced Imaging API base. It seems likely that as the Advanced Imaging API develops and propagates among programmers and imaging experts, Sun and third-party development houses will come up with less abstract imaging libraries that can in turn be used to create powerful imaging applications.

Design Goals

Sun's stated objectives for the Advanced Imaging API—which was in preliminary preview release at the time of this writing—include broader image format support, extreme simplicity of design that facilitates extensibility, and design flexibility that enables programmers to adapt to various operating environments and conditions.

Broader Image Format Support

Java long has supported GIF and JPEG image files—these are the most popular image file formats on the Internet. But GIF and JPEG are severely limited in their capabilities. There's a demand in the imaging community for broader image file format support. The Advanced Imaging API attempts to satisfy this demand.

Simplicity and Extensibility

Programmers are paid to solve problems, and frequently ideas about what is elegant and what is professionally correct—no matter that such ideas frequently do derive from efficiency studies—get cast aside when there's an urgent problem. Lots of programmers will neglect to create efficient inheritance schemes, for example, because they're not always the most intuitive things.

Imaging problems are no exception—they're complicated and often programmers will solve them by whatever means seems most expedient. Sun's goals for the Advanced Imaging API include a very simple design, the framework of which is very easy to comprehend. The theory is that such simplicity will encourage programmers to write their own reusable imaging libraries rather than manipulate pixels in brute-force assaults on particular problems.

Further, Sun claims that the Advanced Imaging API will be extensible with varying degrees of complexity. Stronger programmers will be able to extend deeper, more abstract classes, and less-skilled programmers (and perhaps visual development environments) will be able to extend more refined classes that handle more internally. It remains to be seen whether Sun's plans for the extensibility will work out as planned or not.

Design Flexibility

Imaging applications tend to be hungry for resources—raster images are made up of pixels, which are numerous almost by definition. Each pixel, of course, has its own brood of bits that define its characteristics, including color and transparency.

Sun's engineers want to make it possible for programmers to trade memory use for processing power and processing power for feature richness. This triangular arrangement of resources is nothing new to programmers, and the Advanced Imaging API should make it possible to find more than one way to accomplish some task. With a selection of solutions available for a given problem, you ought to be able to find one that meets your design criteria, whether you're short on memory, long on processor power, or whatever.

Reviewing AWT Image Processing

Under the AWT, image manipulation can be compared to the editing of text streams. There's an image source and an image sink, and images "flow" from the source to the sink. Filtering—image modification—can take place on the way from source to sink, just as stream-oriented text editors like sed can alter character patterns as the characters flow in a stream from one file to another.

Under the AWT, image sources implement the ImageProducer interface. Image sinks implement the ImageConsumer interface. Filters, like physical devices that fit into pipes, take a stream in one end and output it from the other end. Therefore, filtering objects that modify images en route from source to sink implement both ImageConsumer and ImageProducer interfaces—they undertake both functions. When the image data has passed through all the appropriate filters, it's fed into an Image object, which contains the data for display (or further filtering, if necessary).

To render an Image object on a monitor or other output device, the program must instantiate a Graphics object, which incorporates information about the physical device to which the image data are to be written. The method Image.getGraphics() does this. Then, the method Graphics.drawImage() handles the actual rendering of the image data on the output device. The AWT also supports ImageObserver classes, which can be used to monitor the progress of raster data from their various sources to their various sinks.

This is an efficient and easy to comprehend system of getting image data to an output device. The trouble here, as with many simple systems, is that the AWT's imaging capabilities are limited. There's no way, for example, to identify a piece of an image as a "region of interest." Being able to do that is key to image-editing routines and programs that perform, say, edge detection. It's also not possible for an image sink to send out a request for image data—it's dependent upon image sources sending information to it.

Although this system works reasonably well for online applets and applications that simulate the behavior of Web browsers, it's not well suited to more difficult tasks. Java programmers who want to manipulate images with a finer degree of control require better technology—technology that the Java2D classes provide to a limited degree.

Comparing Java2D Imaging

Java2D's imaging additions to the AWT—they're not really separate entities anymore, since Java2D's imaging facilities are a subset of the AWT—are important but few in number. Essentially, the Java2D scheme sticks to the source/sink arrangement.

Persistent Image Objects

However, where the old AWT system didn't have any facilities for persistent image data, Java2D allows for persistent allocation of memory to contain graphic information in the form of an Image object. Java2D also adds better color modeling, better means of defining graphics hardware capabilities, improved filtering, and broader image format support.

Separating the Abstract from Its Representation

Importantly, Java2D supports what's called *rendering independence* or *resolution independence*. These terms refer to a system in which images can be conceptualized and manipulated in the abstract, before the real-world constraints of output devices are considered, for example. The process is similar to the mind of an artist who is thinking about his next painting. He imagines a landscape, say, that brings to mind the conflict between good and evil and the vastness of eternity. He can imagine the scene all he wants, but at some point he must translate his abstract idea into a physical object made of canvas and paint. The physical object must have absolute dimensions, and it must fall within the realm of what it is physically possible to build. The artist, no matter how grand his vision, could not paint a canvas a mile tall or construct a sculpture that defies the law of gravity. His vision is theoretically unlimited, but his means of implementing his vision is constrained by a variety of factors.

Java2D enables you to separate the abstract from the concrete. One of the key benefits of this is that your programs can be less hardware-dependent than they might otherwise be—your image-filtering logic can be separate from your rendering logic. In theory, any abstract image information you send to a rendering device will be depicted as attractively as possible on that device.

Renderable versus Rendered

Java2D refers to the abstract, "processable" image information objects as *renderable*, and context-specific image information objects as *rendered*.

How the Advanced Imaging API Differs

This section introduces some of the features that distinguish the Advanced Imaging API from its predecessors. With a few key additions, the Advanced Imaging API is much the same as standard AWT and Java2D imaging, so there's no need to drop everything and relearn. Furthermore, many Advanced Imaging API methods can be used to alter any object that implements the RenderedImage interface.

The old source-and-sink model doesn't apply under the Advanced Imaging API, though. Rather, this more advanced system employs a "pull" scheme in which an image sink requests image data—which may represent an entire raster image or just a portion of one, making region selection and area masking possible.

Multiple Sources

The Advanced Imaging API supports image processing on a network, as in the case of a powerful server computer working with a number of relatively weak clients. By taking advantage of Remote Method Invocation (RMI) features that are integrated into the Advanced Imaging API, it's possible to take image data from one machine, process it on another machine, and otherwise distribute processing chores across the processors in a networked environment.

Regions of Interest

Every image-editing application features a selection routine—a way to indicate that the user is working with *this* area of the image and not *that* one. The programs' back ends have ways to work with specific regions, too. Those regions are called regions of interest (ROI). The Advanced Imaging API includes the ROIShape class, which enables you to superimpose a shape—a Java2D Shape object—on an image. You can then manipulate the ROI with transforms, or apply image-manipulating operators to the area inside or outside the ROI border shape.

Image Property Management

The Advanced Imaging API supports image properties, which are objects associated with an image and identified by a unique name. You might use properties, for example, to hold information about brightness and contrast operations that have been performed on an original image, or even to hold copyright data associated with an image's owner.

Potential Future Improvements

The final release of the Advanced Imaging API may include some additional features that weren't covered much, if at all, in early versions of the API. These features probably will include the following, though they may not see the light of day until future versions of the Advanced Imaging API come out.

- Three-dimensional imaging
- Image collections and sequences
- Custom coordinate mapping and transformation
- Image compression and decompression

Advanced Imaging API Resources

Looking for more information on the Advanced Imaging API? Take a look at these resources on the network:

- The Java Advanced Imaging API Home Page (http://java.sun.com/products/java-media/jai/index.html)
- The Java Advanced Imaging API Interest Group (http://java.sun.com:81/products/java-media/jai/forDevelopers/interest_group.html)
- The Java Advanced Imaging API FAQ (http://java.sun.com:81/products/java-media/jai/forDevelopers/jaifaq.html)
- The Java Advanced Imaging API White Paper (http://java.sun.com/products/java-media/jai/jai-wp.pdf)
- JavaOne 1998 presentation: "Java Advanced Imaging API: Extensible Imaging for the Java Platform" (http://java.sun.com/javaone/javaone98/sessions/T605/)

What's on the CD-ROM?

The CD-ROM that accompanies this book contains all the programs you read about in these pages, in source and compiled forms.

We've organized the files into directories named after the chapters. The files that have to do with Chapter 5, for example, appear in the folder named Chapter5. All the chapter folders are in the Chapters folder, so the Chapter 5 material appears in the Chapters/Chapter5 directory.

If a program or other file is used in multiple chapters, a copy of the program appears in all the relevant directories.

In addition to the software written for this book, you'll find a copy of Java-Soft's Java Development Kit, version 1.2 (JDK 1.2) for Microsoft Windows. The JDK installation file appears in the folder named JDK1.2.

Hardware Requirements

The Java Development Kit works well on any computer that isn't strained by running Windows 95, Windows 98, or any version of Windows NT 4.0.

On a Windows 95 or Windows 98 machine, you'll want a Pentium 90 MHz or better processor, 16 MB or more of RAM, and 50 MB or more free hard disk space. On a Windows NT machine, the same specifications apply, though you'll want at least 32 MB of RAM.

Installing the Software

To install the JDK, follow these steps:

1. Start Windows on your computer.
2. Place the CD-ROM into your CD-ROM drive.
3. From Program Manager, Select File,Run, and type **X:\SETUP** (where **X** is the correct letter of your CD-ROM drive).
4. Follow the screen prompts to complete the installation.

You may find that you need to modify your AUTOEXEC.BAT file in order for the JDK to work properly.

Add this line to AUTOEXEC.BAT:

```
CLASSPATH .;C:\jdk1.2\bin
```

where C:\jdk1.2 is the folder in which you installed the JDK.

User Assistance and Information

You can get help with the JDK from JavaSoft, on the Web at http://www.javasoft.com. You may have better luck with the participants in various Java newsgroups. If you have a question for the authors, contact Arthur Griffith (arthur@xyz.net) or David Wall (david@davidwall.com).

Other than that, the software accompanying this book is being provided as is, without warranty or support of any kind. Should you require basic installation assistance, or if your media is defective, please call our product support number at (212) 850-6194 weekdays between 9 A.M. and 4 P.M. Eastern Standard Time. Or we can be reached via e-mail at: wprtusw@wiley.com.

To place additional orders or to request information about other Wiley products, please call (800) 879-4539.

A

Abstract/representation, separation, 362

Acyclical color gradient, 45–48
  code, 46–47
  commentary, 47–48

add() method, 136

addAttribute() method, 157

addEdge() method, 278

addFace() method, 278

addHole() method, 272

addTriangle() method, 278

addVertex() method, 278

addVertexID() method, 272

Adjustable wire frame, 283–286
  code, 283–285
  commentary, 285–286

AdjustableWireFrame, 290, 341
  class, 326
  object, 289

Adjustment Listener, 36

Advanced Imaging API, 19. *See also* Java.
  design flexibility, 360
  design goals, 359–360
  differences, 362–364
  future improvements, 364
  image format support, 359
  interest regions, 363
  multiple sources, 363
  resources, 364
  simplicity/extensibility, 359–360

Advanced imaging API, 357

Affine transformations, 12

AffineTransform, 29–31, 59, 60, 96, 99,
    105, 110, 111, 130, 154, 159, 166–168,
    192, 230, 237, 263, 265, 321, 322
  class, 26, 55–57
  object, 24, 26, 61, 69, 77, 112, 150,
    153, 265

Affinity, 26

Alpha-channel values, 21

Alpha component, 241
AlphaComposite
  class, 247
  object, 21, 246
Alpha values, 249, 250
Animation, performing, 169
Anti-aliasing, 19, 230
append() method, 130, 132
Arc2D, 127
  class, 108
  object, 108
arcAngle, 210
ArcFillDraw, 110
Arcs
  102-105
  code, 102–104
  commentary, 105
Arcs, scaling, 105–108
  code, 105–107
  commentary, 108
Arcs2D.Float class, 102
ArcScale, 110
Area averaging images, scaling, 217–219
  code, 217–218
  commentary, 218–219
Area filling, texture usage, 49–51
  code, 49–50
  commentary, 50–51
Area object. *See* Java2D.
  usage. *See* Shapes combination.
ASCII files, 182
Asymmetrical cubic curves, 119–121
  code, 120–121
  commentary, 121
Asymmetrical quadratic curves,
    drawing, 115–117
  code, 115–116
  commentary, 116–117
attach() method, 127
AttributedString, 157

AutoHide, 338–341
  code, 339–341
  commentary, 341
Automatic rotator, 286–291
  code, 286–288
  commentary, 289–291
AutoPerspective, 349–356
  code, 349–352
  commentary, 352–356
AutoRotate, 341, 352
  class, 289
AutoRotatePanel, 289
AWT, 18
  image processing, 360–361

B

Bar graph, 205–209
  code, 205–207
  commentary, 207–208
BarPanel, 207
BasicStroke, 89, 92
  line style, 81
  objects, 20, 79, 83
Bevelled corners. *See* Wide lines.
Bezier curves, 4
BezierPath, 20
  object, 17
Bicubic algorithm, 230
Bilinear algorithm, 230
Bitmapped images, 211
  rendering, 11–12
brighter(), 42
BufferedImage, 50, 51, 226, 241, 244,
    245, 249
  object, 12, 49, 50, 225
Buffering, 12
Butted line endings. *See* Wide lines.

C

Canvas, 176, 192, 253, 353

class, 191, 251
object, 147, 207
window, 149
Caps, 5–6
CGM file-reader, 211
Characters, 10
Checkboxes, 238
CIEXYZ color model, 13
Circularity, 64–65
    code, 64–65
    commentary, 65
Circularity2, 66–68, 67
    code, 66–67
    commentary, 67–68
CircularPlacement, 68–70
    code, 68—69
    commentary, 69–70
Clipping, 170
closePath()
    method, 94, 133
    statements, 80
CMYK color model, 13
Color, 7, 12–13
    conversion, 12
    definition, 13
    fills, 19
    handling, 33
    model. *See* CIEXYZ color model;
        CMYK color model; RGB color
        model.
Color display
    code, 39
    commentary, 40
    graphics object usage, 38–40
Color gradient, 42–45, 47. *See also*
    Acyclical color gradient; Cyclical
    color gradient; Diagonal color
    gradient.
    code, 42–43
    commentary, 43–44

Color objects, 36, 38, 40–42. *See also*
    Predefined color objects.
    code, 34–35
    commentary, 35–36
    creation, RGB values usage, 33–36
ColorCanvas
    class, 35
    object, 38
ColorModel, 222
combine(), 314
compareTo() method, 299
Complex fills, 20
CompositeContext interfaces, 21
Compositing, 21, 241–247. *See also*
    Images.
    code, 241–244
    commentary, 244–247
    constructor, 244
CompositingPanel, 244
computerTo() method, 270
Constructor, 140, 271, 303, 307, 313
CONTRAST matrix, 229
Convolution, 12
ConvolveOp, 225
    class, 226
    filters, 226
    object, 225
Convolving, 222–230
    code, 223–225
    commentary, 225–230
Coordinate mapping/transformation,
    364
Coordinate plane, 55. *See* Two-
    dimensional coordinate plane; User
    Coordinate Plane.
Coordinate points, 76
Coordinate spaces, 16–17. *See also*
    Device coordinate space; User
    coordinate space.
Coordinates, 23, 24

Coordinates, *Continued*
  circular movement, rotation usage, 27
  straight line movement, translation
    usage, 27
  understanding, 23
Corners. *See* Mitered corners.
createBackground(), 244
createEdge() method, 249
createPointChoice(), 146
createTransform(), 167
Cross fading, transparency usage,
    247–250
  code, 248–249
  commentary, 249–250
CrossFadePanel object, 249
Cube. *See* Oblique cube-like thing.
Cubic curves. *See* Asymmetrical cubic
    curves; Double cubic curve;
    Symmetric cubic curves.
CubicCurve2D, 117, 119, 127
CubicCurve2.java, 121
CubicCurve3, 123
CubicCurve.Float class, 121
Cursor objects, 261
cursorTypeArray, 261
Curves. *See* Asymmetrical cubic curves;
    Double cubic curve; Quadratic
    curves; Symmetric cubic curves.
  drawing. *See* Asymmetrical quadratic
    curves.
  fitting, 93
curveTo() method, 132
Cyclical color gradient, 48–49
  code, 48
  commentary, 48–49
CyclicGradient.class, 48
CyclicGradient.java, 48

D

darker(), 42

Dash array, 88, 90
Dash pattern, 88
Dashed lines, 87–89
  code, 87–88
  commentary, 88–89
Data files, reading, 182–185
  code, 182–185
  commentary, 185
Data item, 205. *See* Single data item.
Data stream, 182
Default stroke, 81–82
  code, 81
  commentary, 81–82
defaultVertex, 278
Degrees, 31
deriveFont() methods, 147
Device Coordinate Plane, 17
Device Coordinate Space, 17–19
Diagonal color gradient, 44–45
  code, 44
  commentary, 45
DisplayImage, 212
DisplayImagePanel class, 214
Double cubic curve, 121–124
  code, 122–123
  commentary, 123–124
Dragging. *See* Locating/dragging.
draw() method, 98, 100, 110, 119, 129,
    154, 193
drawChars(), 149
drawImage(), 162
Drawing figures, dashes, 89–92
  code, 89–90, 91–92
  commentary, 90, 92
drawLine() method, 55, 57
Drawn letters, 158–160
  code, 158–159
  commentary, 159–160
Drawn letters II, 160–162
  code, 161–162

commentary, 162
drawString(), 150, 157
Dynamic resizing, 166–168
    code, 166–167
    commentary, 167–168
Dynamic ZigZag, 98–100
    code, 98–99
    commentary, 99–100

E

Edge class, 278
Edge objects, 270, 273
Edge of a shape. *See* Shape edge.
Edges, 274, 328
Electrons, 177–180
    code, 177–179
    commentary, 179–180
Ellipse2D, 4, 127, 135
    object, 80
EllipseAround, 111
Ellipses, 2, 3, 111–112
    class, 102
    code, 111–112
    commentary, 112
enableEvents() method, 55, 57, 59
Endpoints, 296, 303
Ends. *See* Squared ends.
EPSILON value, 314
Equations/matrixes, 25–26
Events, sequence, 62
exclusiveOr() method, 136
Execution loop, 77
expandingText(), 158

F

Face class, 278
Face object, 325, 333
Faces, 137, 274, 333
False arguments, 130
Figure size change, scaling usage, 28

File, shape description, 273–274
fill() method, 43, 50, 93, 98, 102, 105,
    110, 125, 154, 166, 195
Fills. *See* Colors; Complex fills;
    Textures.
FillTrace, 196
FillTrace2, 196
filter() method, 225
FilteredImageSource object, 221
Filtering, 360, 361
firstFrame(), 173, 180
firstFrame() method, 321
FollowMousePanel, 253
Font, 9, 11, 18, 137, 141–143
    code, 141
    commentary, 141–143
Font families, 138–141
    code, 138–139
    commentary, 139–141
Font names, 145
Font objects, 141
fontArray, 146
FontChoice(), 146
FontDemoCanvas, 147
FontRenderContext, 150, 153, 159
Fonts showing, 143–147
    code, 143–145
    commentary, 145–147
fragment() method, 313
Frame, 225
    class, 40
FrameTriangleCanvas, 333

G

gc(), 185
GeneralPath, 96, 127, 132, 133, 165, 193,
    195, 199, 208
    class, 94
    object, 4, 80, 93, 127, 129, 130, 132,
        162, 165, 307, 326

GeneralPath, *Continued*
usage. *See* Rectangle building.
GeneralShape, 130
object, 160
GenPath object, usage. *See* Shapes
appending.
getAllFonts(), 141, 146
getAlphaRaster() method, 245
getBasicStroke() method, 190
getBounds() method, 154
getColor() method, 190
getCommonVertexCount(), 305
getComponents() method, 222
getFloat(), 185
getFontRenderingContext() method,
153
getGeneralPath(), 190, 195, 199
getHole() method, 272
getImage() method, 165, 213
getInteger(), 185
getIterator(), 157
getOutline() method, 154, 160
getPredefinedCursor(), 261
getScaledImages(), 216
getScaledInstance() method, 218
getSegment() method, 328
getSegmentCount() method, 328
getShapeArray(), 81
getSource() method, 221
getTokenType() method, 185
getVertexByID() method, 348
getVertexCount() method, 272
getVisibleSegments() method, 308, 313
GIF display utilities, 357
GIF files, 19, 211, 213
GIF image files, 359
Glyphs, 10, 11, 137, 138
GlyphSet, 11
GlyphVector, 150
Gradient fills, 7–8

GradientPaint
constructor, 48
object, 43, 44
Graphics environment, 13
Graphics hardware support, 13–14
Graphics object, 40, 94
usage. *See* Color display.
Graphics2D, 81, 119, 157
class, 96
object, 42, 43, 77, 89, 94, 95, 99, 112,
149, 150, 153, 154, 167, 168, 190,
192, 193, 247
usage. *See* Transforming.
GraphicsDevice object, 13, 14
GraphicsEnvironment
class, 146
object, 13, 139, 141
Graphing, 181
gtkn() method, 185
GUI interface, 259

H

Hidden line suppression, 295
HiddenLineWireFrame, 326–329,
337, 341
class, 329
code, 327–328
commentary, 328–329
object, 333
Highlighting, 2–3
HTML document, 172

I

Identity matrix, 226
Identity transform, 26
Image collections/sequences, 364
Image compression/decompression,
364
Image objects, 214, 216, 217. *See also*
Persistent image objects.

Image processing. *See* AWT image processing.
Image property management, 363
Image transformation, 230–240
    code, 231–236
    commentary, 236–240
ImageConsumer interface, 361
ImageFilter, 219
ImageProducer interface, 361
ImageProducer object, 216
Images, 19. *See also* Bitmapped images; Raster images; Time-sequential images.
    compositing, 8
    rendering. *See* Bitmapped images.
    scaling. *See* Area averaging images; Replication images.
Images, loading/displaying, 211–214
    code, 212
    commentary, 212–214
init() method, 172
intersect() method, 136
Inverse transform, 28
Irregular paths, 4–5
Irregular shapes, 4–5
isInBack(), 314
isInFront(), 314
isInOrder(), 304
Item object, 205
items.data, 207
itemStateChanged(), 147

J

Jaggies, 216
Java
    classes, 358
    graphics, 1–2, 53
    window, 268
Java Advanced Imaging API, 358–359, 364

Java Development Kit (JDK), 172, 365, 366
Java Foundation Classes (JFC), 1, 15
Java Virtual Machine (JVM), 173, 177
Java2D, 93, 100, 170, 211
    API, 124
    Area object, 325, 326
    discovery, 15
    imaging, comparison, 361–362
    scheme, 361
    usage. *See* 3-D work.
Java2D package, 267
    understanding, 2–14
Java3D, 1
JDK. *See* Java Development Kit.
JFC. *See* Java Foundation Classes.
Join style, 85, 86
Joins, 7
    types, 19
JPEG display utilities, 357
JPEG files, 19, 211, 212
JPEG image files, 359
JVM. *See* Java Virtual Machine.

K

Kernel, 225, 226
    object, 222
Kerning tables, 18

L

Layers, 102
Layout, 18
    capabilities, 11
Least squares. *See* Scattergram/least squares.
LeastSquares.class, 200, 202
LetterPictureCanvas class, 166
Letters. *See* Drawn letters; Drawn letters II.
Letters/pictures, 162–166

Letters/pictures, *Continued*
    code, 163–165
    commentary, 165–166
Lex, 186
    object, 189
Ligatures, 10, 137
LIGHTEN matrix, 227
Line drawings, 79
    code, 80
    commentary, 80–81
Line segments, 300–304, 337
    code, 301–303
    commentary, 303–304
Line splitter, 308–314
    code, 308–313
    commentary, 313–314
Line suppression. *See* Hidden line
    suppression.
Line2D, 4, 127
    objects, 80
Line-drawing graphic
    programs, 53
Lines, 3
    drawing, 2–8. *See also* Threshold.
    obscuring. *See* Triangle.
    styles, 5
Lines, scaling, 96–98
    code, 97–98
lineTo() method, 80, 94, 96
Link, 304–305
    code, 304–305
    commentary, 305
    object, 305, 325
LoadableWireFrame, 279
    class, 283
    object, 280
LoadableWireFrame class, 278
loadPicture() method, 165
LocalGraphicsEnvironment(), 139
Locating/dragging, 261–265

code, 262–263
    commentary, 264–265
Lookup-table modification, 12

M

makeArea(), 325
makeEdgeArray() method, 273
makeLinkList(), 326
makeNewLinks(), 325, 326
makeParts() method, 135
makePerspectiveVector() method,
    348, 349
makePlaneEquation() method, 307
makeTriangles(), 325
makeTriVector(), 326
makeWidget() method, 132
makeXYZPoints() method, 313, 314
Manual rotator, 292–294
    code, 292–294
    commentary, 294
ManualHide, 334–338
    code, 335–337
    commentary, 337–338
mappedGlyphVector(), 150
Matrixes. *See* Equations/matrixes.
MediaTracker, 59, 165, 213, 214
META key, 258
Mitered corners, 83–85
    code, 84–85
    commentary, 85
mixedColors(), 157
mixedFonts(), 157
Monotonic, 189
Mouse, understanding, 251
Mouse cursors, changing, 259–261
    code, 259–261
    commentary, 261
Mouse events, dissection, 255–259
    code, 256–258
    commentary, 258–259

Mouse events, reading, 251–253
    code, 252–253
    commentary, 253
Mouse motion, 254–255
    code, 254–255
    commentary, 255
MouseEvent, 255
MouseListener interface, 251, 253,
        255, 258
MouseMotionListener interface, 255, 258
mouseMoved(), 255, 264
mousePressed(), 253, 264
mouseReleased(), 253, 265
MoveDownRight, 58–59
    code, 58–59
    commentary, 59
moveTo() method, 80, 94, 96
MovingPoint
    class, 321
    object, 321
Multiple traces (one window),
        190–193
    code, 190–191
    commentary, 191–193
MultipleTraces constructor, 191

N

Nearest-neighbor, 238
    algorithm, 230
Nested loop, 249
next() method, 321
nextFrame(), 173, 180, 289, 321
Non-MacOS computers, 13
Nonrotational translation, 27
Non-Windows computers, 13

O

Object face. *See* Space object face.
Object-creation statement, 92

Oblique cube-like thing, 279–281
    code, 280
    commentary, 280–281
On-and-off sequence, 89
Origin, 24–25, 64, 71, 73
outlineFace() method, 334
outlineTriangle() method, 334

P

pack(), 192
Page-layout tools, 8
paint() method, 43, 50, 57, 59, 61, 63,
        65, 69, 81, 135, 147, 149, 159, 162,
        168, 173, 180, 192, 203, 208, 246, 290,
        321, 322
Parent class, 347
Paths, 17. *See also* Irregular paths.
pc(), 185
Persistent image objects, 362
Perspective, 343
PerspectiveWireFrame, 346–349
    code, 346–347
    commentary, 347–349
pgc(), 185
Pictures. *See* Letters/pictures.
Pie chart, 209–210
    code, 209–210
    commentary, 210
Pixel algorithms, 231
Pixel by pixel, 219–222
    code, 219–221
    commentary, 221–222
Plane in space. *See* Space plane.
Plotting, 181
Point in space. *See* Space point.
Point2D, 4
Points. *See* Vanishing points.
    movement, transform usage, 24–28
    understanding, 23

Polygons, 127, 195, 297, 322, 323
Pong applet, 170–173
    code, 170–172
    commentary, 172–173
Pong application, 173–177
    code, 174–176
    commentary, 176–177
PongPanel, 176
    object, 177
Positioning. *See* Two-dimensional
    positioning.
ppVisibility() method, 313
Predefined color objects, 36–38
    code, 36–38
    commentary, 38
processWindowEvent(), 55, 59
Pull scheme, 363
pVectorSort(), 314
pVectorTrim(), 314
Pythagorean theorem, 303

Q

QuadCurve, 114, 115
QuadCurve2D, 4, 117, 127
    class, 112
QuadCurve2D.Float object, 114
Quadratic curves, 112–115, 127
    code, 112–114
    commentary, 114–115
    drawing. *See* Asymmetrical quadratic
      curves.

R

Radians, 31
RAM-resident trace, 185–190
    code, 186—189
    commentary, 189–190
Raster graphics, 211
Raster images, 11, 12

RecolorImageFilter, 221, 222
RecolorPanel, 221
Rectangle building, GeneralPath
    usage, 93–95
    code, 93–94
    commentary, 94–95
Rectangle2D, 127, 135
    object, 80
Rectangle2D.Float object, 125
Rectangles, 2, 3, 127
    drawing. *See* Round-cornered
      rectangles; Square-cornered
      rectangles.
RectangularShape, 127
Region of interest (ROI), 363
Regular shapes, 3–4
Remote Method Invocation (RMI), 363
Renderable, rendered comparison, 362
Rendered, comparison. *See* Renderable.
Rendering, 19–20. *See also* Bitmapped
    images.
    independence, 362
RenderingHints, 237
repaint() method, 166, 238, 258, 337
ReplicatePanel, 216
ReplicateScaleFilter, 215
Replication images, scaling, 214–216
    code, 214–215
    commentary, 215–216
Representation, separation. *See*
    Abstract/representation.
rescaleCount, 289
Resizing. *See* Dynamic resizing.
Resolution independence, 362
RGB color model, 13
RGB components, 33
RGB triplet, 189
RGB values, 35, 186
    usage. *See* Color objects.

RMI. *See* Remote Method Invocation.

ROI. *See* Region of interest.

rotate() method, 286, 289, 348

rotateAroundX(), 286, 348

rotateAroundY(), 286, 348

rotateAroundZ(), 286, 348

Rotation, 75. *See also* Two-dimensional
    rotation; Wire frame.

    usage. *See* Coordinates.

Rotator. *See* Automatic rotator; Manual
    rotator.

Round-cornered rectangles, drawing,
    125–127

    code, 126

    commentary, 126–127

RoundRect, 125

RoundRectangle2D, 127

RoundRectangle2D.Float class, 126

run() method, 173, 177

Runnable, 172, 176, 321

S

Scale factor, 75, 208, 337

scale() method, 285, 289, 348

Scale transformation, 71

SCALE_AREA_AVERAGING, 218

SCALE_DEFAULT, 218

ScaleDownTurn, 74–75

    code, 74–75

    commentary, 75

ScaleDownTurn2, 75–77

    code, 76–77

    commentary, 77

scaleFactor, 208

SCALE_FAST, 219

SCALE_REPLICATE, 219

SCALE_REPLICATION, 218

SCALE_SMOOTH, 219

ScaleUp, 70–72

    code, 70–71

    commentary, 71–72

ScaleUp2, 72–74

    code, 72–73

    commentary, 73–74

Scaling, 12. *See also* Arcs.

    usage. *See* Figure size change.

Scaling variations, 108–111

    code, 108–110

    commentary, 110–111

Scattergram/least squares, 199–203

    code, 200–202

    commentary, 202–203

Screen projection, 344–346

S-curve, 121

Segment objects, 307, 308

segmentize() method, 328, 337

Segments, 322

Set, attention, 61

setAngleX(), 286

setAngleY(), 286

setAngleZ(), 286

setColor() method, 40, 193

setComponents() method, 222

setCursor() method, 261

setFrontBack() method, 314

setHints() method, 221, 237

setIdentity() method, 237

setInitialValues(), 146

setPaint() method, 43

setPixels() method, 222

setRect(), 126

setRotate() method, 237

setRotationCenter(), 285

setScaleDown() method, 237

setScaleUp() method, 237

setShear() method, 237

setSize(), 214

    statement, 68

setStroke() method, 193
setToRotation() method, 65, 67
setTrace(), 202
setTransform() method, 31, 77, 100
setValues() method, 35, 147
setView() method, 348, 353
setWindwingRule(), 160
Shading. *See* Simple shading.
Shape array, 82
Shape edge, 268–270
   code, 269
   commentary, 270
Shape interface, 94
Shape objects, 127, 160
shapeArray, 80, 83
Shapes. *See* Irregular shapes; Regular
   shapes; Wire frame.
   description. *See* File.
   drawing, 2–8
   loading. *See* Three-dimensional
     shape.
   making, 93
Shapes appending, GenPath object
   usage, 127–130
   code, 127–129
   commentary, 129–130
Shapes combination, area object usage,
   133–136
   code, 133–135
   commentary, 135–136
Shapes connecting, 130–133
   code, 130–132
   commentary, 132–133
SHARPEN matrix, 229
show(), 192
showEvent() method, 258
showHighlight(), 154
showOutlining(), 154
showShear(), 154
showTiltedOutline() method, 154

Simple shading, 40–42
   code, 40–41
   commentary, 41–42
simpleAttributedString(), 150
simpleCharArray() method, 149
SimpleLine, 53–56, 58
   code, 54
   commentary, 54–55
SimpleLine() constructor, 54
SimpleLine2, 55–59
   code, 56–57
   commentary, 57–58
simpleString() method, 149
simpleTextLayout(), 150
Single data item, 203–203
   code, 203–204
   commentary, 205
Size methods, 304
skewX() method, 326
skewY() method, 326
SOFTEN matrix, 227
Source-and-sink model, 363
Space object face, 271–273
   code, 271–272
   commentary, 272–273
Space plane, 270–271
   code, 270–271
   commentary, 271
Space point, 268
   code, 268
   commentary, 268
Special appearances, creation, 5–8
Spin, 62–64
   code, 62–63
   commentary, 63–64
Splitter object, 321–322, 328
Square-cornered rectangles, drawing,
   124–125
   code, 124–125
   commentary, 125

Squared ends, 83–85
   code, 84–85
   commentary, 85
SquareRect, 124
SrcOver rule, 246, 247
start() method, 172, 177
String drawing, basics, 147–151
   code, 147–149
   commentary, 149–151
String object, 137, 149
Strings, 9
Strokes, 20. *See also* Default stroke.
   width, 19
subtract() method, 136
Swing Set, 1
Symmetric cubic curves, 117–119
   code, 117–118
   commentary, 119

T

Text, 17
   fields, 353
   file, 182
   fitting, 137
   transforms, 11
   usage, 8–11
Text attributes, mixing, 155–158
   code, 155–157
   commentary, 157–158
TextAttribute, 157
TextLayout, 154, 160
   class, 151
   object, 150, 159, 167
TextLayout operations, 151–154
   code, 151–153
   commentary, 153–154
TexturePaint() method, 50
Textures, 8
   fills, 19
   handling, 33

usage. *See* Area filling.
Third-party development, 359
3-D work, Java2D usage, 14
Three-dimensional coordinates, 345
Three-dimensional display, 267
Three-dimensional drawings, 326
Three-dimensional form, 303
Three-dimensional imaging, 364
Three-dimensional object, 269, 271, 273,
   274, 281, 295
Three-dimensional operations, basic
   tools, 267
Three-dimensional rotation, 279. *See
   also* Wire frame shapes.
Three-dimensional shape, 286, 334, 338
   loading, 274–279
      code, 275–278
      commentary, 278–279
Three-dimensional space, 270, 297, 299,
   300, 352
Threshold, filling/lines drawing, 196–199
   code, 196–198
   commentary, 199
TIFF files, 211
Tiling, 12
Tilt, 60–63
   code, 60–61
   commentary, 61
Time-sequential images, 357
Toolkit(), 165
Toolkit.getDefaultToolkit(), 213
TracePanel, 202
   class, 192
   object, 191
Traces. *See* Multiple traces; RAM-
   resident trace.
   class, 185, 186
Traces, filling, 193–196
   code, 194–195
   commentary, 195–196

Transform(), 100
transform() method, 57, 63
Transform object, 20
Transformations, 20–21
TransformDialog, 238
TransformImage class, 236
TransformImageCanvas, 236
    class, 237
    object, 238
TransformImageDialog, 236
Transforming, Graphics2D usage, 95–96
    code, 95–96
    commentary, 96
Transforming, world/window process,
        28–31
Transforms, 23–25. *See also* Identity
        transform; Inverse transform.
    understanding, 23
    usage. *See* Points.
Translation. *See* Nonrotational
        translation.
    usage. *See* Coordinates.
Transparency, 13, 21, 241, 250
    control, 247
    usage. *See* Cross fading.
Triangle, obscuring lines, 315–322
    code, 315–321
    commentary, 321–322
TriangleFace, 322–326, 328
    capabilities, 329
    code, 323–325
    commentary, 325–326
    object, 328
TriangleMetrics, 305–308
    code, 306–307
    commentary, 307
Triangles, 296, 314, 333
    class, 278, 305
    objects, 323
triangulate() method, 328

Triangulation, 343
    demonstration, 329–334
        code, 330–332
        commentary, 332–334
triVector(), 325
Try/catch block, 214
Two-dimensional components, 307
Two-dimensional coordinate plane, 16
Two-dimensional plane, 300
Two-dimensional positioning, 53
Two-dimensional rotation, 53
Two-dimensional space, 305
Two-element array, 69
Typefaces, 9

U

Unicode character, 137
update() method, 173
User Coordinate Plane, 17
User Coordinate Space, 16, 18–20
Utility classes, 202

V

Vanishing points, 343–344
Vector, 205
    object, 328
Vertex, 269, 271, 273, 333
    class, 268, 278
    ID numbers, 270, 272, 274
    lines, 273
    objects, 278, 300, 304, 305, 307, 348
    values, 349

W

waitForAll(), 165, 214
Web browsers, 361
Wide lines, bevelled corners/butted line
        endings, 85–86
    code, 86
    commentary, 86

Wide lines rounded off, 82–83
    code, 82–83
    commentary, 83
Winding rule, 100–102
    code, 101
    commentary, 102
Wire frame, 349. *See also* Adjustable
        wire frame.
    class, 346
    object, 338, 346
    shapes, three-dimensional
            rotation, 283
WireFrame class, 283
wordInversion(), 157
wordStrike(), 157
wordUnderline(), 157
WritableRaster object, 245
write() method, 279

X

X-axis value, 267, 315
XYPosition, 299
x-y-z coordinates, 299
XYZPoint, 297–300, 304
    code, 297–299
    commentary, 299

Y

Y-axis value, 267

Z

Z-axis value, 296, 315, 345
ZigZag. *See* Dynamic ZigZag.
Zposition, 299

NOTES

NOTES

NOTES

Sun Microsystems, Inc.

Binary Code License Agreement

READ THE TERMS OF THIS AGREEMENT AND ANY PROVIDED SUP-
PLEMENTAL LICENSE TERMS (COLLECTIVELY "AGREEMENT")
CAREFULLY BEFORE OPENING THE SOFTWARE MEDIA PACKAGE.
BY OPENING THE SOFTWARE MEDIA PACKAGE, YOU AGREE TO
THE TERMS OF THIS AGREEMENT. IF YOU ARE ACCESSING THE
SOFTWARE ELECTRONICALLY, INDICATE YOUR ACCEPTANCE OF
THESE TERMS BY SELECTING THE "ACCEPT" BUTTON AT THE END
OF THIS AGREEMENT. IF YOU DO NOT AGREE TO ALL THESE
TERMS, PROMPTLY RETURN THE UNUSED SOFTWARE TO YOUR
PLACE OF PURCHASE FOR A REFUND OR, IF THE SOFTWARE IS
ACCESSED ELECTRONICALLY, SELECT THE "DECLINE" BUTTON AT
THE END OF THIS AGREEMENT.

1. **License to Use.** Sun grants you a non-exclusive and non-transferable license for the internal use only of the accompanying software
and documentation and any error corrections provided by Sun (collectively "Software"), by the number of users and the class of computer hardware for which the corresponding fee has been paid.

2. **Restrictions.** Software is confidential and copyrighted. Title to
Software and all associated intellectual property rights is retained by
Sun and/or its licensors. Except as specifically authorized in any Supplemental License Terms, you may not make copies of Software,
other than a single copy of Software for archival purposes. Unless
enforcement is prohibited by applicable law, you may not modify,
decompile, reverse engineer Software. Software is not designed or
licensed for use in on-line control of aircraft, air traffic, aircraft navigation or aircraft communications; or in the design, construction,
operation or maintenance of any nuclear facility. You warrant that
you will not use Software for these purposes. You may not publish or
provide the results of any benchmark or comparison tests run on
Software to any third party without the prior written consent of Sun.

No right, title or interest in or to any trademark, service mark, logo or trade name of Sun or its licensors is granted under this Agreement.

3. **Limited Warranty.** Sun warrants to you that for a period of ninety (90) days from the date of purchase, as evidenced by a copy of the receipt, the media on which Software is furnished (if any) will be free of defects in materials and workmanship under normal use. Except for the foregoing, Software is provided "AS IS". Your exclusive remedy and Sun's entire liability under this limited warranty will be at Sun's option to replace Software media or refund the fee paid for Software.

4. **Disclaimer of Warranty.** UNLESS SPECIFIED IN THIS AGREEMENT, ALL EXPRESS OR IMPLIED CONDITIONS, REPRESENTATIONS AND WARRANTIES, INCLUDING ANY IMPLIED WARRANTY OF MERCHANTABILITY, FITNESS FOR A PARTICULAR PURPOSE, OR NON-INFRINGEMENT, ARE DISCLAIMED, EXCEPT TO THE EXTENT THAT THESE DISCLAIMERS ARE HELD TO BE LEGALLY INVALID.

5. **Limitation of Liability.** TO THE EXTENT NOT PROHIBITED BY LAW, IN NO EVENT WILL SUN OR ITS LICENSORS BE LIABLE FOR ANY LOST REVENUE, PROFIT OR DATA, OR FOR SPECIAL, INDIRECT, CONSEQUENTIAL, INCIDENTAL OR PUNITIVE DAMAGES, HOWEVER CAUSED REGARDLESS OF THE THEORY OF LIABILITY, ARISING OUT OF OR RELATED TO THE USE OF OR INABILITY TO USE SOFTWARE, EVEN IF SUN HAS BEEN ADVISED OF THE POSSIBILITY OF SUCH DAMAGES. In no event will Sun's liability to you, whether in contract, tort (including negligence), or otherwise, exceed the amount paid by you for Software under this Agreement. The foregoing limitations will apply even if the above stated warranty fails of its essential purpose.

6. **Termination.** This Agreement is effective until terminated. You may terminate this Agreement at any time by destroying all copies of Software. This Agreement will terminate immediately without notice from Sun if you fail to comply with any provision of this Agreement. Upon Termination, you must destroy all copies of Software.

7. **Export Regulations.** All Software and technical data delivered under this Agreement are subject to US export control laws and may be subject to export or import regulations in other countries. You agree to comply strictly with all such laws and regulations and acknowledge

that you have the responsibility to obtain such licenses to export, re-export, or import as may be required after delivery to you.

8. **U.S. Government Restricted Rights**. Use, duplication, or disclosure by the U.S. Government is subject to restrictions set forth in this Agreement and as provided in DFARS 227.7202-1 (a) and 227.7202-3(a) (1995), DFARS 252.227-7013 (c)(1)(ii)(Oct 1988), FAR 12.212 (a) (1995), FAR 52.227-19 (June 1987), or FAR 52.227-14(ALT III) (June 1987), as applicable.

9. **Governing Law.** Any action related to this Agreement will be governed by California law and controlling U.S. federal law. No choice of law rules of any jurisdiction will apply.

10. **Severability.** If any provision of this Agreement is held to be unenforceable, this Agreement will remain in effect with the provision omitted, unless omission would frustrate the intent of the parties, in which case this Agreement will immediately terminate.

11. **Integration.** This Agreement is the entire agreement between you and Sun relating to its subject matter. It supersedes all prior or contemporaneous oral or written communications, proposals, representations and warranties and prevails over any conflicting or additional terms of any quote, order, acknowledgment, or other communication between the parties relating to its subject matter during the term of this Agreement. No modification of this Agreement will be binding, unless in writing and signed by an authorized representative of each party.

For inquiries please contact: Sun Microsystems, Inc. 901 San Antonio Road, Palo Alto, California 94303

JAVA™ DEVELOPMENT KIT VERSION 1.2

SUPPLEMENTAL LICENSE TERMS

These supplemental terms ("Supplement") add to the terms of the Binary Code License Agreement ("Agreement"). Capitalized terms not defined herein shall have the same meanings ascribed to them in the Agreement. The Supplement terms shall supersede any inconsistent or conflicting terms in the Agreement.

1. **Limited License Grant.** Sun grants to you a non-exclusive, non-transferable limited license to use the Software without fee for evaluation of the Software and for development of Java™ applets and applications provided that you: (i) may not re-distribute the Software in whole or in part, either separately or included with a product. (ii) may not create, or authorize your licensees to create additional classes, interfaces, or subpackages that are contained in the "java" or "sun" packages or similar as specified by Sun in any class file naming convention; and (iii) agree to the extent Programs are developed which utilize the Windows 95/98 style graphical user interface or components contained therein, such applets or applications may only be developed to run on a Windows 95/98 or Windows NT platform. Refer to the Java Runtime Environment Version 1.2 binary code license (http://java.sun.com/products/JDK/1.2/index.html) for the availability of runtime code which may be distributed with Java applets and applications.

2. **Java Platform Interface.** In the event that Licensee creates an additional API(s) which: (i) extends the functionality of a Java Environment; and, (ii) is exposed to third party software developers for the purpose of developing additional software which invokes such additional API, Licensee must promptly publish broadly an accurate specification for such API for free use by all developers.

3. **Trademarks and Logos.** This Agreement does not authorize Licensee to use any Sun name, trademark or logo. Licensee acknowledges as between it and Sun that Sun owns the Java trademark and all Java-related trademarks, logos and icons including the Coffee Cup and Duke ("Java Marks") and agrees to comply with the Java Trademark Guidelines at http://java.sun.com/trademarks.html.

4. **High Risk Activities.** Notwithstanding Section 2, with respect to high risk activities, the following language shall apply: the Software is not designed or intended for use in on-line control of aircraft, air traffic, aircraft navigation or aircraft communications; or in the design, construction, operation or maintenance of any nuclear facility. Sun disclaims any express or implied warranty of fitness for such uses.

Java™ 2 Platform (formerly code-named JDK 1.2)

Copyright 1998 Sun Microsystems, Inc. 901 San Antonio Road, Palo Alto, CA 94303-4900 USA, All rights reserved. Java, JavaBeans, JDK and other Java related marks are trademarks or registered trademarks of Sun Microsystems, Inc. in the U.S. and other countries.

Use of this software is subject to the Binary Code License terms and conditions found in this book and on the CD-ROM. Read the license carefully. By opening this package, you are agreeing to be bound by the terms and conditions of this license from Sun Microsystems, Inc.

Use, duplication or disclosure by the United States government is subject to the restrictions as set forth in the Rights in Technical Data and Computer Software Clauses in DFARS 252.227-7013) (c) (1) (ii) and FAR 52.227-19(c) (2) as applicable.

To use this CD-ROM, your system must meet the following requirements:

**Platform/Processor/
Operating System:** To install the Java Development Kit, a 486/DX or faster processor.

RAM: 32 megabytes RAM minimum, 48 megabytes RAM recommended

Hard Drive Space: 65 MB free hard drive space.

Java™ 2: Copyright 1998 Sun Microsystems, Inc. 901 San Antonio Road, Palo Alto, CA 94303-4900 USA, All rights reserved. Java, JavaBeans, JDK and other Java related marks are trademarks or registered trademarks of Sun Microsystems, Inc. in the U.S. and other countries.

Use of this software is subject to the Binary Code License terms and conditions found in this book and on the CD-ROM. Read the license carefully. By opening this package, you are agreeing to be bound by the terms and conditions of this license from Sun Microsystems, Inc.

Restricted Rights: Duplication or disclosure by the United States Government is subject to the restrictions as set forth in the Rights in Technical Data and Computer Software Clauses in DFARS 252.227-7013(c) (1) (ii) and FAR 52.227-19 (c) (2) as applicable.